Marvellously Helped

Marvellously Helped

The Trials and Triumphs of Blanche Brenton Carey

by A Russell

Acknowledgements

A Coronavirus pandemic walk through a local churchyard made me wonder who had influenced the lives of the people who had such evangelistic Bible verses added to their grave stones. This thought improbably led me to Karachi and Miss Blanche Brenton Carey, whose motto was "Marvellously helped".

I never set out to write a book, but my research of Brenton Carey led me to a wealth of information at the Cadbury Research Library in Birmingham. Although the pandemic lockdown meant I couldn't attend the library in person, the librarians were extremely helpful to me and allowed me to access the Church Missionary Archives online.

I also owe a debt of gratitude to local church historian Dr Lesley Rowe, who encouraged me to write the story of Blanche, painstakingly proof read my drafts and gave really helpful feedback and advice.

Finally my heartfelt gratitude goes to my wife who patiently bore with me during this project. She read and commented on all the content and helped me enormously.

Contents

Acknowledgements v

Foreword.. 1

Formative Years 3

New Beginnings - Karachi 17

No Longer a Second 29

Orphans and Villages 45

Widows and War.. 67

Trials and Honour 90

Financial Pressures and Jubilee....................................127

Journey's End 154

Epilogue 180

Appendix A..181

References..182

Bibliography..197

Foreword

One of the most well-known of all the women missionaries to go to India was Amy Wilson Carmichael who served in Southern India from 1895 until her death in 1951. A year before Amy's death another former pioneer missionary to India also died. Her name was Blanche Louisa Mary Boleyn Brenton Carey. Both of these great ladies served their Lord on the Indian subcontinent for over fifty years under trying circumstances and faced social and cultural ills, which limited the opportunities of women and girls. They both worked to improve the lives of countless children, and most of all they were passionate in their desire to speak to others about the glorious gospel of the Lord Jesus Christ.

Blanche Brenton Carey may not be familiar to many of us today but she was a pioneer missionary who served the people of Karachi in the late nineteenth and the first half of the twentieth century. Blanche arrived in Karachi in November 1885, living and working there until her death in Karachi on 25th May 1950. Her missionary service in then India now Pakistan covered the period of two World Wars, the global financial crisis of the Great Depression, and political upheaval which ended with the partition of India and the creation of the state of Pakistan. Blanche Carey and Amy Carmichael were both members of the Church of England Zenana Missionary Society (CEZMS). The CEZMS was a society that sent out hundreds of single women to live and work in foreign lands, facing many personal dangers. They were courageous women of faith who had a love for their fellow "sisters" and had a deep desire to see them come to know their loving Saviour Jesus Christ.

When Blanche arrived in Karachi there was one mission school which had fifteen pupils, and the language was still unknown to her. By God's good grace the mission work expanded until at its height Blanche was responsible for nine schools in Karachi, with about 900 pupils, establishing a Widows' Industrial Class, a Training College, an Orphanage, and a ministry visiting hundreds of women and reaching out to the villages around Karachi.

1

Blanche was a great advocate for the women of India at a time when women were mainly illiterate, when girls would be married at twelve years old, when many women were separated from the outside world, when superstition was rife and the caste system governed every aspect of people's lives.

Blanche saw great growth in the work but like any other ministry there were many trials, much opposition and a lot of sadness. Through it all Blanche trusted her Saviour to overcome all the obstacles that were put in the way of His work. A great woman of prayer and with a strong commitment to evangelical truths, she went forward with humility and love for the people whom she earnestly wanted to come to know her Lord and Saviour. She often wished she could have done more for the people, such was her love.

This story is first and foremost a biography of Blanche Brenton Carey but due to her long years in service it also serves as an illustration of a life in ministry which encompasses all the ups, the many downs, the joys and the sorrows. Blanche endured the race set before her until she reached the finishing line. There is much to learn from how Blanche coped with such trials during a life of service to her Lord and how she managed to display much grace at times of adversity.

The individual experiences of Blanche are also set against the background narrative of a world in turmoil, and a steady decline in the spiritual life of England. In the mid nineteenth century England experienced a revival of religion and God was pleased to raise up great ministers of the Gospel such as Bishop J C Ryle and the Baptist minister C H Spurgeon. This helped stimulate the missionary movement as many people went overseas to spread the good news of Jesus Christ. But as the nineteenth century ended and the twentieth century began, the spiritual life in England started to wane. There were fewer faithful Christians to support the missionaries, in terms of finance and workers. This becomes evident in Blanche's cries for more workers to spread the good news and the need for funding to sustain the cause of the gospel. But above all this there is a God who is sovereign and rules over all and His purposes are sure and certain. This is the God whom Blanche trusted in and prayed to and the Saviour whom she served. Blanche's life challenges us to recognise and adapt to the changing circumstances of our own times whilst trusting God to supply all our needs.

Formative Years

Family Background

Blanche Louisa Mary Boleyn Brenton Carey was the second daughter of the Rev. Adolphus Frederick Carey and Harriet Mary Carey (nee Brenton). Blanche was greatly influenced by her parents and it was no ordinary family.

Adolphus Frederick Carey was born on January 19th 1824, the son of Thomas Carey, on the Island of Guernsey in the English Channel. Adolphus' family traced their descent to Mary Boleyn, sister of Anne Boleyn and her husband William Carey, which would explain the use of the name Boleyn in Blanche's full name. Adolphus was an highly educated man as he attended Wadham College in Oxford from where he graduated in 1845.[1]

In his early years Adolphus was greatly influenced by his mother, and she approved of him becoming a minister of the gospel. Adolphus was a man of great energy and without his mother's influence he may well have joined his brothers in a military career. Adolphus performed his duty in the service of his King the Lord Jesus Christ. This he was able to do with the support and guidance of his Saviour and the love of his mother.[2]

Adolphus entered the ministry of the Church of England being ordained at Peterborough Cathedral in 1847 and served as a curate from 1848 to 1852 in many places including the Somerset parish of Badgworth and the Leicestershire parish of Aston Flamville and Burbage.

He moved abroad and served in Belgium and Switzerland before returning to England to become the assistant minister of St. Matthews, Spring Gardens, London in 1859. He then settled in Devon to become the Vicar of Brixham in 1861.[3]

The first Bible text he preached to the Brixham congregation was 1 Corinthians 2:3, "I determined to know nothing among you, save Jesus Christ, and Him crucified." He consistently preached the gospel throughout his many years of ministry there. The Primitive Methodist preacher Mr C Briggs said that he was an "earnest preacher of the pure Gospel of Jesus Christ."[2]

Adolphus was a low churchman and was always against ritualistic practices in the church. He had great sympathy for the Nonconformists and he felt at home in their company. He took a keen interest in the religious and secular education of children and became the first chairman of the School board in Brixham.[2]

He worked in the parish for nearly forty years and had a great influence on his parishioners. The welfare of the Brixham community was upper most in his mind. Adolphus was a friend and help for those in need and he "endeared himself" to all, those who were difficult, those who were easy going, the rich and the poor. A representative of the local council said that Adolphus, "had been a pattern for truth and righteousness". People warmed to his person and character. The local community held him in high esteem, love and respect.[2]

Adolphus showed a great interest in overseas mission work, which almost certainly influenced his children as he had connections with a number of missionary agencies such as the British and Foreign Bible Society, the Church Missionary Society, the South American Missionary Society, and he had a particular interest in the mission to the Jews.

He was not averse to change and controversy. A news paper article in *The Press* in 1877 from New Zealand ran a story about the Rev. A Carey in Brixham who wanted to introduce the Sankey hymn book to the congregation at the expense of the Prayer Book hymns; this caused quite a stir and it was reported that only one member of the congregation supported him. Nevertheless, as Adolphus continued to serve in Brixham until his death in 1900, the situation must have been resolved.

Adolphus Carey married Harriet Mary Brenton in 1846. Harriet was born in Bath, Somerset in 1824 and was the youngest daughter of Vice Admiral Sir Jahleel Brenton and Isabella Stuart. Vice Admiral Sir Jahleel Brenton was born in America in 1770 and lived on Rhode Island. He relocated to England after the outbreak of the American War of Independence, he served in Nelson's navy, and was a Christian who had a "firm confidence and lively hope in the merits of his Redeemer ... Free undeserved grace was his only hope; to that he looked, and it was on that he rested; but it was in the full assurance of faith that he did so."[4]

Harriet was an educated woman and was described as a 'lady of distinction', being a poet, and an author of fiction for young and old.[5] Harriet wrote books such as *Evenings with Grandpapa, Naval Stories for Children* and *Echoes from the Harp of France* where the author is described as the 'Corresponding Member of the Imperial Academy of Sciences, Arts and Belle Lettres of Caen, Normandy.'

Adolphus and Harriet made their home in Brixham and they had nine children. The family must have enjoyed a somewhat privileged position with their distinguished heritage and the society contacts they would enjoy. Several of their children in addition to Blanche had very influential careers overseas.

Jahleel Brenton Carey, born in Burbage, Leicestershire in 1847, became a captain in the British Army and fought in the Zulu Wars. He became infamous for an incident, chronicled in many military history books of that period, where Louis Napoleon Bonaparte Prince of France (who was living in exile in England) died at the hands of Zulu warriors. Jahleel was court-martialled for his actions during this incident and was found guilty (cowardice in the face of the enemy would have warranted the death penalty) but later he was exonerated for having been responsible for the Prince's death. This incident was well publicised in the national and international press and the close family would have suffered a great deal of stress.

Although Jahleel did not court publicity, after he was exonerated he wrote a letter to a newspaper called the *Christian*:

"My dear Sir,

May I ask you to kindly insert a request for praise on my behalf in the next number of your journal? Since the first moment of my arrest I took the whole matter to my heavenly Father. I left it in His hands, reminding Him constantly of His promise to help. He has borne my burden for me. He has sustained me, my wife, and family, in our distress, and He has finally wiped away tears from our eyes. There were certain circumstances at first that it seemed, owing to the bewildered statement of the survivors, difficult to explain; but though my faith wavered His promised (sic) endured, and He in His good time brought me to the haven where I would be. I feel that it would be wrong to keep from my fellow-believers such a wonderful example of God's goodness and power influencing the hearts of men; and though I hate publicity, I feel compelled to add my testimony to the power of prayer." J Brenton Carey Captain 98th Regiment, Southsea, 25th August 1879.[6]

Jahleel died in Karachi in 1883. He had a daughter named Edith Isabella Brenton Carey who later joined Blanche in missionary service in Karachi.

Reginald Orme Brenton Carey was born in 1848 and became a captain in the Royal Navy. He went to South America to look after British interests during the Peru-Chile war. He left the British Royal Navy and became the Admiral of the Mexican Navy. After his naval career Reginald became a Brethren Missionary to South West Mexico where he distributed many Bibles. Reginald died in 1921. A memorial plaque for Reginald in Ometepec read, "The entrance of your Word gives Light ... A servant of God and men, who left his homeland to dedicate his life to Christian service in Mexico."[7]

Another brother Cranstoun born in 1852 became the Inspector of Constabulary in Jamaica.

Harriet Carey died on the 3rd of June 1886, shortly after Blanche went to Karachi. Adolphus remarried in 1890 to the widow Mrs. Gaches.

After many years service in Brixham Adolphus became unwell, and despite his infirmities he continued to faithfully perform his duties. On Sunday 29th April 1900 Adolphus preached his last sermon from Psalm 17:15 "When I awake after Thy likeness I shall be satisfied." At the end of the sermon Adolphus "broke down", which shocked the congregation and moved many to tears. They managed to carry him back home and call for help, but despite medical attention his condition deteriorated and his family was urged to come.[2]

On the Thursday Adolphus offered this prayer, "O, God I thank Thee for Thy watchful care over me and my children, I humbly ask Thee to continue to watch over them and all my parishioners. I have fought the fight; my work is done. I pray Thee look upon my successor, and grant that he may preach the word in sincerity and truth, for Jesus Christ's sake. - Amen".[2]

Then on 6th May 1900 Rev. Adolphus Carey died peacefully at home, he was seventy six years old. The bell was rung out to announce his death to his parishioners and the flag on the tower was put at half mast. The funeral took place on the 9th May. There was a great number of people who attended his funeral, an hour before the service started the Church was full, and hundreds of people had to be turned away. Many clergy from the surrounding area including Nonconformist ministers came to remember Adolphus and to pay their respects. All the Sunday school children and their teachers attended numbering one hundred and fifty persons, Firemen came dressed in their uniforms, boys from the orphanage, teachers from the boys school, Royal Navy reserves and Coastguards and many others, he was much loved and appreciated by the whole community he had served. The funeral procession was said to be a mile long. It was evident that Adolphus' ministry had remarkably affected the population of Brixham.[2]

Early years

Blanche was born in 1856 in Bath, in the county of Somerset, England and was baptised there on the 14th March 1856. Five years later she moved with her family to Brixham in the county of Devon. Blanche spent the rest of her childhood in this fishing town, on the south coast of England. She grew up in a very busy home with her many brothers and sisters. Her mother would recount tales of naval adventures told to her from her Admiral father, Blanche's grandpapa. These stories of far-flung places must have been very exciting for the children and the tales of overseas travel would live long in the memory. The thought of travelling to foreign lands would have expanded their horizons and going to such places would not have been frightening to them.

Like many girls of the time from her social background, Blanche did not attend school but was home-schooled and she found that she enjoyed learning different European languages. She learned to speak French, German and a little Italian. When asked on her missionary application form if she had the ability to learn languages, with humility she replied, "I like them, but do not know."[8] Her humility remained with her; she was often self deprecating.

Spending this time at home, Blanche would have been greatly influenced by her mother and father, watching her mother writing and her father working in the parish church and hearing stories of missionaries abroad. It seems as if Blanche inherited her own writing skills and story-telling from her mother.

We do not know when Blanche was converted when she first came to trust in the Lord Jesus Christ as her Saviour, but we do know she was confirmed on the day before Whit Sunday 1868 in Brixham aged twelve. We also can deduce from her missionary application form that she was of an evangelical persuasion with a servant heart. Blanche wrote what she thought it meant to be a real Christian, "to be trusting only to the finished work of the Lord Jesus for pardon for sin and acceptance with God, to have taken the gift of salvation by faith, and to have given oneself up body and spirit to God's service desiring, and striving day by day in His strength to follow the steps of the holy life of Jesus Christ. Christ Jesus came into the world to save sinners - therefore to save me."[8] She had a desire to learn more about the Scriptures and the Christian life as she read a number of Christian books which included William Paley's *A View of the Evidences of Christianity*, Matthew Henry's *Commentary on the Whole Bible*, Richard Baxter's *The Saints' Everlasting Rest*, and sermons by Melville, Aitkin, and Spurgeon. Blanche was a diligent and prayerful student of the Word of God, declaring that she did not think, "the Christian life can prosper without it."[8]

From the age of twelve Blanche wanted to tell others about the Gospel of Jesus Christ, and so she taught the children in the Sunday school. Soon after at the age of fourteen she was able to superintend the Sunday school. Blanche even went on to write out the lessons for the other Sunday school teachers. It was at the early age of fourteen when she started to feel a call to the mission field. She became interested in missionary work overseas, taking a special interest in missions working with women. Blanche started to raise funds for a mission society and became a local secretary, but she did not apply to become a missionary at that time. Her long interest in mission work enabled Blanche to gain a good understanding of the main Hindu gods in India and a knowledge of the Muslim religion.

Blanche developed a character which was to be tested in foreign fields. She believed that her character was not of a "very gloomy or despondent nature." She trusted in the biblical promise that, "as thy day is so shall thy strength be."[8]

She believed and trusted that God would supply all her needs in those times of trials and hardships. Blanche also had a good sense of humour even in her application form she couldn't resist answering the question; 'what is the state of your health?' with the answer; "Very good as far as I know."[8] More of her humour will be seen later in her written articles and in her letters even during the hard times.

Blanche helped around the family home and when she was old enough she was able to continue to serve and help others as she assisted her father with his parish work in Brixham. She would visit young ladies in the community and she led a young women's Bible class for eight years in the parish. Blanche's zeal to tell others of Jesus took her to the Miss Daniell Home in Plymouth to work for a few months amongst the armed service men who were stationed there.

All this service and knowledge served as a great training ground for Blanche, waiting for the time when she believed God had called her so that she could put her name forward to become a missionary. Blanche expressed her chief motivation for becoming a missionary; "That God's way may be known upon the earth, his saving among all nations and the prayer answered 'Father glorify thy Son." [8]

Eventually Blanche asked for an application form to become a missionary but the prospect seemed hopeless due to the expense of the training and her mother's objections, so she did not apply at that time and the papers were returned. She must have been very discouraged and wondered what was happening to her but the Lord removed those obstacles and in 1884 Blanche offered herself as a missionary of the Church of England Zenana Missionary Society. Blanche explained why she believed she was called by God to this work; "I have always thought hitherto that my work lay at home and have constantly given that as a reason for not accepting repeated invitations to offer myself for Zenana mission work in which I have long been interested, having been local secretary for some years." She goes on to describe what has changed:

"This objection has lately been done away with as I find myself obliged to leave home owing to the great expense which my father has incurred in the education and putting into professions of six brothers and to assist him, with the youngest now preparing for the army. I now therefore feel free to offer myself to this work and a friend having come forward and offered to defray the expense of the training just at this time, it seems to me as if God had been over-ruling all for this end and having called me from my work at home which others have undertaken, I do not think I am wrong in supposing that it is His will that I should obey His call and seek to serve Him in India."[8]

Blanche's application form to become a missionary and the subsequent reference letters, some of which are reproduced at the end of this chapter, provide a good picture of Blanche's early life and character.

Church of England Zenana Missionary Society

Many missionaries from Britain went out to the different parts of the unevangelised world from the late-eighteenth century to the twentieth century, reaching out to the indigenous peoples with the Gospel as preachers, teachers, doctors and nurses.

The first English single woman missionary sent out to India was Mary Ann Cooke. Mary went out to reach women and girls with the gospel through use of education and she faced criticism from some men who told her, "All who know most about the country regard her attempt to bring Hindu girls together into schools as idle as any dream of enthusiasm could be." The pioneer missionary women needed great faith, courage and perseverance in the face of such criticism.

The Ladies Society for Promoting Education in the East, which was formed in Calcutta in 1824, initially opened some day schools for girls. In 1852 the India Female Normal School and Instruction Society was formed to help reach the women who lived in seclusion. This society later changed its name to the Zenana Bible and Medical Mission (ZBMM).

The Church of England Zenana Missionary Society (CEZMS) was founded in 1880 when the Church of England separated from the interdenominational Indian Female Normal School and Instruction Society.

Zenana comes from the Persian word for woman; in India it refers both to the women's quarters in a Hindu home and the more general meaning 'belonging to women'. The Zenana was accessible only to women.

The CEZMS sent out single women onto the mission field with the main aim of telling other women the good news of Jesus Christ. But when the women missionaries arrived in India they saw the particular conditions under which indigenous women were living in India, Mrs. Weitbrecht a wife of a Church Missionary Society (CMS) missionary wrote, "the daughters of India are unwelcomed at their birth, untaught in childhood, enslaved when married, accursed as widows and unlamented at their death." Under such circumstances the Society also desired "as God may enable us and bless our efforts" to alleviate the misery of their sisters. The CEZMS missionaries saw this as a privilege to help their sisters suffering in these circumstances. They evangelised the people by means of 'normal schools' (teacher training colleges), zenana visiting, medical missions, Hindu and Muslim female schools and the employment of Bible women. These means would also help develop and educate the Indian women in order to alleviate some of their suffering.[9]

Astonishing changes in the role of women were seen in India during the life time of the CEZMS. Initially many women were illiterate but they became educated and some even "leaped across the political chasm" to become elected representatives of Legislative Assemblies, "which it took Western women generations to bridge."[10]

The CEZMS had a significant impact on many thousands of lives of the people of India who came under their influence, God acting through the great faith of these single women missionaries. At its height there were over 200 women working across many parts of the world spreading the good news of Jesus Christ. The Society worked in close co-operation with the CMS.

Various sources help to build up a picture of Blanche's life and missionary service, including the annual reports from the missionaries and the extensive library of correspondence between the Society's committees home and abroad and the missionaries themselves. In addition the CEZMS produced a monthly periodical called *India's Women and China's Daughters* for their supporters to read and it would update them on all the work that was being done overseas by their women missionaries.

A lot of the information about Blanche's life comes from the articles written in the periodical mainly by Blanche herself and her colleagues in Karachi. However, as fellow-CEZMS missionary Amy Carmichael writes in her book *Things as They Are*, there was a pressure on missionaries to write encouraging stories for their readers. Even today not many of us want to be discouraged by what is happening in the mission field, especially when we are reviewing what missions to support financially. The missionary might write about a positive gospel conversation they had with a woman or child, which may have led to a commitment to read the Bible and to pray, and people back home might assume that this was a conversion to Christianity. But this was not necessarily the case, for Indians to come out publicly and follow Christ was very hard. We see this evidenced in the many references made to the lack of baptisms in Blanche's reports. Many of the converts in India tended to come from the lower uneducated castes, those of higher castes were less common.

Training

Blanche applied to become a CEZMS missionary on 8th February 1884. When her application to become a missionary was accepted Blanche trained at The Willows in Stoke Newington, it was here that the English women candidates for mission work were prepared for their service. Many hundreds of women enjoyed the opportunity to be trained at this facility in readiness for the foreign mission field. In 1893 there were forty six women there. It had spacious accommodation and pleasant grounds. The cost of the training was to be met by the candidate, and the length of the course was normally one to two years. The candidates received instruction in the entire range of Christian work i.e. the Scriptures, the country's history, geography, climate and religions, one or more languages of the mission field, the life, work and health in tropical climates, housekeeping, and accounts.[11]

Letters from missionaries who had left The Willows to work abroad were read on Sunday afternoon, to help the trainees appreciate the rigours and joys to come. They would listen to the letters being read whilst looking at the maps of the countries to locate the towns and villages mentioned. The missionary prayer meeting was well attended on Tuesday evening. They would pray for former students and the letter reading helped them to pray intelligently for the needs of the mission stations. The prayer meeting was precious to the candidates, they were not moved by any romantic adventurous notions, but they were women who had heard their Father's call to tell others of the good news of the Lord Jesus Christ. When the missionaries were on the mission field they knew that they were being remembered by the women at The Willows and were being prayed for, which was a great encouragement to them.

There seemed to be a warm and loving spiritual atmosphere amongst the candidates. Harriette Cooke writes, "You cannot be with these happy Christians without feeling the power of Christ."

Many of the girls who attended The Willows were well educated and came from wealthy homes. Some came from other European countries. If any of them struggled in an area of education, a class was formed to support them and to provide what was lacking.

After the morning classes there was practical hands on work to do in the afternoon, this included mothers' meetings, district visiting, and mission work. Many of the women taught in the Men's night school during the winter months. Some were employed in the medical mission or attended a training school for teachers. Some studied languages such as Hindustani and some learned practical skills such as sewing. They were all taught to sing, and drill.

The most important training was the study of the Bible, Old and New Testaments. The chaplain gave a Bible lesson three mornings each week, one morning was taken up with the history of the Old Testament, another with the Gospels, and another with the comparison of the Articles of the Church of England with the Bible. The women were expected to write out and submit their notes for correction.[12]

Blanche recalls one of the speakers at The Willows; "Mr Karney ... when speaking of the taking of Jericho, and comparing it to the Christian missionary warfare, impressed upon his hearers the importance of fives "S's": Silence, Sound, Surround, Shout, Self-surrender. The lesson drawn from the third "S" was that the Gospel was for every creature, and every part of the world must be surrounded by the soldiers of Christ.

"If this is true of the world as a whole, it is equally so of that small corner of it in which any one of the warriors of God may be stationed, and I want to show the readers of *India's Women* the efforts which have been put forth in the last ten years by CEZMS workers to surround the Fortress of Sin in Karachi - efforts which we are sure will in due time be repaid by the walls falling down flat, and the Kingdom of this world becoming the kingdoms of God and of His Christ."[13]

Blanche retained fond memories of The Willows and appreciated the preparation she had received there.

Farewell Meeting

On the 8th October 1885 Blanche attended the Annual CEZMS Farewell meeting held in the Mildmay Conference Hall, London, with a large gathering of sixteen outgoing missionaries and their praying friends who were there to wish them well on their departure. The missionaries were addressed individually and publicly given their instructions by the Society. One of these was Miss M T Condon an experienced missionary who was chosen to go to Karachi in India with Blanche. "You Miss Condon, after several years' service in our Normal School at Calcutta are now intrusted by the Committee with a solemn and responsible charge. They have long desired to place their work in Karachi upon a permanent and satisfactory basis, and, after much prayerful consideration, they have concluded that the best way to do this will be to appoint one of their senior missionaries to the station, and to associate with her such younger workers as the Mission may from time to time require."

Blanche and another new missionary were then addressed: "... Miss Carey and Miss Bloomer, are going to Sindh. Your stations will be Karachi and Hyderabad respectively, with which, by personal or family associations, you are already connected.

"The work at Karachi, you will find, has its special difficulties. Much consecration, discernment, wisdom, firmness, and zeal will be needed on your part, in order that our Mission there may rise to the occasion, and that the work which Mrs. Ball has, in the absence of a regular staff, so long kept together, may be greatly developed and expanded.

"The good Lord supply all your need!

"The Committee are confident that you, Miss Carey, will cordially co-operate with Miss Condon in taking up the work at Karachi, which has been already referred to in these Instructions.

"... We ask all to remember that the study of the language is the first year's business. It is most natural that an over-pressed missionary should desire to enlist at once the services of a junior colleague, and that the newly arrived sister should pine to get to work; but a missionary who has not mastered the language is like a workman who goes to his task without his tools ...

"Secondly. Do all you can to strengthen the unity of our body. Though you be in India, and we in England, you and we are one. Write often, freely, fully. Think of us, pray for us, trust us ... Look back often to your time there [Training Home], to the many blessings you received there, to the precious truths you learned there. Pray much for those in charge of it, and for the fourteen young sisters now preparing there for the Society's work in India, China or Japan. The American Missionary Review lately said of us: 'It has given us great pleasure to notice how personal and warm is the sympathy and love between the missionaries and the workers at home.' Be it ours to strengthen that sympathy by every means in our power, so that all may see that we 'stand fast in one spirit, in one mind striving together for the faith of the Gospel.'

"Thirdly. Cling ever fast and firm to the distinctive principles of our Society. Never be ashamed of the words 'Protestant' and 'Evangelical,' which are emblazoned on the very forefront of our Constitution. We live in difficult and dangerous days; both at home and abroad the tendency is to throw down landmarks, to rub out dividing lines, to mix together light and darkness, truth and error, to dilute the Gospel rather than to deny it or oppose it, and to blend in hopeless confusion the symbols of superstition and the shibboleths of truth. Be you clear, consistent, unmistakeable. See to it, beloved, that Evangelical doctrine be no mere shibboleth with you. Let your Protestantism be a witness against sacerdotal error, because it is a witness for scriptural truth revealed in your own souls by the indwelling of the Saviour, and worked out in your lives by the Holy Ghost ...

"Fourthly. Our last word of counsel is this: Cherish very watchfully the closet life. Let nothing, no pressure of work, no urgency of engagements, clash with the silent hour. Public means of grace are no substitute for private communion with God. Nothing can take its place. And let it be real communion, not one-sided, but complete; you speaking to God in the confidence of prayer, and listening for God to speak to you in the pages of His Word. This is the real remedy for that worldliness which is such a snare in many parts of India. A soul living in communion with God, and walking in the light of His countenance, will have no taste for worldly society. This, too, is the real secret of power. That, the overawing power of holiness is the 'open reward' of the 'secret life of prayer'.

"And now, beloved in the Lord, we bid you farewell. That your voyage may be prosperous, that your dear ones in sparing you may reap a rich reward, that you may be kept in full health of body, mind, and soul, is our fervent, constant prayer."[14]

Correspondence and Referees

Some of the correspondence in the Cadbury Research Library, Birmingham, England gives further insights into Blanche's character. Amongst the letters there is one written by Blanche's sister Ella on behalf of her mother who was concerned for her daughter. The letter raised some practical concerns to the Mission organisation regarding payment for Blanche and what would happen if Blanche fell ill in India and who would pay for the voyage home in such an instance. Her mother it seemed did not want to see her daughter Blanche leave.

21st November

My mother who is quite an invalid wishes me to write for her to ask you a few questions about the zenana mission of which you spoke to my sister when at Torquay last. Could you let her know the rules and regulations. Whether in case of health failing a free passage is given to England, & for how long one is bound to work without returning home – also whether the salary is sufficient for comfortable support.

My sister is again working under Miss Daniell at the Plymouth Soldiers Home, but having a wish to try zenana work, my mother is willing to withdraw her objections, provided she sees no insuperable obstacles in the way ... [15]

Two months later Blanche herself wrote to the Secretary, reporting that circumstances had now changed, and requesting another application form:

26th January

My dear Madam

A few weeks ago my sister returned you the papers respecting C of E Zenana society (which I had asked to see) as we found that there were two obstacles in the way which would quite have prevented my offering myself to the work. One was my mother's objection to my going to India and the other the cost of training. Both of these have since been removed, a friend has offered to send me as her substitute and my mother has quite given her consent to the plan.

I am writing now therefore to ask if I may have the papers again and to tell you that I am quite willing, if the society should be in need of workers, to offer myself as a Zenana missionary. Perhaps you would let me know what I ought to do about it. I hardly read the papers which we had then as I then thought it quite hopeless.

Believe me

sincerely yours,

Blanche Brenton Carey[16]

The letter written by Blanche's father to the CEZMS Committee as a referee gives testimony to his daughter's spiritual gifts and service.

Feb 11th 1884

Dear Sir ...

Both Mrs Carey and myself approve the step our daughter Blanche is taking in offering her services to the zenana mission in connection with the Church Missionary Society. God has given us a great blessing in this dear child to whom he has given a good measure of the grace of the Holy Spirit.

She has been a steady and successful worker in my parish for many years and has gained a great influence over many young women & young lads.

I am told by those who have heard her that she has a great gift in evangelistic addresses and the success at Miss Daniell's soldiers home at Plymouth has been very marked. This is shown by the letters of thanks she has received from soldiers acknowledging her as the means under God of leading them to a Saviour. One of her great characteristics is that she does not weary in well doing and never flinches under difficulties.

I am Dear Sir

Most truly yours

A F Carey[17]

However Rev. Allen wrote more cautiously about Blanche's abilities, wisely suggesting the need for her to have the oversight of more experienced colleagues at the outset:

15th February 1884

Dear Madam

I beg to say with reference to Miss Carey, that as far as I can judge I believe her to be a sincere Christian and one who both by conduct and conversation would I should think be likely to further the work of God. She has been a diligent helper in the Sunday school and has also undertaken the visiting of one of the districts in the parish and lately has been doing work among the soldiers at Plymouth.

Though personally I have been unable to judge of the results, yet I have reason to believe her work has been blessed in more than one instance – Yes I should certainly consider her of fair average ability and one who would do thoroughly the work entrusted to her; but I think she would do far more as a second than as the organiser of a new mission; such a feat would I presume be beset with many difficulties and while she has many valuable qualities which would prove of great service to the cause of missions, I think they would be brought out in co-operation with and under an experienced organiser, more fully than if the responsibility of organisation were placed upon her.

Believe me

Your very truly

S Allen [Rev][18]

Departure for India

Blanche boarded the SS Belgravia in Liverpool and set sail on her long journey to India to the province of Sindh stepping ashore in Karachi in November 1885.

New Beginnings - Karachi

The Climate and Geography of Karachi

"The Afghans say that the sun of Sindh will roast an egg and turn a white man black."[1] Blanche on her arrival in Karachi was faced with a very different climate from the one she had experienced in England. In fact many Western missionaries found the climate too harsh for their health and had to leave.

Karachi was situated in the region known as Sindh, at that time part of India. Its situation by the sea accounted for the diversity of its population: it was a city which contained many different nationalities and languages, and so the mission there was known as a polyglot mission. At the time Karachi had an excellent natural harbour, and was about twelve miles from the outlet of the river Indus. There were fine public buildings and dwellings in the suburbs, but the CEZMS mission was in the native part of the town, where the usual flat-roofed houses and narrow dirty streets were.[2] Blanche writes that there were six districts in the region of Sindh; Hyderabad, Karachi, Larkhana, Sukker, Thar and Parka, and Upper Sindh. As well as the oppressive weather conditions, the region of Sindh was recognised by experienced missionaries as a very hard place in which to share the Gospel.

Early Missionary Endeavours in Karachi

The missionary activity of the Church of England in Karachi dates back to 1850. Christian Officers in the British army, such as Captain Preedy, planned a mission to the Sindhi people. They established a school for boys at the commercial port of Karachi, and obtained from Calcutta the services of a converted Bengali Braham Modhu Suda Seal.

However these early endeavours were costly. The Rev. CCT Schreiber was sent out to Karachi in 1850, but within five months his wife had tragically died. He wrote home, "It is as if this mission, like the East African mission, has to be commenced on the grave of a missionary's wife".[3]

The CMS in those early days worked almost exclusively among men. However they found that their work in Karachi was greatly hindered by the lack of female missionaries to work amongst the women of Karachi. Part of the reason for this was the separation of married Indian women in the Zenana, keeping them from the outside world. This meant it was impossible for male missionaries to witness to them but women were allowed to visit them in the Zenana. So they wrote urgently to the Church of England Zenana Missionary Society (CEZMS) begging them to start a women's work in Karachi, so that these women could be reached by the gospel. Sometimes the Indian Christians themselves asked for help from the CEZMS (Appendix A).

The CEZMS Karachi mission was opened in 1880, but only a few years later the station was bereft of missionaries, owing to the marriages and the illnesses of those who had gone out to the city. The parent committee in 1885 decided to send out an experienced Irish lady Miss M Condon, who had been in charge of the Normal School in Calcutta, to take over the work in Karachi. She was accompanied by Blanche Carey and it was hoped that between the two of them they would stabilise the work which had seen so many changes during its early years. Their hopes were steadily realised as Miss Condon remained in charge for many years. Continuity was maintained as Blanche succeeded her, becoming known affectionately by the supporters of the CEZMS as 'our Miss Carey of Karachi'.

The Rev. J J Bambridge was a CMS missionary working in Karachi at the time Blanche arrived and his experience in the city provides an insight into the situation that Blanche would face. Bambridge observed that Karachi was a growing commercial city and therefore had become more prosperous, and because of this he felt the people were unwilling to accept the gospel message, "often the cares of the world and the deceitfulness of riches entering in choke the word and it becometh unfruitful." He went on to say, "... courage to confess Christ openly and boldly seems utterly wanting." The Hindu men seemed to listen attentively to the Word of God and they often admitted to the truth of Christianity but underneath the missionary could see that, "there is a fatal carelessness about their soul's salvation." After ten years experience in the mission field, he thought Karachi was an exceedingly difficult mission.[4]

Challenges facing the Mission Schools

Blanche's first impressions of the CEZMS Salt Gate school were recorded some twenty five years later; the school was in the heart of the city and to get to it she had to walk up a "dirty little lane". The door to the school was old and it creaked open as you went through. Blanche must have wondered what she would find, inside this uninviting entrance. She described the room as "a room of twelve by sixteen feet", there was a hole in the roof to let in the air and sunlight to the space below. Part of the room was taken up with water pots, with a blackboard and maps next to them. The pupils were arranged around a raised surface of twelve-feet square. In front of them there was a table at which the Hindu teacher sat. The teacher was advanced in years, and he wore a distinctive Sindhi hat which was red at the top, with stripes of red and green down the sides. He was clothed sensibly with loose fitting trousers, a white muslin skirt outside of them and a coat of striped cotton. There were ten children present on that occasion sitting around him; there were fifteen in total on the roll.

As she observed that first lesson Blanche was left wondering why there were so many girls at the school: "There are no games, no needlework, nothing to make grammar, geography, or sums pleasant; and the little girls bend over lists of names and places and shout them out, waving backwards and forwards as they commit them to memory." As soon as she had left, Blanche found out that the teacher took off his hat, put his legs up on the table and had a nap. Blanche groaned to see such a sight; there was so much for her to do.

However Blanche was encouraged to find that the children were bright and intelligent, and she longed for an educated Christian woman who could step in and take over the teaching of the school, for Blanche herself was not to serve in this capacity. It was not easy to find Christian teachers in Karachi; many of the more experienced workers in Karachi and in the region of Sindh thought it most unlikely if not impossible for them to find Christian teachers in the area to take on such a role. Miss M Condon had spent many years in Calcutta, a large Christian centre, where Christian teachers could be found, and even she felt bewildered with the challenge in Karachi. Miss M Condon would despairingly cry, "What can be done with no Christian fellow workers?" But she would then respond in faith and hope, "Never mind! If the Lord means us to do the work, He will send the workers." Blanche and Miss M Condon's only hope was to trust in the Lord through prayer for Him to supply the necessary Christian teachers.[5]

Finding teachers was not the only challenge for Blanche and Miss M Condon. There was also great difficulty in persuading the parents that the girls were worth educating. The parents could see the sense of educating boys but not girls; the girls could work and provide income for the family until they were married, often at a young age. Then there was the further complication of which language they would use to teach the children, would it be Sindhi, Gujarati*[1], Marathi, or Urdu? The pupils did not wish to be away from home for such extended periods and the length and breadth of the lessons was a

---

*[1] Gujarati is the contemporary spelling of the word, the missionaries at the time used the spelling Gujerati

puzzle to them, neither could their parents understand why they were gone for so long. The parents often saw the need to learn to read and write but modelling, playing with mud, was much below their dignity and games and object lessons were simply a waste of time. If these were not enough obstacles, there was also the divisions in caste between the pupils, and the pupils and their teachers. Pupils couldn't use sand and water unless the water was from their own homes, it must not be touched by any child of lower caste, even the Christian teacher must not demonstrate how a thing was to be made if she expected the children to touch the sand tray afterwards.

To give an idea of how the caste system affected the development of the children, a brief article entitled the 'iron chain of caste' appeared in the *India's Women and China's Daughters* CEZMS magazine of October 1901: "The two-fold hard bondage of Caste and Custom is wearing out the women of India with cruel servitude. We have known the people of a village watch a poor little child of three gradually sinking in a muddy pool, without stretching out a hand to save her, because their caste did not permit them to touch her, and had not a Christian man been at hand to rescue her, she would have been drowned before their eyes. We have also seen a poor little low-caste baby left out in the blazing sun, because the mother was not at hand to lift her into the shade, and no one else would lay a finger on her." These two illustrations are not used to show that the women of India didn't care they were just as able to show such kindness as others - but the caste system prevented them from acting on their compassion.[6]

There was a pressing need to expand the opportunities to educate the girls of Karachi, as there was only one other Sindhi school open at this time in the city. Miss Condon would lament the opportunities available to the girls for their education, "The Men have advanced with the age, for they have all the advantages of good schools, those of the C.M.S. more especially, where the Word of God is taught, and the moral standard of the young man raised. There has been no similar effort amongst the women, who consequently remain in all their primitive ignorance and superstition, bound firmly as ever with the iron chain of Caste ..."[7]

So these were some of the challenges that Miss M Condon and Blanche faced when they arrived in Karachi, but they believed in a God who answered prayer and so they prayed, for they knew that if their Heavenly Father desired them to do such a work in Karachi He would supply the means.

Learning the Language

Upon her arrival Blanche gave all her time to the study of the Sindhi language and the supervision of the Sindhi girls' school in the Kharo Dar quarter of town, which was in danger of closing. Learning the Sindhi language was made more difficult because she found limited opportunities to practise the language outside of the zenanas she was to visit. This was because Urdu was the commonly used language for commerce and conversation in the streets of Karachi. Therefore Blanche didn't hear Sindhi spoken that often during the course of normal life. But despite this obstacle Blanche made good progress in learning Sindhi.

Blanche visited the little Sindhi school week by week and with the 'Wordless Book' in hand would give a gospel message. She reported that, "The fact that there was a Madam Sahiba who could love and smile at them, even if their loudest shouts could not make her understand, soon made the school more popular". Blanche was proudly taken to the homes of these little pupils and as the language was acquired lasting friendships were formed.

The 'Wordless Book' was introduced by C H Spurgeon in 1866 and was designed with only 3 pages black, red and white. Spurgeon told of an old unnamed minister who had put three pages together to remind himself of his sinfulness (represented by the black page), of Christ's blood shed for him (a red page) and of his cleansing from sin (a white page). It became a very popular book used around the world to explain God's plan of salvation. The 'Wordless' book and picture illustrations were very useful for the missionaries to help them explain the gospel to the women and girls. Blanche would often request the readers of *India's Women and China's Daughters* to supply additional picture illustrations to help them explain gospel stories.

As soon as Blanche had passed her first language exam and could make herself understood, she started to visit the mothers of the school children, and was warmly welcomed: "They 'wished to be my companions and friends'; 'would I not come every day?' It was the desire of their hearts that I should.'"

Some of the boys helped Blanche with the language. Many of the men who had been educated in the CMS Schools were quite willing to send their girls to the CEZMS schools or let them read the Bible to their families. Blanche recalled that in one house to which she was invited a teenage boy came forward saying in English, "'We are so glad you have come to teach our women; they want you to tell them about Jesus Christ.' And he was quite impatient when I began to speak of Adam and Eve and the fall, saying again, 'Won't you tell them of Jesus Christ?'"

One of the women she visited whom Blanche described as "bright and clever", invited her friends every week and they would attentively sit on mats before Blanche's feet as she told them the, "good tidings of peace by Jesus Christ." In many of the homes Blanche visited she would get a gathering of between three to ten women, plus numerous children, and two or three men.

21

Blanche didn't observe many idols in the homes. As Karachi was a port the sea was very important to them and they saw it as very powerful, more powerful than they were and so this most of all seemed to be the object of their worship. One woman said, "If friends go to Bombay offerings must be given to the sea for a safe voyage. If a child is born, something must be thrown into the sea for a thank-offering". In response to this Blanche would tell them the story of Jesus stilling the storm over the sea of Galilee. Blanche found that this illustration was useful to show that the sea had no power of its own, but was only subservient to God's command.

Blanche soon learned the art of telling a Bible story which related to the peoples thoughts and native customs: "One of my women meeting me in a relation's house, said, 'Read her about the sea being God's servant, and obeying His Son's word. Then turning to the woman of the house, she added, 'The Madam Sahiba says that when she came across the water her relations did not pray to the sea, or give it presents, but they asked God to keep it quiet, and He did.'"

One of the most popular stories the women liked to hear was the gospel story of the prodigal son. Blanche was often asked to read it to them: "read about the bad son", they would say and when she got to the words "was dead and is alive again, was lost and is found," the women often repeated the words after her. One woman said, "That is a true word! If a son is ever so bad, there will always be love for him in his parent's heart." The women were also interested in hearing how the Lord is going to come again, while another popular story was the healing of Peter's mother-in-law.

Not all the women were attentive though; some were curious about these white Europeans, "'Why do you wear those pins in your hair? Would it fall down if you did not? Why don't you put oil on your head?' or, 'Did you make that dress yourself ... how much did it cost?'". Blanche described another encounter: "The other day a woman begged me to give her some medicine to make her face white, and would hardly believe that I had not used something to change the colour of mine!" Such responses to white missionaries was not unique to the local community in Karachi, Amy Carmichael experienced similar questions and distractions in Southern India.

Blanche would leave suitable gospel tracts with the women. As most of them could not read, the tracts were left for the husbands with a respectful request for him to read it for himself and then read it to his family. Blanche would look for English tracts that were good and easy to understand, but they were hard to find.[9]

General Haig, the chairman of the CEZMS, commented: "The most encouraging part of the work appears to be Miss Carey's visiting to the women from house to house. She has made good progress in Sindhi, and is heartily welcomed to as many houses as she is able to visit ... They are glad to have her simply to read and explain to them the Word of God."[8]

The Bible seemed to come more alive to Blanche as she served amongst the people in Karachi, she explained, "I think I never understood the Bible so well before; these customs seem so like those of Bible lands. The husbands sometimes tell us how their wives worry them for jewels, and many are in debt because they cannot say 'No.' I try to show them how much better it would be to wear God's jewels."[10]

The Work starts to Grow

So in spite of all the difficulties and distractions, the work in Karachi began to grow and thrive. "Marvellously helped" was Blanche's motto, wrote Miss Condon, as they were very thankful to God for answering their prayers. The work had made steady progress in that first year in Karachi, and was now expanding and developing to such an extent that it could truly be considered as established. Miss Condon and Blanche were able to recruit five Christian workers, which although they felt was not sufficient to cover all that was needed to be done was still a great encouragement to them. They saw this answer to prayer as a sign of great things to come, and Miss Condon wrote that she believed God has "much people in this city." They believed that now the gospel was an open door to the women and girls, they would see great inroads in to the city for their Lord. The visiting of the women and children of the city was purely evangelistic in intent, and Miss Condon and Blanche took every opportunity, despite the alternative motives of some of the local fathers and husbands: the men of the house allowed the missionaries in to speak to their families, not necessarily to accept Jesus as their Saviour but to experience something of the European customs.[11]

Blanche happily writes about what God had done in bringing a small band of Christian women teachers together in Karachi which many thought unlikely: "Writing last year, a few months after our arrival, we could only tell of the 'impossibility' of finding Christian helpers for any branch of the work. I often wish that those who have been remembering this want in prayer for us at home could take a peep into our drawing-room on a Friday afternoon. They would see a little band of workers gathered together to study God's Word with us, while in turn we spread the needs of the coming week before Him, and ask for blessing on the seed already sown ... 'the things which are impossible with men are possible with God.'"[12] Blanche and Miss M Condon saw the great need for themselves and the team of workers to study the Word of God and to pray together so that they might appreciate their utter dependence on God for the gospel to take effect on the people of Karachi.

So the Lord provided the personnel that Blanche and Miss Condon so desperately needed, Christian women who were willing and able to teach and could help them to establish schools in the many different languages spoken in Karachi. Their CMS colleagues thought it was most unlikely that they would find such help in Karachi. However although discouraged Miss Condon trusted that God would provide if this was His purpose and indeed the Lord supplied this need in remarkable ways. Blanche writes, "A casual visit to a next-door neighbour revealed the fact that she had a sister working in Surat who greatly desired to live with her, but would not come unless she could find some Christian work to do. Here was an assistant missionary, knowing Gujerati, sent direct from God."[5]

This lady was Mrs. O'Connor, a young Anglo-Indian widow who came back to Karachi to live with her sister in law and to work alongside Miss Condon and Blanche in May 1886. She worked with Miss M Condon in the Gujarati school which was opened in 1886 and became the superintendent of the school which later changed its name to the Condon school in honour of Miss Condon. Mrs. O'Connor also threw herself heart and soul in to the zenana work and would visit the city every day. A work had started with the mothers of Ranchor Lines and Swami Gari Khata, and Mrs. O'Connor was loved by the girls, the teachers, and by those whom she visited. She had the pleasure and joy of knowing some come to know Jesus as their Saviour.

Mrs. O'Connor wrote of the impact of the Gospel on the women: "It is pleasant, and a matter of thankfulness to know that the women ... who have learned here about Christ, and say how they think and speak of Him to their friends and relations. If they are asked if they have forgotten what they have been taught, they reply indignantly, 'How can I ever forget Jesus and all that He has done for me? I always take the Name of Jesus the first thing in the morning and at night before I go to sleep.'"

One said, "My mother-in-law was so pleased with the books you sent her; if any one comes to see her who is able to read, she makes them read them to her. She had given up idols, and believes only in Christ, but when she tells others to do likewise they laugh at her and say she is mad."[13]

When the missionaries perceived the need to help the women of Sindh develop and give to them educational opportunities their mothers never had, they acted upon it. At the same time at the core of the education of the girls was the Word of God which was taught every day. The gospel was presented to the very young who would take it back to their homes, repeating verses either in scripture or in song and then when the mothers or carers were visited by the missionaries they were able to follow up with gospel conversations.

Whilst the missionaries looked for a Sindhi-speaking Christian teacher, the old Hindu teacher continued at the CEZMS Sindhi school, and Blanche was able to share the gospel with the children despite the teacher's steady opposition. The number of pupils had increased in the school to thirty five, and the homes of the children were visited. The missionaries continued to pray that God would provide a teacher. In 1889 their prayers were answered as an Indian woman named Minna Ghose, who was the daughter of the late Rev. S Ghose, an Indian CMS pastor of Karachi came to help. Minna was highly educated at the Alexandra school in Amritsar, and she had the advantage of gaining much valued experience by working for a short time with Miss Tucker (ALOE - A Lady of England) of Batala. Minna Ghose heard that there was a need for workers in her own home town, and she decided to return to Karachi. Minna soon became proficient in Sindhi and began to work alongside Blanche at the Salt Gate School with the Sindhi girls. At first there was an apprehension at this appointment amongst the Sindhi parents and children because this was quite different from what they had previously known, but this apprehension was quickly replaced with trust and love, such was the character of the missionary women.[5] Minna soon became a most valuable asset to the mission, and when the orphanage was founded it was Minna who took charge. She eventually became a full CEZMS missionary in 1917.

Around the same time as Minna Ghose started, Miss Green and Miss Lizzie Green who lived with their parents in Karachi, came to join the mission work. So gradually Gujarati-speaking Christian teachers were found, and in a comparatively short time a second Gujarati school was opened in 1888. Then there followed the opening of a Marathi school, and by 1889 there were nearly two hundred girls being taught by the mission.

The Work Moves On (1889-90)

The Mission was reinforced by Alice Dawson from Yorkshire who worked in Karachi until 1900. Alice studied the Sindhi language, and it was through her energy and interest that a second Sindhi school was opened in another quarter of the town, Mitho Dar.

The missionaries continued to go from house to house: Alice Dawson visited the women in the Sindhi city, and Miss Green visited a large number of houses and found ready listeners even among Brahmins. Blanche wrote, "I am sometimes really pulled into houses, with the cry, 'Come and tell us of Jesus Christ. You teach others; why not us? Is it because we are poor?'"[14]

"In the Sindhi school there is a class of 58 infants between 3 and 7, of whom Miss Dawson says, 'they quite unconsciously prepare the way for us in the homes, even teaching the Hymns learnt at school to mothers and sisters.'"[15]

Alice described a visit to a zenana as "not like visiting at home". She had to learn not to be distracted or put off by the sights and the smells, and she must be patient and not to be seen as in a hurry. Alice would sit cross legged on a bit of wood lying on the floor, and "without appearing to object to an army of black ants marching round" read and sing. Alice would also learn to handle a baby covered in oil, either clothed or naked. Sometimes there was a large fire in the eight feet square room for cooking which was painful on the eyes. On one occasion Alice visited a woman who was little more than a child herself with a baby. The girl took great care of the baby and Alice was called aunt. The young Indian woman was attentive to the scriptures, and asked, "when my son is able to understand, will you teach him of Jesus? I do not wish him to learn to worship idols?"[16]

Alice vividly comments on the experience of walking the streets in Karachi, the sights, sounds and smells: "It needs a little care to walk in our narrow lanes with any comfort. Cows block up the way, or a big dog barks furiously from a doorway; dozens of carts crawl lazily along; little children are having their morning tub in the open-air; -worse than all, the good ladies of Karachi have not yet learnt the use of drains, but empty refuse into the streets, and it may happen- as it has done to me -that a quantity of black water is thrown over you, making you a funny object for the rest of the morning."[17] To the dismay of all Alice Dawson had to leave Karachi for medical reasons and went to Abbottabad in 1900. The little girls missed her, for they loved their "laughing madam."[18]

Many children who had come to know Jesus died in those early years of the mission, children who had truly accepted Him and confessed Him in their homes. "Do not cry Mother," said one of these, young believers, "I am going to be with Yisu Masih [Jesus the Messiah] and I am so happy."[19]

More Schools More Workers (1891-93)

By 1891 there were four schools, fourteen Christian helpers working in four languages with four home visitors. There were 255 children being taught, 121 in two Gujarati schools, 80 in the Sindhi School and 54 in the Marathi School. The work went from strength to strength and in 1892 the number of pupils rose to 425 children in five schools with a third Gujarati school opened in the Sudder Bazaar. An additional assistant missionary joined to superintend the Christian teacher and also to visit folk from house to house. After six and a half years' work Blanche returned home on furlough for a well-earned rest.

The efforts of the missionaries were earning the trust of the population as thirty native men approached the mission for a school to be opened for their daughters, and an Indian merchant had promised to build two large upper rooms in a more central location.[15]

New recruits continued to join the mission, including Emily Amelia Prance from Plymouth in 1893. She learnt Gujarati as her language and superintended a school and visited in the Gujarati zenanas. Accommodating the increasing number of workers continued to be a real challenge and we read in the CEZMS Annual Report for 1894 that a house for the staff had been found in a better location as regards to health, but not quite as convenient for the work locations.

Still the number of schools being opened increased: in 1895 an additional Sindhi school was opened with a young Bengali Christian teacher overseeing the work. In the Trans Lyari quarter in 1900 a Muslim Sindhi school was started, and then a Marathi school for low caste children was opened. The CEZMS ladies started to work amongst the Makranis, who were a low caste tribe living in straw huts on the sand in Karachi. One of the schools established was for the Makrani girls. A quarter of the people of Karachi lived in this location across the Lyari river. The work continued to expand when in 1905 a school for children to learn English was begun. This made nine schools, with 650 students. The head teachers were Christian, with some non Christian assistant teachers helping them who would also hear the gospel being taught.

So after much uncertainty the mission at Karachi became a going concern full of energy, and potential, led by missionaries whose trust in a prayer-answering God had been signally honoured by the gift of faithful and whole hearted fellow workers.

Miss M Condon and Blanche were together for approximately nine years, during which time the schools multiplied and a great deal of work was undertaken. As an Indian man exclaimed, "the whole city is waiting for your visits." To the Society's supporters the names Karachi and Miss Brenton Carey became almost synonymous.

The Lord had provided the workers and missionaries who were able to educate hundreds of girls in their many native languages. The buildings also had been acquired to house the schools in many quarters of the city which allowed the girls to travel to a local school. A constant supply of materials and equipment had to be procured to enable the teachers to provide lessons to the girls, and the mission station requested many items from the readers of *India's Women and China's Daughters*. This advert from 1911 is typical: "Miss Brenton Carey would be grateful for India rubbers, pencils, foot rulers, drawing books, ruled notebooks, any kind of kindergarten materials, map of the world, map of England, wooden knitting needles, wool sewing needles, scissors, blunt penny ones being useful for paper cutting. 600 children need to be kept supplied."[20]
As the organisation increased so did the monthly expenses and funds were

required to meet these demands. The workers would attend sales to sell work, either gifts from overseas or from the ladies of the station. Their local funds entirely supported their schools.

Even with many potential distractions Blanche continued to prioritise the time set aside to teach the Bible to the pupils in the schools. This approach was strongly vindicated in spite of the fact that some of the girls' parents had threatened to withdraw their children from the schools. Despite this opposition Blanche stuck to what she knew was right, being convinced that the most important thing the girls could be taught was the Word of God.

The Prize Giving day for the girls was one of the highlights of the year and became a regular event in the calendar. Blanche recalls an early occasion: "On the 11th of January our prize-giving took place at our house. The Gugerathi (sic) girls, who are close by, were able to walk; but my Sindhi children were obliged to have carriages, which added much to the delight. The two schools filled our dining-room, where they sat in rows - Sindhis on one side and Gugerathis on the other- and were a pretty sight, with their different coloured potis [unsure meaning perhaps little books or scrolls?]. The Gugerathi girls sang a hymn very nicely, and every one was pleased with the polite way in which each child marched up to receive her prize, putting her hand to her forehead with a 'Madam Sahiba salaam,' by way of 'thank you.' I wish those who sent the many presents could have seen what pleasure they gave, especially the beads! I have been beset by requests for 'beads' ever since; and I have heard the children inviting their little companions to school with the assurance, 'You'll get beads if you go there!''.[12]

Blanche struggled to fit everything into her busy schedule and often lamented what she couldn't do: "Often I am beckoned into houses as I pass along the streets, but I am obliged to refuse because I have no time. The Lord has set before us an open door.

No Longer a Second

The work in Karachi received a setback when the experienced Mission station leader Miss M Condon's health was adversely affected by the climate in Karachi. By 1894 she was obliged to seek a better environment and moved to Abbottabad. Blanche stepped into her shoes as station leader - an even more daunting responsibility since the organisation in Karachi had expanded. One of Blanche's first tasks was to use her language skills to learn Gujarati, "that I may properly take up her work, a necessity which is also a great pleasure."[1]

Blanche knew that she could do nothing without the Lord's power and was dependent on approaching her Lord in prayer. She requested the *India's Women* readers back at home to pray; "we need your prayers as much as ever ... Pray for power from on High to endue us and fit us for our work. Pray, too, that those to whom we carry the message may be convinced of sin."[1]

There were now numerous workers at the mission station in Karachi whom Blanche managed and cared for. Many of them had first to learn the languages which would enable them to visit the women of the local communities near the schools and help them run the schools. The departments of work of the mission were organised by language: Gujarati, Urdu, Sindhi, and Arabic, and split between Blanche, Alice Dawson, Emily Prance, and Edith Brenton Carey (Blanche's niece, who joined in 1894). The five assistants were Mrs O'Connor, Mrs Ghose, Miss Green, Honor Troyal, and Miss Brooks. In addition there were nine teachers who made up the rest of the staff, including Minna Ghose, and Miss Bose. By 1895 there were seventeen CEZMS workers in Karachi.

Blanche's ongoing strategy was to ask her fellow CEZMS missionaries to superintend a school and then visit the homes of the children of these various schools, to befriend these women and to talk to them about Jesus. The Head Teacher appointed to the school would be a Christian.[2]

As leader of the mission Blanche saw growth in the number of schools and in the number of pupils but she also saw growth in the influence of the gospel in people's lives. After ten years' work a woman said to her, "At first we used to hear a little about Jesus Christ, but now his name is noised all over the city and everyone is talking of him; some say what you teach is true and some say it is false but all speak of it."[3]

By 1895 the old Sindhi School which had started with only fifteen pupils had grown to 130 students on the roll, with an average attendance of 110. Minna Ghose had been in charge of the school for nearly seven years, the school had two teachers, and two pupil teachers under her. Miss Green visited the local community near the school. However this work also suffered a great loss when Helen Wredden who was learning Sindhi and preparing to visit in the city died. Her place was taken by Miss Brooks.

In the Ranchor Lines School Mrs O'Connor endeavoured to teach the children and the mothers the one way of salvation. She had the joy of one Brahmin woman expressing a desire for baptism, and another a Beni Israel wife wanted to follow Christ. The Beni Israel in India were a community of native Jews also known by the name Shanvar Telis. It was believed that they had arrived from Arabia and adopted the language and clothing of the local inhabitants. A number then settled in Sindh; a large enough community to have had a synagogue in Karachi. Many of them could read Hebrew, although not many could understand it. They did not seem to be very knowledgeable about the scriptures but the women were happy to read the Old and New Testaments. They liked the hymns which was useful as there were many Marathi hymns. As these Jews assimilated the local customs their rituals became a mixture of indigenous and scriptural traditions. One of the Beni Israel girls who lived near the Karachi mission house and was educated by the missionaries declared herself to be a Christian, resulting in much opposition, but she continued to love and trust Jesus which helped her to overcome these trials.

The Joria Bazaar School was being taken care of by Emily Prance. Emily started to visit the mothers of the pupils every Thursday to pass on to them the message of the gospel. She was often told by the mothers that they knew a verse or hymn she had mentioned because their child had told them when they returned from school. Sometimes this came from the mothers of the children whom she thought were either too young or not concentrating during the lessons. This was a great encouragement to her.

After an earlier visit to her home, Emily returned to the school to find that while she was away the work had stopped because of the plague. She was happy to be back at the school but her return was tinged with sadness as she asked after some of the students, "Where is Gunga? Where is Monji?", and to receive the answer, "She is dead, Mem Sahiba!" This became a familiar story as she visited the houses, all had a tragic story to recount.[4] In 1898 Emily had to return home again under the advice of the doctor, but she was missed by the pupils. One pupil sympathetically remarked "She was so thin and so pale, it is good she has gone." Emily recovered while on furlough to return to Karachi in 1899.[5]

In Sindh the women found it difficult to come out publicly and take the step of baptism, and so the mission saw only a few women baptised, but some were. In the 1895 Annual Report we read, "two girls were baptised, who may thankfully be regarded as the first fruits of many who would, if they could, follow their example. One of such was 'Little Gomi' ... to whose last hours an aunt bore this testimony:- 'When Gomi was dying, her face was very bright. She looked so happy! just as though someone had come to call her to her father's house.' It is added- 'No one who does not know the joy with which the little daughters-in-law welcome a call to go home on a visit can fully understand all that this meant.'"

The struggles that missionaries had to penetrate the barriers of false religion and native culture were widely acknowledged. The Rev. E P Rice from the London Missionary Society in Bangalore, speaking at the 1900 Student Missionary Conference, explained that the Indian people trusted their own religion and customs to meet their heartfelt needs and had no desire for what they perceived as a 'foreign' religion. He said, "They will always listen courteously to what we say, and this constitutes an open door for the Gospel, but of conscious need and hungering for the Gospel there is little or none". He went on to point out that when someone deserts their caste, its customs and the traditional worship, the community becomes hostile and intent on stopping that person from their course of action. They "defend the vested rights of Hinduism." It was very difficult for the people to leave family, friends, neighbours and community. Amy Carmichael gives examples of individuals who would take a great interest in the gospel and wish to become a Christian but when she later went to visit that person they had disappeared and had been transferred to a different part of the country. Amy even tried to track people down but found they had been moved from one place to another.[6]

Blanche's niece Edith arrived in the autumn 1894 in order to take on Alice Dawson's work when she went on furlough the following spring. While in England Alice Dawson spoke about her experience at the CEZMS annual meeting: "Missionary work is very real; it is not excitement; it is hard work, too, there is no doubt about it. You have heard this afternoon what the climate of Sindh is like, but there is one thing I want all, and especially those who are going out as missionaries, to believe, that missionary work in the foreign field is very much the same as at home. The same love that surrounds you here knows how to enfold the missionary in the everlasting Arms, the same love knows how to cover and conceal much that would be repugnant to the feeling of an English lady, and the same love which speaks to your hearts and mine knows how to attract women in Zenanas and children in schools ...

"Little girls are free to come and go until they are eight years of age, so we are able to get them into our schools, where they receive a good elementary education. The schools are inspected every year by the Educational Inspector, and once a year in religious subjects. Last year we had the great pleasure of having the Bishop of Lahore, and he gave as his opinion that he had examined many schools in England and from none had he received clearer answers than from ours ...

"Every child that enters our schools in Karachi first learns the text, 'God so loved the world that He gave His only Begotten Son,' &c., and that text is taken into the houses, and not only taken into the houses, but has even been repeated to men in the streets. I came across a child standing in front of her father's shop. She was quietly repeating the text to him. He asked me the question, 'Who is this Son of God Who came into the world?' And though it was only a few minutes I had to spare, I was able to tell him something of God's love.

"Then they open the doors for us into the homes, bringing invitations to us to go and visit their parents. My senior missionary, Miss Carey, was visiting a village about eighteen miles from Karachi; it was the first time she had been there, and she was wondering where she should go, when a woman said to her, 'Will you come into my house? I have a little child who has been singing a hymn to me, but we cannot understand it. She can only sing the first verse.' Going into the house the heartiest welcome was accorded by a little child who was in the Mission school for two months. The hymn was, 'Jesus loves me, this I know,' and the question was asked, 'Who is this Jesus?' and Miss Carey was free to go and come into the house during the fortnight she was in the village.'"7

With all the responsibilities that Blanche now had and everything that she had to do, she continued to go out to visit and spread the gospel to the women, taking with her Sindhi, Gujarati, and Hindustani Bibles. She commented, "as these are not published in pocket editions, but are more the size of big dictionaries; the missionary book-bag presents a funny appearance!"8

Blanche compared the work in Sindh to walking around the walls of Jericho; "Thus we have been marching round the fortress during the year; sometimes cheered by seeing signs of loose stones and tottering parapets; and sometimes tempted to despair as we look at the massive thickness and strength of those mighty walls; and stirred to fresh prayer and effort by the assurance, 'The Lord hath given you the city,' and the command 'Begin to possess.' May God keep us all looking not on our own armour or weapons, but on the mighty power of our Jehovah Jesus, and surely we shall be able to put on record, 'There was not a city too strong for us.'"[8]

By March 1896, after ten years of work, there were three Gujarati schools, two Arabic Sindhi schools and one Marathi school with 497 names on their books. The houses receiving a weekly visit now numbered 165. The Marathi school replaced the one which had to close at the end of 1893 because of the teacher's marriage. Blanche describes the Marathi children as, "Punctual, clean, and tidy, carrying their own slates and books, the little ones have come pouring in, until our roll has reached sixty. Many of them are Beni-Israel, some Brahmins, and the rest other castes of Hindus."[9]

Alongside the encouragements and growth of the educational work there were discouragements and tragedies. The year 1896 saw the heartbreaking death of Miss Compton. Miss Compton had gone to Hyderabad in 1887 to begin a medical work for the CEZMS, and a dispensary had been opened. While she was on a short holiday to Quetta, Miss Compton and Edith Brenton Carey went for a drive; the horse took fright and bolted, upsetting the cart against a brick structure. Edith was only slightly injured but Miss Compton was knocked unconscious and she passed away into the presence of her Lord.[10] Alice Dawson remarked a year later on Miss Compton's death, "that a Mohammedan gentlemen described her as 'a saint of God, a ministering angel.'"[10] Thankfully Edith Brenton Carey made a full recovery from her injury and was able to return to the mission station in Karachi.[11]

Follower of Jesus and Becoming English

The Sudder School was near the Zenana Mission House and Honor Troyal who visited the local community found a loving welcome in the many houses nearby. But sadly many of the women were under the misapprehension that to become a Christian one had to adopt English customs. To separate the cultural and religious differences at the time of British Colonialism in India was going to be hard work for the western missionaries. One Indian visitor to England gave this view of the English, "in India, we see only one of the sides of the Englishman, and that is the official side - a stiff and unlovely side it is too. An Englishman, when he sets his foot on a foreign land, suddenly becomes conscious of the fact that he is an Englishman, and at once makes up his mind to stand on the dignity of his race."[12]

In an article entitled 'The English in India', from the Zenana newsletter of May 1906, we read "The history of the British Empire in India has, doubtless, been marked by many errors and blunders, and sometimes also by deeds that make us blush for shame. It would not be a human Empire if it were not so."

The CEZMS recognised that the Empire had behaved shamefully at times but from a contemporary perspective, as we look back on some of the atrocities which the British committed in India, we might regard this acknowledgment as inadequate. Despite the fact that many evangelicals at the time were quick to highlight to the British government when they saw injustices in other countries that were part of Empire, there was a danger that some missionaries thought there was a close relationship between Christianity and the British way of life. Some assumed that Britain in the nineteenth century "constituted a model of Christian culture and society", because they believed that Britain had been brought out of paganism and idolatry by the Word of God through the Protestant Reformation. They attributed Britain's prosperous and powerful position to its Christian roots. Thus many thought Britain was the "archetypal" Christian nation, and they let others know it. It was not a surprise then that some of the Indian people thought they had to become English to be a Christian. This was a tragic misrepresentation of the gospel.[13]

Although some made this mistake, it is good to read that the missionaries in Karachi knew that becoming a Christian was nothing to do with becoming British:- all were sinners whether European or Indian and all needed to hear the good news of Jesus, and receive the Saviour as their own. Nevertheless, the missionaries were products of their time and grew up in the Empire, and many had relatives in the armed forces.

Plague

Plague was a constant threat to the inhabitants of Karachi. Many children and parents succumbed to the disease. The schools would close and the people would isolate or go into segregation camps located on the outskirts of Karachi. The loss of life, the loss of friendships built over time and the loss of pupils whom they had taught and had come to love, took a toll on the emotions of the teachers. The plague was devastating to the whole community.

We get an idea of the effect the plague had on the people of Karachi from the Rev A E Ball's letter from Karachi dated January 25th 1898: "The first case of the plague occurred on December 10th 1896, and in spite of all the efforts of the Government and Municipality, the scourge was with us nearly seven months. Out of 4167 reported cases (and many cases were not reported) 3387 died ... A perfect panic seized upon the people in the city, and whole streets and Bazaars were left empty. It was almost like a city of the dead, nearly all work stopped, schools closed for months ..."[14]

Edith Brenton Carey wrote: "A short time after the plague broke out in Karachi, many of the families I had been visiting during Miss Dawson's absence, flying from the infected quarter of the city, came to live in a part of

Karachi not more than a quarter of an hour's drive from the Zenana Mission House. We very soon began to call the Terrace, where our friends lived, 'the Sindhi colony'."[15]

Though the missionaries and workers were comparatively safe themselves each day brought news of the death of a relative or friend living in the old town. Edith continued, "As we visited them we could not help noticing that they were beginning to lose courage, and we longed to cheer them and help them to keep a good heart through it all."

"Speaking of this to a friend one day, she said, 'I have been longing to give a little treat to the children of your school.' We talked it all over, and finally a delightful treat was planned for all the Sindhi women and children living in the 'Sindhi Colony,' which was not far from our friend's house.

"The party was to assemble at her house at 4:30 p.m., so Miss Ghose and I started at 1:30 to 'call' them and tell them that it was time to come. It was only three minutes' walk, but it took three hours' labour to get all our friends safely to the house ... There were fifteen women and thirty-five children altogether, not counting babies. The first part of the entertainment was that they should wander all over the house and see everything. This they thoroughly enjoyed. Then we all assembled in the dining-room, where native sweets and English crackers were distributed. The children, of course, quite enjoyed the fun ... a conjurer performed some wonderful tricks; and then came the crowning point of the evening. By the time the conjurer had finished his performance it was dark enough to see the magic-lantern pictures on the sheet behind. This was something quite new to all but a few of the younger children who had seen a magic-lantern in the boys' school ...

"The last four pictures were special ones. Two were from *The Pilgrim's Progress* – Christian with the bundle on his back, and the bundle in the act of falling off. The elder girls, of course, knew the story almost by heart, and were delighted to watch the picture on the sheet as Mr. Sinker (C.M.S. missionary) spoke to them about it. Then we had a Sindhi hymn and two more pictures - one of the Good Shepherd looking for the sheep who had got caught amongst the thorns. After a few more words on the picture the happy evening was closed with prayer that the Old, Old Story they had heard so often might come to them with new power and that they might believe on the Lord Jesus Christ and be saved.

"It is four months ago that that happy party gathered together. Since then we have been surrounded by death and sorrow on every hand; but one bright spot stands out prominently. Though it made our hearts ache and brought the hot, burning tears to our eyes, yet we can and do rejoice that the Good Shepherd has gathered one of these little lambs who was present that evening into His loving arms and has bid her rest."[15]

Blanche went to help in the segregation camps of the plague stricken city, where they were reaching people they had never spoken to before. When the women were first led to one of the segregation camps, the people feared them because they mistook them to be doctors or Government officials whom they dreaded for many unfounded reasons. Once the peoples' fears were allayed many of them were ready to hear their message.[15]

Blanche wrote, "In December the plague was increasing so much in the lower part of the city that our two Sindh schools had to be closed. Then it broke out in the Joria Bazaar, and Emily Prance felt it would be no longer right to gather the children together, although she was still able to visit, until the rush from the place had left nothing but empty houses and deserted streets. Next the Sudder and Ranchor Lines schools had to go, and last of all the Marathi School was closed by Government order, as cases had occurred close to where it was held. Most of the people we visited regularly had also fled, and many days were spent in wandering about empty streets looking for work.

"However, God had His own plan for us, and early in March He led us to one of the segregation camps, where He had prepared ready listeners ... whenever a case of plague occurred, all the members of the household, and others likely to be affected, were sent to live in huts built for the purpose, until all danger was over. In some cases whole communities were sent away from infected quarters and not allowed to return until the city should be free from sickness and well disinfected. Thus a large camp was formed in a wide plain on the other side of the Lyari River by the Nassapuri community, who filled about five hundred huts ...

"it did not take long to get an entrance into one of the small huts there. Seated on a mat, we were soon surrounded by a crowd of women and able to tell our errand. The Message was received as very new and wonderful. One woman clapped her hands together and said, 'What! you have a peace in your heart and you have come all this way to tell us about it! How kind you have been to us.' Then came the story of their troubles, and it was sad to look round the hut as T--pointed to one and another: 'This woman has lost her husband and two sons; this one has lost her husband, and her brain has been turned ever since; this woman had a dear daughter; she has cried day and night since her death - only to-day she is smiling for the first time, and that is because you have given her comfort.'"[16]

Blanche continued, "Since that day the Nassapuri camp has had the larger share of our attention; Miss Green, Miss Brooks, my niece and I have visited there constantly. Miss Ghose has started a little school in one of the huts, and is supremely happy to be once more surrounded by Sindhi girls ...

"Mrs. O'Connor has done what she could among Gujerati-speaking people - very few of whom have fled to their own country; and Miss Troyal and Miss Bose have given their time to the training and teaching of their pupil-teachers, so as to fit them for work among the little ones when our school re-opens.

"My niece and I have also been taking it in turn to give six hours' help daily in the Plague Hospital, and have found the work most interesting and happy; and although there has not been the time or opportunity for many words to be spoken, we have had the joy of knowing many quite realized that the work was done for them out of love to God."[17]

Many of the men when they entered the hospital feared that their life was at an end, and that the doctor would give them poison because this would give the doctor an extra ten rupees from the Government for the death of another patient with the plague. The convalescing men could now laugh when they told this story. There was much mistrust of the Government which bred wrong views and unfounded rumours.

Blanche continued, "Thus ... our work goes on at present, and we feel it good and pleasant to have to look up to our Master in a very special way to guide our next step forward; and even now we can see that He is bringing to Himself glory, and is working for the good of Sindh even through this terrible affliction which has come upon this land. ...

"Perhaps the death which has caused us all most sorrow has been that of dear little Kakari, who was Miss Ghose's right hand in the Kharo Dar School. She was deformed, and, although she must have been fifteen years old, was not bigger than a child of seven or eight. This had prevented her early marriage, and as she looked so small she was allowed to come daily to school, and proved a most excellent teacher of the first standard ... She was, they say, the constant teacher and adviser of the children, stopping quarrels and making peace among them. We tell them this is because Kakari believed in Jesus, and they agree and say that she has certainly gone to be with Him."[17] It was said of this woman, "For the last two years we have never heard her speak anything but the truth. No woman dared to tell an untruth before her; they were ashamed to do it."[18]

A woman in the Nassapuri plague camp said to Blanche, "You did not know me and I did not know you, but God knows us both, and brought you here."[19]

As the plague was abating it was decided after a day of waiting on God to re-open the two Sindhi schools. The absence of some of the scholars gave to the re-assembling an element of solemnity. Karachi appeared to be recovering from the plague, and people started to return to their homes from the settlements outside the city. The schools were opened and again five hundred students were in attendance. But the plague broke out again, many fled to temporary huts outside of Karachi and the schools had to close. One teacher reported: "I kept my school open, even when I had only nine children. Then my school-servant's husband died of the plague, and she was put into quarantine. Now all my children are gone, and I wonder sadly which of them I shall see again."[20]

At one of the schools the school servant had found a large dead rat in an upstairs room, at which point Alice Dawson was required to close the school. Finding a dead rat would mean the plague had reached that house and cases of the plague in humans were sure to follow.

The teachers wondered which children they would see again. Some had already been carried off by the fatal disease, and many of their dear friends had been left widowed or childless.

All the schools were touched by the plague and large numbers of children never returned. Many of their brightest students were lost to the disease. But the missionaries were comforted in their grief with the knowledge that many of the ones who were lost in death seemed near to the Kingdom of God.[21] Mrs. O'Connor heard about one of her school girls who on her death bed was repeating the Bible lessons she had heard in school.

Amongst the discouragements of the plague came the happy announcement of the engagement of Edith Brenton Carey to the Rev. R Sinker, who spoke at the lantern show which Edith had organised earlier. They were to be married on September 18th 1897.[22]

Itinerate village work around Karachi

In the villages and towns surrounding Karachi there were many thousands of women who had not been reached by the gospel. Blanche's desire to spread the good news of Jesus Christ amongst the people of Sindh led her to travel to such villages with these trips becoming known as their itinerate work. The women missionaries in Sindh were in one mind that they should reach out to these village women. Difficulties seemed to prevent them from achieving their desire, but then an opportunity presented itself to them. A young Christian man who lived at Mirpur Batoro which was several miles east of Karachi, offered to be a guide for them and said he would let them have use of his home if they would share the Gospel with the women there. Emily Prance and Blanche took up this opportunity and went on a two-week scouting trip to reconnoitre the area to share the gospel with the unreached women that they met.

Travelling to Mirpur Batoro encompassed a two hour railway journey to Junghshai station. When they arrived at the station they were met by some friends who had camped there to greet them. They were then driven thirteen miles to the Dak bungalow which was an unpleasant journey. The bungalow was only one and half miles away from Tatta, a small town with approximately eight thousand people.

Emily and Blanche then mounted camels to visit the villages. All the luggage was packed onto spare camels, and cushions were arranged to make the seats of the missionaries more comfortable. These preparations took a long time before they could even set off on their journey. This was the first time the missionaries had ridden camels so they had to hold on for their lives as the animals lurched backwards and forwards when they stood up. They then had to traverse the Indus river by steam ferry, camels and all. After sixteen miles of riding they eventually reached their destination of Sujaval and stayed in a Government bungalow which was set in a lovely garden.

Blanche and Emily visited the women of the village which had a population of approximately five thousand people. Many gathered around to listen to the missionaries. In one place an angry Brahmin woman turned the crowd away but it was too late to stop the crowd from hearing the gospel. Emily was warmly greeted by a former school pupil and then she was taken to two Gujarati homes in the village where she received a similar warm welcome.

Emily recalls the encounter: "I suddenly felt a hand touch my shoulder, and an eager whisper, 'Mem Sahib! my Mem Sahib!' On looking up I found Jayoi standing by me, with her baby brother on her hip. Jayoi was one of the standard children in my school, but had left Karachi on account of the plague. Her face was full of delight, and she pulled me by the arm, begging me to go and see her mother ... I went off as quietly as I could, Jayoi pouring out all the story of the time since we parted. Dear little girl, it was nice to meet her, and made me think how happy it will be when we meet some of these little ones and their mothers in Heaven, for we never can tell how far the Message has been received, and how many we shall meet there. Well, a chair was dragged out, and Jayoi brought her precious hymn-book, which had been carefully kept during all the travels; and, sitting on my knee, we had to go through all the hymns she had learnt. "There was too much excitement to do much teaching, but I had a very nice time with them. As I was returning to Karachi I left Jayoi a Gospel of St. Luke to read, for, happily, she could do this very nicely."[23]

The next day some people from a nearby Muslim village came to see and quiz the missionaries. They were taken into the village and to a home where some of the women gathered. The women seemed bright and intelligent but it was difficult for the missionaries to help them understand how Jesus came to be a substitute for them, and open up the way for them to have their sins forgiven.

Blanche and Emily rode onwards on their camels to Mirpur Batoro. As they travelled the road the camel driver for the missionaries wanted to know if they would like to stop to partake in some shooting, but was taken aback when he found out that this wasn't the reason for their trip. When night started to close in they were greeted by their Christian host, and went to his home which was a mud house on the way into the village. To make the place more homely for them Emily used a red twill cloth to cover the table and then spread a small rug and a camel bag on the mud floor. Many villagers, boys and women, peered over the wall of their accommodation into the courtyard to see these ladies and were amused by their eating habits.[24]

Mirpur Batoro had a population of about five thousand villagers and the missionaries remained there for a week to visit the Sindhi-speaking inhabitants in the village. Whilst there they also met a large number of poor Gujarati speaking peasants whom they assumed had migrated to the area. The school boys in the village bought a number of hymn books, but they often followed the missionaries around as if the ladies were a source of entertainment and amusement. When one day a number of boys gathered to see the ladies, they assumed again it was for the boys' amusement, but on this occasion they brought along with them a Brahmin lad who desired to purchase a hymn book for him to read to some people in a distant village. The missionaries were thrilled by this and gave the lad some tracts too.

Blanche and Emily met one literate girl who, when she had heard the gospel and was shown how to pray, came to the ladies the next day and said, "I have been watching for you since day dawn; I am so glad you have come." The ladies enquired if she had prayed to God. "Yes, I said, Oh God, I am a sinner; I have heard that Jesus died for sinners; give me a clean heart for His sake." The girl noticed that the missionaries closed their eyes when praying and she wondered if they saw God with the eyes of their heart when they did this. The missionaries left her with many books to read and said that God would help her to understand them.

With sadness the missionaries got back on the camels to leave the people they had met. One man remarked, "You should stay here longer to teach the women; what you have done is only like pouring water upon sand", and another old Gujarati man said to Emily, "you have the light but we are in darkness." Blanche left wondering if schools could be established in the villages and who would teach in them. She longed for workers to be raised up.

Emily and Blanche returned to Tatta and remained there for several days visiting different homes. Such was the impression made by the ladies that some of the inhabitants wished for them to stay. They left with them a number of books including hymn books to read. They also taught a hymn to the people for them to learn off by heart. By using the Wordless Book they were able to teach them some simple Bible texts such as 'All have sinned', 'One died for all', and 'Wash me and I shall be whiter than snow.' Blanche knew this was just scratching the surface and she desired that they could do more to reach out to them with the gospel.[24]

In Irene Barnes' 1897 book *Behind the Pardah* which tells the story of CEZMS work in India, Blanche speaks about this visit, "Daily during our visit to Tatta, we visited a dear old woman who has wept herself blind in sorrowing for her three sons, and who listened eagerly to the story of a True Guru, who could give peace to the broken hearted. Great was her sorrow when we told her that we must go away.

"'Since your feet came into my house, joy and rest have come,' was her cry. And it was sweet to hear her pray the prayer for a new heart which we had taught her, adding, 'O God, show me thy face!'

"'When will you come again?' asked a polite Hindu boy, who had taken us to see some of the ladies of his family, whom he was most anxious we should visit. 'I hope to do so next cold weather,' was the reply. 'Next cold weather!' he echoed; 'why, who will be alive then? We want a lady to live here and teach.'"[25,26]

In 1898 Eliza Georgina Vacher arrived in Karachi and helped for several years with the Sindhi work. Georgina was particularly keen on the itinerate work in the colder months combining it with some medical care. She proved to be one of the most enthusiastic evangelists they would have.

Return from Furlough (1898)

Following a furlough in England Blanche returned to India in 1898 with Agnes Fox Grant. Agnes had a short time to unpack and look around the schools before she got to work studying her assigned language Marathi. She was to superintend the growing Marathi school and was to visit among the Marathi-speaking people. At the time there were about three thousand Marathi speaking inhabitants in Karachi.

Sundabai Vishwasrao, a Marathi Christian was the head mistress of the Marathi school when Agnes went to Karachi, and 'Bai', as she was known, had done a great work. Bai was the daughter of Christian parents and had come to Karachi from Bombay at the invitation of some of the Karachi workers. Blanche welcomed the young teacher and gave her charge of the Marathi School. There were only a small number of pupils when Bai took over and the number steadily increased to over a hundred. She was much loved by the pupils and their parents. She visited many of her former pupils and found a very warm welcome among them. When Agnes arrived Bai "took her under her wing" and called her "Marathi Miss Sahib." Bai helped Agnes especially with the language and was constantly prepared to help others. Bai was always ready to do God's work. Even when she was unwell Bai would go for hours to the outskirts of town to tell others about Jesus. She eventually gave up school work and devoted her time to visiting the Zenanas where she still received a generous greeting. One day Agnes was "touched" to see a young boy help a now much-aged Bai up the stairs to visit his mother. Sundabai continued to serve God until she was taken ill and "passed into the presence of the Saviour she loved" in 1930.[27]

When Blanche returned to Karachi she was heart-broken to hear the stories of loss due to the plague. She recalled leaving many "happy, smiling wives and mothers" and now she found them "sitting apart on a mat with tearful, sad faces, in mourning garb, grieving over the husband who was so suddenly snatched away." The story would go, "He was well and went to his work in the morning, at mid-day he came back saying he had a headache, and the next day - the rest of the sentence is an expressive gesture which means, he was not." Blanche told the story of a "little curly-haired Bachi, whom I left with her little fat arms folded, singing 'Jesus loves me' in our Kharo Dar school," who "has been called away to sing on high."

Blanche reflected, "Perhaps you wonder how a missionary feels when, after talking of the work and looking at it from the distance, she is once more face to face with the reality. I can only say for myself, I feel more than ever man's utter helplessness and the utter weakness of all human effort. How well one can understand Moses' question when sent to deliver Israel: 'Who am I that I should go?' How comforting is the Royal answer: 'Certainly I will be with thee.' Oh, 'Ye that are the Lord's remembrancers (sic)', pray on, pray earnestly, hold up your hand towards the throne of the Lord; for those in the battle sorely need the help which your prayers can and shall bring down upon them."[28]

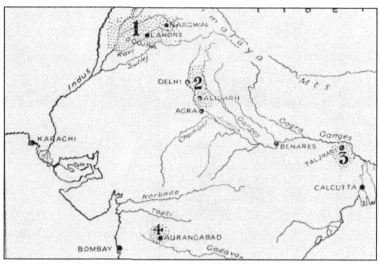

CMS Sketch of the cities in Northern India[29]

The Karachi mission staff in those early days.[30]
Left to right front row: Miss E Dawe, Miss E Brenton Carey, and Miss M Brook.
Middle Row: Miss Compton, Miss Brenton Carey and Miss Redman.
Back Row: Miss M Prance, Miss A J Dawson, and Miss L Gordon.

Front row sitting on the ground left to right: Massih Charran teacher, Joira Bazaar School, Pani Bai teacher, Sudder Gujarati School, Elizabeth Charran school helper, Amarith Bai teacher, Ranchor Lines Gujarati School.
Second row sitting left to right: Miss Troyal assistant missionary working among Gujarati women and children, Sudder Bazaar, Mrs. Ghose wife of the pastor, Blanche Brenton Carey, Emily Prance, Mrs O'Connor assistant missionary working amongst Gujarati women and children, Ranchor Lines.
Third row standing left to right: Mary Ai second teacher, Sindhi School, Miss Dawson, Miss Green assistant missionary working amongst Sindhis, Miss Ghose head teacher of the Sindhi School, Miss Wreddon assistant missionary preparing to work among Sindhis, Elisa Bai teacher, Gujarati School, Chandurnal Munshi who teaches Sindhi to all new-comers. Published in 1894.[31]

Agnes Fox Grant with Sundrabai Vishwasrao published in 1930 [27]

Orphans and Villages

Despite the devastating effects of the plague, by 1901 the six CEZMS schools in Karachi had 557 children on their rolls. Honor Troyal and Miss Panibai were in charge of the Gujarati Sudder Schools, and Mrs. O'Connor looked after the Gujarati Ranchor Lines School. Emily Prance with Miss Inglis and Sarahbai were responsible for the Joria Bazaar School. Agnes Fox Grant with Sundrabai superintended the Marathi Gari Khata School. Ella Ghose headed up the Sindhi School at Mitho Dar and Minna Ghose looked after the Sindhi School in Kharo Dar.

Then a tragedy hit the mission station. Blanche's niece Edith Sinker (nee Brenton Carey) died on the 22nd July 1901 after undergoing an operation. Edith Sinker had enjoyed a few short years in India having arrived in 1894. Following her marriage to Rev. Robert Sinker, she had served faithfully alongside her husband as he moved to Hyderabad in 1899 to be the Principal of the High School and Edith had shown a special interest in the CMS school there. Edith had given birth to three children during her marriage, the youngest of whom was only three months old at the time of her death. Blanche had lost a close relative and companion; the widowed Robert Sinker resigned from the CMS in 1902 for family reasons.[1]

The Church Missionary Intelligencer for December 1901 reported Edith Sinker's death: "Her last illness was a long one, but she was very cheerful and bright through it, and the end was a very peaceful one. When she was informed of the necessity of an operation, she took it quite calmly. Before the operation, she asked Miss Brenton Carey (her aunt) to read the 53rd and 26th chapters of Isaiah to her. And she kept repeating the words 'perfect peace' to herself ...

"On the following day - her last on earth - she was quite cheerful and bright, and when told she was soon going Home she was quite happy ... Her nurse was much struck by her patience, and brightness, and her thoughtfulness for others even in illness. Her Hindu friends are much impressed when told of her peaceful end and readiness to go. And we shall yet some day see in what other ways God was glorified by her death.

"The one thing above all that her Indian friends noticed in her during her few years in India was how she strove to be one with the Indian people and they valued her for that. During her last hours she sent a message to the Indian Christians of the place: 'Tell them', she said, 'I am thinking of them all'." [2]

Orphanage

A new branch of ministry to add to the already long list of work at the CEZMS mission was beginning. One day a mission worker asked Blanche, "Will you take a baby?" Blanche was taken by surprise by this request and wondered how they could possibly start caring for babies. There was already so much to do, so many existing challenges which faced Blanche as leader of the mission team; schools to superintend, homes and villages to be visited, all of which involved so much organisation, paperwork and funding. How could they take this child in? But the worker showed Blanche the little emaciated baby who was wrapped in a curtain. Her mother was dead, and to help keep her quiet the father had given her opium so he could go to work. The worker said to Blanche, "Let us keep her, else she will die." Blanche finally agreed that they must take the baby. The child was so ill that she had to go to hospital and it was touch and go for many months whether she would live. But the little girl survived and returned to the missionaries to be loved and cared for. The orphanage in Karachi had begun.[3]

Soon after the arrival of the first baby, a homeless child of two and a half whose mother was a victim of the plague, was brought to them. When the child grew up she trained to become a nurse and worked in a CEZMS Hospital, but later she also sadly succumbed to the plague.

Blanche reported, "A letter came one morning to the Senior Missionary, asking if she would take charge of a two-year-old, whose mother had died of consumption and the father of plague. Off went the missionary to the plague hospital and found the little one hiding behind some matting. She wore nothing but her birthday dress, and with matted hair, huge mouth, and a body far out of proportion to the rest of her, was certainly not a fascinating spectacle. How was she to be conveyed through the streets in that condition! The kind Hindu doctor came to the rescue by wrapping her in an old tattered sheet and by tenderly placing her in the ghari [carriage] beside her new mother." She became a teacher.[3]

Blanche reflected on the year of change since the orphans arrived: "Looking down the long verandah where twelve happy children are eating their evening meal, we exclaim, 'How little we expected, at the beginning of 1902, that the end of the year would see us with so large a family!' ... For two years Suvta reigned as the CEZM baby, but last February two more little girls were thankfully passed on to us from an over-full orphanage. A week after that a sweet plague orphan of two and a half was given to us, and four big girls from the Katni-Morwara Children's Home came to be trained as teachers in our schools and were able to take charge of the babies. In September the Collector asked us to take a child who had proved unmanageable in the Hindu houses where she had been put to live since the death from famine of both parents. ... A month after Dya's arrival, a police constable brought Bachi, who had been a sort of stowaway on board ship and, so far as any one can find out, seems to have been cast off after the death of her father, which she says took place a few days before she came to us. A little Goanese girl was added to the list last month. She was deserted in Karachi by people who had brought her from her own country; and I have just been asked to take in another.

"We feel so thankful to have been in our present house before our family thus increased. Now we are most anxious to buy it, that we may be able to make alterations which make it more suitable to our purpose."[4]

The need to house these destitute children led to the addition of an extra room to the new buildings, which proved the beginning of the orphanage and in 1904 fourteen little girls were settled into their new quarters, under the charge of Minna Ghose. Minna proved to be very gifted in this sphere of work supporting, guiding and developing the children of the orphanage, which in years to follow was to prove of great value to the growth of the Kingdom of God in Sindh. Many young lives would come to know Christ at the orphanage, and would go out in to the world working for Him in school or at home as teachers or wives, and mothers. They would be able to look back and see that their spiritual and intellectual growth was influenced by the wise and loving 'Go-ji' Minna Ghose.

Minna asked one of the old girls whom she had not seen for years, "Do you remember all you used to learn about the Lord Jesus?" She replied, "Remember? Do I forget my father and my mother?"[5]

The orphanage would become the Girl's Hostel and Children's Home where many of the younger teachers lived. Priti Piyarelal, who was orphaned during the 1900 famine and brought up in the mission, later became the Matron.

Blanche wrote, "As these girls advance in their teens the question of 'What shall they become?' crops up. Here as far as possible, their own tastes are followed. Some elect to be trained to teach; others become nurses; some specialise as needlework teachers. Each one, from the time she comes here, is given care, education and finally training in some branch of work. Then marriages are arranged with much care and prayer and with the consent of the girl herself.

"Seven of our little ones have been handed over by officials. As to the money for their support, some of it comes from friends in England and some from friends out here."

Many years later Blanche looked out of her window on to the compound, and confessed that "watching the girls still holds its fascination for me. There are the 'big sisters' to whose care three or four little ones are given. They mend their children's clothes, see they are clean and tidy, and mother their flock. Then there are the 'middle aged' children the 11 and 12-years olds, who apparently delight in washing their clothes, cooking, and tidying their boxes. Of course, by far the most fascinating are the 3 and 4 and 5-years-olds-who scamper round the compound, or who sit down to make the most delicious mud chapatties. Should anything cause 3-years-old to cry, how quickly does a 4-year-old kiss away the tears!

"Yes, our children are quite human and natural; they have their naughty and their good days; their tears and their smiles. Our aim is to train them in body, soul, and spirit that they may live to the honour and glory of Him Who once 'called a little child unto Him and set in the midst.'"[3]

Itinerant village work around Karachi

Blanche continued to visit the villages around Karachi, and kept a record of her experiences: "Miss Young (of Hyderabad) and I left Karachi by an early-morning train and were landed in half an hour at a little roadside station. We expected to find the bungalow which had been kindly lent to us quite close, but the station-master was a stranger from Upper Sindh, and the camel-men only told us it was miles away, hoping to make a good bargain, for they refused to take us unless we promised a large sum. This we would not listen to, and as we could do nothing else, we spread our breakfast on two chairs, and I sat on the book-box and Miss Young on the small medicine-chest and we began our morning repast, seemingly not caring if we spent the day at the station or no. This had the desired effect, and we saw the camel-men were beginning to load our goods, and at last, after much of the weary bickering as to pay which drivers of vehicles and animals seem so to delight in, we got off. The bungalow, which turned out to be six miles off, was indeed a haven of rest after the hot ride".[6]

Some ex-students lived in some of the villages, and they gave the missionaries a warm welcome dispelling the neighbours' fears as to who they were and what they wanted. The box of medicines Blanche and her colleague had brought with them contained simple treatments which would have been common to European householders. Using these medicines helped the missionaries access people's homes. One woman asked for something to treat a fever and after that the villagers came to their tent morning and evening. They were able to run a "Sunday school" for the children.

Blanche continues, "Mirpur Sakro, our next halting-place, we had visited before. The headman was civil, and let us have some big meetings in his house, and we had some good Mahommedan congregations, especially among the potters, who seemed simple, quiet people, and listened to the Gospel, without any attempt at argument."

The missionaries went on to Boharo on the banks of the River Bughar, through which they waded on the camels, all the time fearing that the camels would sit down in the water, which they often did. Blanche reported that, "The many sore eyes which were getting better from the effect of our lotion made us quite famous in the villages for four or five miles around from which patients came to us, generally going back with a book to give to the one man in the place who could read. It is cheering that we hardly found a village where there was not a single man able to read.

"In Boharo the tapedar, or headman under the Government, was very polite, and we were welcomed to his house, the secret being that his wife had been a patient of Miss Compton's many years before, and she was never tired of speaking of her loving, gentle care, 'just as if she had been my mother'. What a joy it was to find that that unselfish, beautiful life was yet bearing fruit in Sindh, where, indeed, she 'still speaketh' in many ways.

"Here we were delayed by not being able to persuade the camel-drivers to carry our baggage and tent to Keti Bandar. 'It was a desert,' they said, and they and their camels 'would die of hunger,' and so on. At last some consented to go, and we started on our march. Our way lay over desert salt sand, and we saw the most beautiful mirage which I have ever seen. We were quite taken in, and even one of our camel-drivers could hardly believe that it was not the Indus which he saw, cool and sparkling under the shade of the distant trees ...

"Garho was a small place, and we meant to stay only over the Sunday, but, alas! on Sunday morning we heard much talking, and the words Badji vio (run away) coming in very often, and it was not long before we were told that the perfidious camel drivers had fled and we were stranded in this place, where our patiwala (servant) feared it would be next to impossible to get camels. We could not move without our tents and baggage, although we had our riding camels; so there we were prisoners for the time being! On Sunday we visited the few Hindus and received Mahommedan men, women and children all day long, and a visit from a neighbouring landowner, who took away a Gospel; so we felt that God had work for us, and were glad we had not to leave on Monday morning...

"We sent back to Boharo in the faint hope of getting camels, but in the meantime our evening stroll had revealed to us that we were only about a three minutes' walk from the river, and as we watched the boats go up and down, a bright thought struck us- 'Why not go by water?' We secured a boat owned by a mother and two sons, and were intending to start for Keti, but the wind blew strongly in the other direction, and we feared with wind against us we could never accomplish the journey in time to be in Karachi at the date on which we were due ... We were praying for guidance, and perhaps God would give it through His wind. If in the morning it was fair for Keti, we would go; if not, we would go up the river to another place we had heard of. The wind did blow the other way, and the end showed how much the wiser course it was not to take too long a voyage in our very slow old boat ... Once the wind blew rather strongly-it had turned against us again soon after we started, and the poor old lady came to us saying 'I am so frightened.' 'You frightened, and a sailor's mother!' I said laughing. 'Yes, I am,' she said, 'for we have lost twelve boats, and how do I know this will not go over?' This was cheering news for the passengers, and soon after our pilot confessed that he did not know that part of the river very well, and had no idea where we were, and as it was dark he thought we had better anchor for the night!"[6]

In the morning Blanche and Miss Young went to see the women who lived in a small village next to the river bank where they were anchored, "Some listened, others were afraid; but we found men who could read, and a man with toothache. These gladly followed us to the boat for medicine and books."[6] Whilst they were in that village they saw a number of people who needed serious treatment which they could not give to them. Some people had broken bones which had been set by a local carpenter or potter.

The missionaries then came to a landing place which led to a village called Sanvalpur. They wondered how they would pitch their tent, but nearby they found an empty government bungalow which they could use. They stayed here until they could obtain some animals to carry their belongings from Kotali which was two and half miles away. In the village of Sanvalpur they tried to speak to the women and hand out tracts but they experienced some opposition; a Hindu man who had received a tract at Baharo said in a loud voice "These people have come to tell you that there is no Guru but Jesus Christ; you must leave all and obey him". The women didn't let the mission workers come into their homes and some shut doors in their faces.

But one old woman cautiously opened her door and with some persuasion allowed the missionaries to enter. Some boys who were not allowed in banged on the door of the house showing their displeasure. Despite this distraction the visitors were able to speak to the women, and then the Hindu man came in to the house who had dismissed the women previously. The old woman tried to get him to leave but he wouldn't be persuaded and he closed the door behind him and loudly told the women what they were going to teach. The missionaries heard him speak the gospel message and they were thankful that the message was heard even if it was with hostility.

Following this the old woman pleaded with the missionaries to go, but her daughter wanted them to stay saying, "Mother, don't send them away, they are telling us the words of God." The missionaries left to go to other houses. The daughter of the old woman followed them and they were able to have a good conversation with her and finding that she could read they gave her the Gospel of Luke. She was one of the few who seemed hungry for the Word. The 'tract man' who had appeared so aggressive now seemed to help as he explained to any women who didn't understand.[7]

On another occasion in 1904. Blanche accompanied by Emily Prance returned to a number of villages. They rode to the river side and came to some huts, where some of the women listened but they treated what the missionaries said as a joke. They then visited an old man whose camel they had used previously on their first trip to the villages. The women there recognised the missionaries: Blanche related, "They remembered that we had visited them two years before, and asked after Miss Vacher who was with me then. When I took out the wordless book they remembered it, and I was able to read the whole of 'Reconciliation' to them."[8]

The last time Blanche went to Jhirak with Emily Prance they had looked down on to the village and yearned for a school and a gospel work to be established. To do such a work here seemed impossible to them, so they prayed earnestly to God that he would make the way possible. The subject became a matter for special prayer. Then two of the workers in Karachi, Miss Green and Miss Brooks volunteered to set up the work in Jhirak. Emily went out to get the work started. She found a mud house with an upper floor near the village entrance. On the lower floor there was one room for a kitchen, one for a servant and one for a small schoolroom. The upper floor consisted mainly of a verandah and accommodation for the two assistants.

So the school was opened, and regular house visits for gospel sharing began in Jhirak notwithstanding the unknown hazards which come along with the start of any new ministry. Miss Green and Miss Brooks courageously persevered in the work. They received intermittent visits from Emily Prance, and took the occasional trip back to Karachi.

After seven months Blanche herself went out to Jhirak to observe the progress and wrote, "It had been a long camel ride. We had left the railway station about an hour before sunset, and had jogged along very slowly. The camel was not a good one, so I feared to ask that the pace should be quickened, and let the jat (camel-man) take his time and spare his camel and me! ... We had started at half past four, and it was nearly eight o'clock when the welcome cry was raised that Jhirak was in sight!

"Our first day was Sunday, and we enjoyed reading the Service together. In the afternoon I was present at Miss Green's interesting Sunday-school for boys. Over thirty were present and answered well. They are encouraged to come by the gift of old Christmas cards, and we gave some specially big ones to those who did best. These boys can all read and write as there is a good boy's school ... In most of the villages one man is both school master and postmaster. In the evening we wandered down the pretty road towards the river Indus, watching the parrots and other birds of bright plumage flying among the trees, or the camels straying about on the strand, and the curious boats plying their way up and down the river, or perhaps sticking in the mud in shallow places. Whatever the road leading to it may be, Jhirak itself is a pretty place ...

"Monday's work was examining the little school taught by Miss Brooks. Seventeen girls presented themselves. In spite of big days and other drawbacks, they had made very good progress. At first the parents had been afraid to send their children. A report had arisen that as soon as they were educated they were to be sent to the war! And other stories equally absurd alarmed the people. But confidence has been won, and I was much struck by the friendliness of the women. 'Our little Madam is so good.' 'She has taught me this;' and 'She has shown me how to do this;' and 'If we do not see her face for a week we are quite unhappy,' were the comments all round. A bright, old Brahmin woman has become a firm supporter of the school and sets aside all foolish reports with authority. Miss Green has treated a number of patients during her stay in Jhirak. The remedies given have been quite simple, but the difference they have made to the comfort and happiness of the people has been untold and they are very grateful. In this way also love and confidence have been won.

"We thought our first prize giving a great success. Only one doll's leg was broken in spite of the perils of camel riding. And such dolls we hear, had never before been seen in Jhirak. The mothers were invited (so that all fear as to the girls being despatched to be soldiers might be finally removed), and a goodly number arrived. They were seated on one side of the room with the children who had got tired of school and had left off coming. The girls sang and said some of their lessons, to show what they had been learning, and then the mothers were told that the prizes had come from the king's country, to show the love of English sisters, who wished the Sindhi girls to learn, and above all to know and believe the love of God. The mothers were harder to keep in order than the children, but our Brahmin friend used her authority with success every now and then. The prizes gave great delight, and the children who had left school began to beg that their names might be put on the roll again and to promise attendance in the future. All the regular comers got a doll, and some a special prize as well - a cholo (a short jacket) or a bag. Next came sweets as the crowning joy, and then the children were dismissed. The mothers had to be left to retire at their own sweet will, while we scrambled up the ladder leading to the living room to be greeted by the welcome sound of a boiling kettle!

"On the last evening we sat at the door of my little tent and received visits from the women who had come from the distant villages consisting of tiny huts made of palm leaf matting. First came a mat-maker with her dried palm-leaves arranged as a cloak around her. She seated herself before us and began her tale of woe - 'Constant fever - someone in her house with a sore foot,' &c, &c. Medicines were promised on the morrow and she cheered up and began to ply us with questions and to tell me how good the 'Madams' were. Others joined her and sat talking or asking for medicine until they realised that the sun had set and that they must hasten homewards."[9]

After two years of work at the Jhirak outstation there were changes in personnel; the following article was written for *India's Women* in March 1907: "Miss Green and Miss Brooks have lived and worked at this outstation for two years, and now Miss Brooks has left and Miss Ella Ghose has taken her place.

"Miss Green, who undertook the Zenana visiting, was partly supported by the British and Foreign Bible Society, and in the report sent to that Society she said, 'In February there was some opposition to the school work in this place but I am thankful that the people in the houses still like me to visit them, and they are willing to listen to the Bible lesson.

"'It is encouraging to hear one woman after another say she prays for pardon. In one house there was a sick man, and after talking about his illness he said, 'Tell about God.' He seemed to enjoy hearing.

"'A woman and her daughter heard the Bible story in a house where I was visiting and came and listened again in the bungalow. The mother remembered the prayer I had taught. The girl returned another day and did not wish to go until she had heard about God; she kept repeating the prayer over and over again.

"One visit often leads to another. After teaching in one house Miss Green was called to a woman who was ill next door and who had heard something of the Gospel story. After speaking with her she offered prayer. The woman became unconscious and died the next morning. On visiting the neighbour later Miss Green was told that before losing consciousness the sick one had prayed for forgiveness in the way she had been taught.

"Miss Green adds that she often has the opportunity of selling Testaments and Gospels. She has a class for boys on Sundays, as many as thirty or forty are sometimes present; these lads save their pocket money to buy tracts.

"While the visiting has in many ways been so encouraging, the school work under Miss Ghose has been carried on amidst many difficulties. A new mission house has been built through the generosity of a member of the Mission, but before the school house was completed most of the children left and the school was closed. Miss Green and Miss Ghose left lately for a holiday, and prayer is asked that God will definitely guide future work at Jhirak."[10]

Emily Prance provided the accommodation and school room in Jhirak for Miss Green and Miss Ghose. There were twenty children who went to the school and they were mostly from Muslim families, because the parents of the Hindu children at the time were frightened that the missionaries wanted to steal their children.[20]

Blanche wrote again about visiting the villages in 1910: "All journeys have to be taken on camel-back, so every move from twelve to sixteen miles is not only tiring, but takes up a good deal of precious time and is expensive. It is therefore found better to stay a week or some days at least at each big village and to ride out in the early morning to little hamlets, two, five, or six, miles away, returning to the tent for the heat of the day, and visiting in the near villages in the afternoon ...

"We visited another village this year, which Mrs. Day and I went to three years ago. We had found the women in the Mukhi's (Hindu headman) house most interested. This time they gave Miss Vacher and me a warm welcome. We asked for one woman whom we specially remembered, and were told that she had gone back to her husband's village. 'How much she thought of you,' said her mother; 'she was constantly repeating the words you taught her, over and over again.' How we longed to know what words! In this house Miss Vacher showed the picture of the Broad and Narrow way, which to my surprise was well understood and created great interest. 'Look!' cried one of the daughters-in-law, 'there is a woman on the road to Heaven; our shasters [a shaster is a book containing the institutes of the Hindu religion] tell us that women have no inheritance there!' How glad we were to point out that the Road opened by the Great Substitute was for all - men, women and children."

Sometimes in Muslim villages the men would bring gospels with them and the missionaries were able to read the story of the Cross to the whole village. Once a man listened "with politeness and attention" but replied "This is your religion, but we have our own Prophet." They asked him, "Brother where is your prophet now?". "Oh, he is dead and we worship his grave", he answered. "And where is Hasrat Isa?" [Isa in Arabic meaning Jesus] they continued, "He sits in the fourth heaven until he comes again," he replied. The missionary left him with a question, "Well, brother ... Is the dead one or the live one best able to help and save you?" All the folk they met spoke of Christ with 'respect and honour', but they longed to see the people give Him the full honour He merited. They began and ended their two month tour at Jhirak their small outstation.[11]

Georgina Vacher and Miss N Theophilus later took over the work at Jhirak, with Georgina leading the Sunday service in Urdu. Georgina writes a short account of the work at Jhirak, "It is certainly most cheering to see how the whole village has been more or less influenced by Miss Green's long stay there. She has indeed given a faithful witness for Christ which we trust must surely be as 'bread cast upon the waters.' I may safely say that there is now hardly a house in the village where we should not be gladly welcomed.

"One family especially I must mention; they are potters, and the men and women alike are most interested. One of the daughters has just learnt to read Arabic Sindhi with me. She was well up in Persian and in the Koran, and so learnt very quickly. Now, if she wishes she can read the Gospel for herself, and I have given her a simple Gospel story which, I trust she will read to the other members of her family.

"It is a great point to teach the women to read. I might mention here that in a village we visited about four miles from Jhirak, there was only one person who could read, and she is a woman who had been taught in the Municipal School in Karachi. I sold her a Gospel of St. Mark and a simple Gospel story, and she promised to read these to the neighbours. I hope to visit this village again as soon as I get back to Jhirak.

"We are also much interested in three young men of low caste, who are baptised Christians. One is, I trust, a very true Christian; he seems greatly in earnest. These young men love singing bhajans [a devotional song]. Feroz came to us a few days after we arrived, on November 10th, and asked us to teach him to read Hindustani; so reading lessons were started by Miss Theophilus, and the three brothers came regularly every day. In about six weeks' time Feroz, the sharpest of the three, could read fairly well; now he is able to read the Bible and to learn fresh bhajans. I shall be glad when we are able to have settled workers in Jhirak for the sake of these three Christian men, as well as for many other reasons.

"There is also an old chaprasi [messenger] who is much interested in Christianity; he first became interested through Miss Green telling him about Christ as he was driving her on the camel from the railway station to Jhirak. Now he is so glad to learn more. I must not forget to tell you about our school. The building is conveniently situated close to our bungalow, and is very nicely fitted up. The trouble is that so few girls attend. One reason for this is that, owing to the illness of our head teacher, the school has had to be closed several times, and the children's parents have got discouraged, and think it is of no use to send them. But now we hope to start regular work, and then I believe there will be no difficulty."[12]

Mountains of Difficulty

The work was hard and exhausting due to the resistance of the people. On one occasion, following a baptism, the zenana visitors faced great opposition which led to one of the Indian castes withdrawing their pupils.

Also it was not easy to teach the women to read and write, it was very time consuming. Many of the Sindhi women who began to learn to read often got weary of it when they entered into difficulties. After four months of teaching, one student had only just got to grips with the letters and vowel marks. At other times a woman would be doing very well and making good progress but her mother in law would put every possible obstacle in her way to disrupt her learning. The lessons were often cut short and interrupted which slowed their progress. The main purpose for the missionaries in teaching the women to read was that the Sindhi women might read the Bible for themselves, but this was a long-term goal and took a lot of time and energy. Despite these struggles they were encouraged by the women who desired for them to come and visit them again and again. There were also others who showed a great interest in the Word and who had dropped some of their long held customs when they saw that they were wrong.[13]

A Brahmin widow called Janki Bai had heard the gospel message from one of the missionaries in Karachi and was very interested in becoming a Christian, but the men in the household were concerned by her desire and eagerness and so they acted. They stopped the missionary from coming to teach Janki the good news of Jesus. The men didn't mind Janki talking to the European women but they took exception when she showed a real earnest interest in the gospel. However the story didn't end there, God had other plans.

Soon after Janki caught the plague and became very ill but thankfully she recovered. Janki, still interested in her spiritual life, went on a pilgrimage. She took all her Hindu books, and the Bible she had and threw them into the river. She had decided to start her spiritual journey afresh. She went to Multan in the Punjab, and stayed there for about six weeks, and then she continued by foot and by rail stopping to worship in temples or to bathe in special sacred rivers, in an effort to receive enlightenment.

In one place a Rani (a princely ruler or wife of one) became fascinated with her, and arranged for clothes, cooking vessels and money for a ticket for her to go to Juggernath*². When Janki saw the idol of Juggernath she said, "This cannot be God's Work." Janki's journey to find what she was looking for led her to Calcutta. In Calcutta she heard some people in the streets preaching the gospel, she responded to the message and made her way to them. She spoke to one of the preachers and confirmed that she believed what she had heard and asked to be baptised. However as she was going with the preacher they were separated by the busy crowds in the streets and she lost him.

She then went on to Benares. A day or so after she had arrived she found the CMS Church in the city, where a service was being held and she went in and stayed until the end. When all the people had left she remained and spoke to a catechist (teacher which may have been a native catechist), and Janki explained how she wanted to be a follower of Jesus. Janki went to have a meal with him and his wife at his home that evening: by doing this Janki was breaking her caste and demonstrating her sincerity to believe.

The next day she visited Miss Mathews (a Zenana Bible and Medical Missionary). Janki was by now wearing very dirty clothes, and after much discussion and with many questions Miss Mathews was sure that Janki was a genuine seeker. Janki had been on pilgrimage for three years, and for all that time she had found "No love", only "Give: give". Miss Mathews taught Janki from the Hindu New Testament, which she could read, about the love of Jesus, and His sacrifice on the Cross, and Janki broke down in tears. Janki was baptised and changed her name to Prabhu Dasi.[14]

Although the ministry in Karachi came with hardships and disappointments. The seeds which were sown by God's good grace could be harvested by others in His own good time.

Another recurring problem was the dreaded plague which would not go away and year on year Karachi was disrupted by the disease. School attendance was at its highest in the autumn but in the plague time months of March, April and May the number of scholars declined. The whole city might go into segregation camps and many schools had to close. The fearful disease took away some of their brightest students, but the missionaries continued to hear testimonies from the local community of how their dying pupils kept a level of happiness during their final trial.[15]

Honor Troyal paints a picture of the transient nature of life in Karachi at that time, and the dangers faced by the pupils which must have had an adverse effect on their caring teachers.

---

*² Juggernath festival - Vishnu's title was Jananath meaning lord of the world. A giant carriage transported an image of the Hindu god Vishnu through the streets, and some devotees would throw themselves underneath the huge carriage and be crushed to death

The Sudder Bazaar Gujerati School, Karachi.

"This is a group of the elder girls in the Sudder Bazaar School, with Panibai, their former teacher, in the centre. I superintend the school and visit the parents of the children who are nearly all Hindus. Pani-bai looks very happy with her girls around her, and they all love and respect her . It is nearly a year and half since she had to give up work on account of ill health. The girl on her left hand is little Ganga; she died suddenly of cholera in July. The girl behind her is Paimu, who left to be married; and to the left of Ganga is Kesi, who will leave for the same reason in about two months' time."[16] Many girls would leave their schools and teachers to be married at a very young age. Their future would be very uncertain and it was often an unhappy one.

Accommodating all the workers was a constant problem, and they were housed separately in different locations. The need for a new mission house became urgent and through the generosity of a friend it became possible to acquire more suitable buildings. A mission house in which all the teachers and their assistants could live under one roof was procured by Blanche.[17]

In 1904 the mission was reinforced by Sophia Morrison and Ellinor Roberts, however Ella Ghose had to leave owing to her mother's death. There were now seven schools, with an average of 608 students on the rolls, and the orphanage contained fourteen girls. One of the girls requested baptism and four of the elder girls were confirmed. Zöe Bose had also joined the work.

Blanche wrote in April 1905, "As we count up all the subjects for which we have to praise God, our difficulties fade away as a morning mist. Each department of work has its mountains of difficulty, but many of these have disappeared as we got up to them, and those which we have had to climb have not proved as steep as we expected."[18]

As the importance of education grew in India the government introduced stricter educational standards, which impacted the CEZMS schools as they needed to conform to these new requirements. Blanche wrote to supporters, "Our schools present another difficulty at present about which we would ask you to pray. The difficulty of getting teachers is very great and Government requirements are increasing, so that much time is taken up in keeping them up to the mark. We feel that Mission Schools, if carried on at all, should be as good as possible, and should show that Christian work is the best, but to do this we need a good staff of teachers, and expenses daily increase. The time has not yet come when we can charge fees for girls' schools."

Prayer was continually requested, "that we may be guided, and that, if it is God's will that our schools, should be carried on, and He will raise up trained teachers with a true missionary spirit, ready to accept the lower salaries which the Mission has to offer, instead of seeking Government employment ..."[19]

A number of changes were seen in 1907 when Emily Prance was married to the Senior CMS Missionary Rev. A E Day in the spring and Agnes Fox Grant left for England in December for family reasons. Emily had been serving with Blanche for thirteen years, and they were sad to lose her, although they could still enjoy her company as she was staying in Karachi. Miss Brooks and Miss Troyal retired which left vacancies to fill so that the work could continue. Blanche explained, "Keeping up the staff of teachers is always difficult. The Sudder school has suffered from being without a head teacher for some months, but the need is at last supplied. Miss Mark was called back to Alexandra, and left Kharodar School without a head teacher; but one of our 'Home' girls passed the first year's course examination of the Hyderabad Training College in December, and is now able to take her place with Miss Ghose to superintend and help. We are hoping that others may be able to do this later. We all agree as to the importance of having Christian teachers; but none, except those on the spot, realise the difficulty of obtaining them! Our Bible lessons this year have been on the life of Christ. It was cheering to hear how well the children remembered the great facts of that wonderful story. Almost everyone seemed to grasp that Christ suffered 'instead of us.' May that knowledge be of the heart and not of the head only."[20]

As the work of the mission increased there was a need to obtain specialist help to improve the educational standards of the schools. Blanche had interviews with the committee urging the appointment of a woman with some practical knowledge in modern methods of teaching for training teachers in the schools at Karachi.[24] This need for a trained educationalist was filled by Catherine I Davidson who joined the missionaries in Karachi in 1909. Catherine learned to speak Sindhi as her first language, and began the Widows Industrial work. She also took on the roles of Superintending the schools and the training of the teachers.

By the start of the next decade in 1910 there were 688 girls on the rolls of the nine elementary schools. There had been promising advancements in the work in the Liari quarter where the school had been moved to a more central location among the villages and the numbers of pupils had increased to ninety.

The mission faced constant financial pressures which would become more and more difficult during Blanche's time in Karachi, especially during the catastrophic events that were to unfold during the first half of the 20th century. Blanche explained the situation: "During 1906-7 our expenses increased and our supplies from home fell off, so we were obliged to draw heavily upon a sum which we called our 'Reserve Fund.' ... Many of our workers, having been with us for a long time, expect their salaries to rise as they become more useful; and they find living in Karachi becomes more expensive year by year. We can, therefore, only retrench by cutting off some definite work or workers.

"When we consider which school or branch of our work shall be given up, we feel like the poverty stricken parents whose friend offered to take one of their many children off their hands! ... Indeed, the many openings which we see on all sides make us wish rather to extend. After prayer and consultation together, we have therefore decided not to retrench this year.

"We have not the least doubt that He is able to give us just what is needed, and will do so, as long as the work is pleasing to Him. Therefore, we are in no way anxious, but only ask for your prayers, that in all things He may be glorified, and that even if 'the work' must be less, 'the power' may be correspondingly greater."[20]

In the midst of trials the missionaries were encouraged by the interest shown in the gospel, as Blanche notes, "'More interest than formerly,' seems to be the report of most of our visitors. It was the same in our Itinerating Tour when Miss Prance and I visited many old and new villages on the other side of the Indus. We never had such attention, never sold so many books."[20]

In the orphanage Blanche records a time of spiritual blessing: "A slight wave of blessing swept over our "Home" last autumn, the effects of which have certainly been lasting, but far from all we could wish; only enough to let us see what God can do and make us long for more. The number of children remains the same i.e. eighteen. None have left us this year, but one has been promoted to rank as teacher, and a little one from Sukkur, who was sent to us in July, has filled the gap. She and Miri are an amusing pair. Roda was a visitor from Quetta. She suffered from fits which seemed to be better in the warmer climate of Karachi, so Miss Warren asked us to take her in for the winter. It was partly through this bright little Christian that our girls got a lift Heavenwards in the autumn. In spite of her sad state, she was such a happy, patient child, and was loved by all the others. Two months ago she left us for her Heavenly Home. It was such a release for the poor little sufferer that we could not but rejoice for her, though she was much missed. She used to read the Bible to a woman who took care of her when the other children were out at their schools, and had also taught her a hymn. I once heard her pray, 'O God, I thank Thee that my uncle turned me out, or I should never have gone to the Quetta Miss Sahiba, and learnt to know Thee.' Thus our Master picks up the jewels which man casts aside as useless."[20]

Blanche Defended the Schools' Work

Blanche went on furlough in Spring 1908.[22] On her return to England Blanche began to see a positive change in supporters' attitude towards education, noting that "We used to find that people said it was no good to have Mission Schools; that was not the way to do missionary work, and we have even had missionaries who have come out, and when asked to superintend a school, have replied: 'We have come out to preach the Gospel, and do not know anything of school work.' But generally, before they have finished learning the language, they write home to their friends saying they consider the school work the most telling!"

Blanche was able to supply evidence of how educational work was having a real impact for the gospel in the lives of children who could now read the Word of God for themselves: "Another young girl, who is dying of consumption, when told by her people that she must give up reading the Bible replied: 'It is the only thing which gives me comfort'.

"I could tell you if I had time of some baptisms that we have had at Karachi. One very bright girl of 13 or 14, baptised in August, and has just been confirmed. Her sister was baptised at the same time. They are the fruit of our Marathi school."[23]

Blanche reported four baptisms during the year, and she heard this testimony from a family who lost a child, "The mother of one child told Mrs. Day that her little daughter said when she was dying, 'Why do you cry, I am happy. I am going to God, the one true God. He is calling me and He will take care of me. I am not afraid, it is like going to my country, I rejoice.'"[24]

The missionaries faced many interruptions when visiting and speaking to the women of Karachi and Blanche would compare this to the full attention given by the pupils at the schools to highlight one of the benefits of the educational work: one woman said to her, "I have my work to do; I have my children to look after and my husband's food to cook; I cannot read and I forget so soon." Blanche continues, "A woman sat by the tent door and seemed to listen well, but I had just got to the most important part when she remembered her household cares and that she was on her way to buy food, so she quickly bustled off. It is often the same in the city, most difficult to get uninterrupted quiet. Babies cry; spoiled children fret and whine round their mothers; neighbours come in; husband wants his dinner, so that the lessons are often broken off at the most important part.

"But come with me to one of our CEZ schools. The bell has rung for prayers; the girls are standing quietly; a hymn is sung; a short prayer offered while all stand with covered eyes. Then the children file off to their classes, and for half an hour you have girls before you who are able to read, trained to remember, to listen and to think, to whom you can point out the truths of the Gospel.

"Do you wonder that we say school work, if rightly carried on is the most helpful? Very, very important is the Zenana visiting, the village itinerating, and the teaching in dispensaries, but all these are greatly helped if the hearers have even had a very little education.

"It is sometimes said: 'You should teach the young certainly, but gather them into Sunday Schools and do not waste Mission Funds upon secular education.' Our answer to this is that no knowledge which opens and improves the mind, and is imparted by a Christian, should be called purely secular. Arithmetic teaches the little Hindu girl that much-needed lesson of how to think and observe. Geography, history, and object lessons enlarge the mind. She can no longer believe that an eclipse, or an earthquake, is caused by some of the absurd reasons to which her mother and grandmother attribute it ...

"Not long ago a member of a Hindu Household in Karachi was struck down by a severe illness. It was the young educated daughter-in-law who then came to the front among the women. She remembered what the doctor advised; she gave the medicine at the proper intervals by the clock, not only whenever she happened to think of it! She persisted quietly and firmly in having food and medicine taken, in spite of the protests of the patient, remembering how her school teacher had been able to make her take quinine, when no one in her family could persuade her to look at it! All the house were ready to acknowledge that it was to her care and attention that they owed the life of the sick one. 'And it was you who taught her all this,' they said gratefully to her teachers. 'You have given me a good daughter-in-law, we like the girls who come from your schools,' is high praise from a Hindu mother-in-law, and we much rejoice at hearing it, especially when it is said of those who are trying to walk worthy of the Lord in Whom they believe.

"The daily Bible lesson taught, not as a task, but by the lips of a teacher in whose heart the truth she is trying to impart to others has taken root downwards and is bearing fruit upwards, does affect the minds and lives of the hearers. We try to give that lesson at an hour when all pupils will be present. With the help of pictures and maps, the Bible story is made as real as possible. The application to daily life is not forgotten, either during the lesson or afterwards, when childish faults and failings give occasion to refer to it again. Whenever it is possible to find quiet for talk and prayer the little one is pointed to the only true power by which sin can be overcome.

"'But we want to hear of results,' you say, 'are there any?' Not, as a rule, those that can be counted or written about. While men missionaries can point to many schoolboys who have come out to become the truest, the best taught and the most spiritually-minded of their converts, we zenana missionaries can only speak of such girls as very rare cases indeed. A woman is not a free agent in India. She is married before she is of age to choose for herself, and then has no freedom of action.

"Her case is one of great difficulty. 'Is it right for a young wife to leave her husband even had she the power to do so?' is a question over which there are grave talks in the mission field ... We can therefore believe that she is carrying out the Gospel command even when she can only 'confess with the mouth Jesus as Lord' in her home and among the members of her own family ... 'You must allow me to read the Bible, it is my only comfort,' said a delicate young wife to her father-in-law lately. 'You say I am a good girl in every other way, and your only wish is that I should not follow Christ,' said another, 'but it is obeying Him which has made me able to please you by my conduct.'

"Many refuse to bow to idols. Many have passed away from this world with words of faith and trust on their lips. 'Why should you cry? I am going to God. Jesus Christ died for me and my sins are forgiven,' are last words which are often repeated to us by the relatives of some young girl, who has been a pupil in our schools.

"Then there are the secret believers. They fear to confess, but their faith is true and deep. Dare we say that the loving Saviour does not draw near and listen to the silent cry which goes up to Him from them, even though their lips hardly dare to frame the words of prayer lest any should hear and be angry ...

"Are these results sufficient to justify our efforts? We missionaries think so, Christian sisters ... Listen to this extract from a paper of the Christian Literature Society which I came across the other day. 'Of every 1,000 persons in India 947 cannot read or write. The illiterate women and girls are more numerous than the men and boys. One person in 10 of the males has an elementary education; but only 1 in 144 of the females. This vast multitude is beyond our reach ... The paper goes on to say that the Government is making greater efforts than formerly for the education of women. But what will that be? A Christ-less education! Shall we not be the first in the field, and offer in all the towns and villages of India an education teaching the fear of the Lord which is the beginning of wisdom? ...

"We are longing to put on our 'seven leagued boots' to march around the villages, starting new centres and new efforts, but are drawn back by the reminder that we 'must not look only at our work, but at the limitations of finance'" Blanche appealed, "English Christians! will you not unbind our feet and set us free to carry the Gospel of Peace to all who need it, ere it is too late and the opportunity has been lost?"[25]

By the turn of the century Blanche had become an experienced missionary in India and she became more prominent in the CEZMS. For example at the Decennial Missionary Conference in 1902 (an interdenominational missionary conference), it was Blanche who introduced the resolution under Baptism for Women which was adopted by the conference. Attending these conferences would expose Blanche to other missionary ideas and would help her discover what others mission societies were doing in different countries. At this conference resolutions were discussed on such subjects as setting up Industrial work and Teacher Training classes for the native women.[21]

Some of the children, Phulmani, Hyaten, and Amarit [26]

A Sindh bullock cart which was used for transport published in 1903.[27]

Sindh river boat published in 1904. [28]

Children in the Orphanage [29]

A Muslim family home in Sindh published in 1904.[30]

Widows and War

The struggle of the great European nations including Britain for power and pre-eminence resulted in war in 1914. This caused devastation not only in Europe but in many parts of the world. The effect of the war was felt in India, and many Indian troops went to the support of Britain and died on foreign fields. War costs money and Britain and its people had to fund the war effort. Everyone was working for the troops so finance was diverted causing a shortage of funds and physical supplies for the mission stations. There was intense pressure from the Home Committee to cut back the work of the mission in Karachi, and with no doubt sadness one school had to close because of a lack of funds. As the head of the mission station, Blanche felt these tensions keenly. The decade 1911-1920 also experienced heightened political tensions, and a devastating riot and massacre in Amritsar in 1919.

Widows' Industrial Class

The plight of widows in India was often desperate. Amy Carmichael in her 1905 book *Things as they are* described some terrible cases of cruelty, although she worked in a different part of India from Blanche and in a village setting there were many parallels to the situation in Karachi. Amy tells the story of a young girl who was an "innocent, playful little child", but who married at a very young age and became a widow at nine years old. She lived with the mother of her deceased husband. The family took her jewellery away from her, and she was forced to wear clothes made from rough material. At the time she didn't understand what was happening, but her predicament caused her to weep for which she was punished and called harsh names. Then she came to see she was not like the other girls; she had brought bad fortune on the family.[1] A widow was often considered accursed and was reliant on others for food and shelter. If there was no family or she was disowned by them how would she provide for herself and her children?

The plague had left a countless number of widows in Karachi. A Sindhi man suggested to the CMS that they should start an industrial class for these desperate women so that they could learn a trade and thus support themselves and their families. In 1911 Blanche took on this challenge and the Widows' Industrial School was started by Catherine Davidson to help the many Sindhi women widowed by the plague. The widows, the missionaries wrote, had become "dull, inert, sorrow stricken, with empty minds and aching heart. The paste, the pins, the scissors were brought to bear, in the form of discipline, education and a new interest in life. And the chiefest, they were given a vision of the All Great Being the All Loving and human Son of Man, planning, purposing, caring for every creature He has made."[2]

The Widows' Class was located in a large native-built house up a quiet lane, with two signs outside which read the "Widows' Industrial Class" and the "Teachers' Training Class", for both were housed in the same building. The Widows' Class was held in an upper room. The widows would be seated around the room, and when any visitors came they would display their finished work spread out on a low table. They made decorative velvet bands for women's hair or necks, of different colours and decorated with gold or silver material. Items were often produced to order so that they would match a particular garment. The widows were taught how to use silk or gold thread with their needles and worked in coloured silk to make cushion covers, book holders, mats, needle cases, card cases and table cloths. They produced items to suit both European and Subcontinent styles.

Half of the women's day was devoted to education - reading, writing, arithmetic and looking at scripture - and the other half to learning needle work, a trade which would help them provide for their families. For this day's work a fixed wage was offered to all the widows. At first many didn't believe the wage would be paid and so in the beginning only a few came but one widow tried and the money was given. There was no need for persuasion after that; crowds came to beg for admission, but not many could be taken.

One of the widows who was twenty-six, had attended one of the CEZMS schools and was remembered as a happy child. She had been married but her husband died due to the plague, as did her brother-in-law, and her brothers. Her sister then had to return to her parents. The widow was left in a household of three women, with three small girls and one old man who was to support them all. Before the plague the young widows would make garments for their husbands and themselves but now they couldn't make a living. The widow became a teacher in one of the CEZMS schools on a low salary, and when the Widows' Class started she was able to use her skills and was put in charge of the class with a salary increase. All of the widows had experienced similar tragic events.

Many of the widows studied so hard at reading, writing and arithmetic that they decided to continue their studies and achieved the Government Teachers First certificates. Some of the widows became capable teachers at the CEZMS Schools.

Catherine Davidson went home for a 'well-earned holiday' after improving the efficiency of the schools and her absence was relieved by Mary Brenton Coward who was a niece of Blanche. Mary gave this impression of the work among the widows; "In November I arrived in Karachi ... to be plunged into facing the crying needs of Sindhi widows in Karachi city. It is among them my work chiefly lies. There are now twenty-three on the roll and the daily attendance is good.

"Their mornings are spent in learning to read and write, and during the afternoons the industrial work is carried on." Mary described the process by which this was done: the Class received the order, purchased the material, measured and cut it to size, chose the colours and patterns, and finally produced the item. When the order had been completed the item would be carefully wrapped up.[3]

The Widows' Industrial Class could not increase its numbers during the war years because of the economic situation, even though there were many on the waiting list. However the items produced by the Class increased in number, variety and quality, two of the most interesting orders being a "marvellous sash for the drum major of the British regiment here; and a piece of church work which now adorns the CMS church."[4] Then the government introduced a code for the training of the needlework mistresses, and many of the widows from the Class decided to sit for the examinations.

One of the more encouraging consequences of the CEZMS Karachi Widows' Industrial Class was that it greatly influenced some of the Indian men to the point that they also started up two similar enterprises by themselves.[2]

Lillie Oldfield arrived in November 1922 and took over the responsibility for the Widows' Industrial Class with the help of Mrs. Mansukhani. The inhabitants of Karachi loyally supported the Industrial Work among the widows, and it was often a challenge to decide what orders took priority. The Widows' Class continued to produce a large amount of work to sell.

The 1935 report from Karachi contained some encouraging remarks from the visitors to the Widows' Industrial work. These are some of the excerpts:

"The main fact which is obvious to everyone, is that, while many people talk about improving the lot of Indian widows, the CEZ ladies have set to work to do it, and are doing it most effectively." P Ireland Jones CMS

"Such work as this, causing 'the widow's heart to sing for joy' is surely a service owned and blessed of Him Who so tenderly had compassion on her who 'was a widow.' May it go on and prosper, even under His eye!" A G Sutherland ZBMM

"I always find an account of the work done in Karachi by the CEZMS an unanswerable argument when anyone speaks unkindly of the value of Mission!" N Wentworth Stanley

"I am indeed much impressed with the good work which is being carried out in the Church of England Zenana Mission, Karachi. I think a few moments spent in the Widows' workroom well worthwhile. The hand work is beautiful, but the kindly atmosphere of the room more so. All the rooms are bright and airy, and the impression one carries away is that of a great endeavour being carried out most nobly and efficiently." H Whitely, (wife of the late Speaker of the House of Commons.)

"We were all greatly interested in this work, and felt it a great privilege to be shown around, and were impressed by the nearness of Christ and His great Love, the power of a noble and good influence." Mrs Cameron Scotland.[5]

Many women who professed Christianity were forced to flee their homes, leaving them without a means of income and a place to shelter. These Industrial Classes also helped the women converts in providing skills to enable them to earn a livelihood.

To provide shelter for some of the converts who had to leave their family and community Converts' Homes were opened by some of the CEZMS mission stations. In 1916 the mission station at Karachi opened a hostel for destitute women which consisted of one room, that would house women in desperate need of temporary or permanent shelter. It was hoped that this would become the Women's Hostel. In 1918 the missionaries in Karachi were able to establish a proper 'Converts' Home' which accommodated four women at a time. A friend's legacy and a personal donation enabled them to purchase the home.[6]

War Work 1914-1918

The missionaries were loyal supporters of the British war effort, and to their home country which was so far away. During the war there were many false rumours containing anti-British sentiment circulating in Karachi. The majority of the local women in Karachi could not read the newspapers and so the missionaries found themselves reporting the state of the war to their communities, calling this their "war work." So although they couldn't perform any actual direct war work they contented themselves with "becoming a kind of weekly Times to the city women". The girls at the Karachi schools collected money for the Red Cross, and the missionaries spent two hours each week working and supporting the Soldiers' Institute and Hospital.[7]

The CEZMS widows and the teachers at the schools all joined the War League, and contributed small monetary monthly amounts. They also spread the news they heard in the schools to the people in the city. These workers and teachers were often laughed at by the women of Karachi during their conversations, for believing what was reported by the missionaries. When the war came to an end they were happy that the "tables are turned."[8]

While their fellow country-men were fighting each other in Europe, the British missionary societies showed their love and concern for the German missionaries and ministers living abroad in British or French territories. They offered prayers and sympathy for their brothers and sisters in Christ of "German birth" who were "alien subjects in an enemy country."[8] Many British missionary societies helped the German missionaries in India when they hadn't received finance or supplies from their homeland. Some supported the German mission stations when the Germans had to leave. These brothers and sisters in Christ continued to love one another, and many missionaries sacrificially took money from their own pockets to assist them, and this despite spiralling costs.

Herr Oehler, Chairman of the German Mission-Ausschus, wrote thanking their British counterparts, "Our hearts have been touched by the kindness of our British friends in offering their fraternal help to German missionaries in distress, wherever such help is possible. Please express ... our sincerest appreciation and gratitude ... May God abundantly bless your labours for the supra-national Kingdom to which we all belong, and may He soon grant us renewed fellowship of peaceful work." On this occasion they did not accept the gift but suggested giving it to the French missions.[9]

When the German missionaries were at risk of internment, the British missionaries interceded with the government on their behalf. Murray J Lovell wrote, "Other bonds broke, but the missionary bond held. It was a beautiful display of the spirit of Jesus and a mighty apologetic for Christianity in the presence of a great non-Christian people."[10]

The 1917-1918 CEZMS Annual Report highlighted the external difficulties the missionaries faced at this time amidst freak weather conditions and political tensions in the Sindh and Punjab regions, "At several of the stations work has been seriously hampered during the past year by the abnormally heavy rains and consequent outbreaks of fever, which has been very severe in certain localities. In some places an increasing opposition has caused anxiety, but "holding on" has been the keynote of our work in these districts. It has gone on steadily and an increased readiness to listen on the part of the women, who have given their sons for the King Emperor, is noted. Among the Christians a keener expectancy of the coming of the Lord is begetting a deeper life and a greater longing to be used in His service ..."[11]

The war had some unexpected consequences for some of the mission workers. In 1919 in the Hyderabad district a number of young Punjabi men from one of the villages who had enlisted in the 71st Punjabi regiment had been baptised. Mr Harper from the CMS requested help from the CEZMS to send some ladies to speak to the wives and children of these young soldiers. Georgina Vacher and Mrs. Isaac were able to take on this task and went to see these women, which resulted in a happy reunion of the families when the men returned home to their villages, as they discovered Christian women awaiting them. The missionaries reported, "The husbands and wives were able to praise God together."[12]

The fighting finally came to an end with the armistice of 1918 and in Sindh there seemed to be a "Special friendliness shown to visitors in Zenanas and houses." There was great rejoicing over the news of the war's end, and many non Christians joined the Christians in thanksgiving to God.[13] During the celebrations for peace the mission children were taken to the Tamasha (A sight/puppet show) and led the girls' school procession.[14] Now there was peace the difficulties and constraints faced by the CEZMS home base during the war years had disappeared, and there were hopes for a period of "expansion and development."[15] To add to the good news of peace, the Sindh region also saw a large number of baptisms which must have been a cause of great joy in a place where such open evidences of faith were often sparse.

India's Women in June 1919 reported "There is much cause for thankfulness at Karachi in the generous help given by the English population. In spite of very heavy calls upon them for help in war service, they were more than kind in supporting the schools and industrial work. A 'Sale of Work Replacement Fund' restored the mission's finances to more than enough to meet the monthly expenditure of about 1,700 rupees. The widows' class, with grants and gifts from friends, was self-supporting."[16]

Reflection on 25 years work

After 25 years of service in Karachi Blanche reflected on the work which started with the ten children present on her first visit to the Kharo Dar or Salt Gate School: "... [today] peep into Kharo Dar school, you would find three fair-sized rooms, filled with nearly a hundred children, taught by five Christian teachers. These teachers have been trained and taught by the one who first gave herself to the work; and now is able to spend much time in helping and cheering her old girls who have married into new homes.[17]

"May 1886, saw a Gujerati school opened ... among the mothers of Ranchor Lines and Ram Swàmi Gari Khata. In 1888 a second Gujerati school was opened in Goria Bazaar and also a Marathi school in Gari Khata ...

"A third school for Gujeratis was opened in 1892 in the Sudder Bazaar ... It was not until 1895 that a new Sindhi school was opened, under the name of 'Chapar Para School' ... In 1900 a Sindhi school for Mohammedans was begun in the Trans-Liari quarter, and a small Marathi school for low caste children in the CMS compound,

"A school for girls who wish to learn English was commenced in 1905. This brought the number of schools to nine with six hundred and fifty children on the rolls. All the schools have Christian head teachers and these are assisted, in some cases, by under teachers who are non-Christians in name only, and who thus have an opportunity of hearing the Gospel message with the elder girls.

"Parvati, one such teacher in the oldest Gujerati school, refused a place where she could have got higher pay, saying, 'I shall not hear the Word of God in that school, I will stay here; never mind about the pay, I must hear God's word.' ...

"The Karachi Municipality have granted us two sites, one for the Marathi school and another on which we hope to build a really good Sindhi school, where we can combine the two now being carried on. They have also given us a grant in aid of our nine schools ... We long to see the foundations laid and the walls rising ..."[17]

Catherine Davidson's arrival in 1909 helped to increase the efficiency of the schools, which became increasingly important. School attendance which had remained fairly level had now risen to 686 students. There were twenty-four children in the Orphanage, and three hundred zenanas were visited. The dispensary in Jhirak was reopened and 350 patients had been attended to. The missionaries continued to see openings amongst the Marathi people, but the work as a whole was far greater than the resources available to the mission. Some of the women from the local communities asked earnestly for visits each week but they had to wait for a monthly call to receive their Bible lesson.

Changing Attitudes to Girls' Education

In the early years some parents didn't see the need for some of the classes the children were taking, but now there were signs that the attitude towards the education of girls was changing in India. Annie Saunders of Jandiala, Sindh, wrote; "The people are beginning to see the need of teaching their girls and in many villages they are asking for schools."[18]

Many people external to the CEZMS organisation bore testimony to the benefit of the work undertaken in Karachi; a report in the *Sindh Gazette* of July 16th 1913 at the time of the CEZMS sale of work at Karachi Frere Hall declared, "The truth is that the Mission is unostentatiously doing a work of charity, piety, and usefulness unexcelled anywhere in the Indian field of Christian endeavour. I don't make this statement on hearsay evidence but on the testimony of my own eyes. The five ladies at the head of the mission whose acquaintance I have the honour to claim – Miss Brenton Carey ..., Miss Fox Grant, Miss Ellinor Roberts, Miss Vacher and Miss Davidson – are five of the gentlest, kindest, and most gracious souls it has ever been my good fortune to meet, and their loveableness of character is reflected in all that they do.

"Every Indian girl who comes under their influence - there are hundreds and perhaps thousands of such girls – shows some new refinement, some new grace of manner or of character as the result. If I had the pen to describe what I have seen of the educational philanthropy of the CEZ Mission in the native city of Karachi, I believe that I should interest and impress not only my fellow Christians but all right minded people of whatever religion who admire the uplifting of human standards of thought and conduct."[19]

However, despite signs of encouragement, progress was not universal. The Muslim School in the Liari quarter continued to face challenges as the teachers found it difficult to sustain the number of pupils in their classes. This was mainly because of the poverty experienced by their parents which required their children to begin earning for themselves, at the expense of their much-needed education.

Evangelism and Education

Blanche was a great advocate for mission schools as an evangelistic means to reach the pupils and subsequently their parents. She often voiced this to the audience back in England through her speaking engagements and her magazine articles, as we have already seen her doing on her furlough in 1908. However, it is obvious that the doubts expressed by home supporters about the value of education work persisted, and she returned to the subject again in an address of August 1915.

"Is it only the educational missionary who is told, 'You cannot expect to keep pace with government demands; you must be content to let your school work lag behind, and to know that the mission schools are below the average; this is secular work, and you must not be too keen upon it.'

"We answer 'No - a thousand times No.'

"We absolutely deny that education is 'secular' work. It is the holiest, purest work to which the woman missionary can put her hand; for is it not to tend the Shepherd's dearly loved lambs? ... Is it not to train, discipline, and strengthen a nature which when mature, may have courage to enlist as a good soldier in the army of Him who goes forth conquering and to conquer? ...

"Let us be as anxious that the school should be fitted with drill apparatus as that the hospital should have its operation table. Is it not at least as important to strengthen the limbs as to amputate them? ...

"Let the mission trained teachers be the most up-to-date in their work; let the buildings, apparatus and furniture be what is really needed by Government Codes.

"Then is it not a solemn duty laid upon us of the Christian schools, to show to an impartial Government and a critical world that this great aim can only be attained where the Holy Spirit of God is the unseen Head of the School? Where the co-workers are those who have given their lives to his service. Where the secular and the spiritual, the earthly and the heavenly, know no dividing line, because 'Earth's crammed with heaven, and every common bush afire with God.'"[20]

Now that many more of the women and girls were able to read, the missionaries saw an increase in the desire for literature. One missionary wrote, "One of the chief features has been the very ready sale of books, little cheap hymn books, gospels and catechisms. A large number of these are bought by the little school girls, and as I go about in and out of the houses, men and boys and women too, ask for such little books. It is most important that good literature should be supplied now that so many women and girls can read."[21]

By 1916 the mission had approximately 930 pupils. The CEZMS now educated nearly fifty percent of the total number of girls in school in the city. What a responsibility now on the shoulders of Blanche, and what influence she would have on the future generations of girls in Karachi.[22]

Visiting the Zenanas and Villages

The review of 1919 gives this insight into the visits to the Gujarati women, supplying a description from the one worker who carried out the task: "The Bible lessons in the 2 Gujerati schools last from 11 to 12:30 at which time the women are just beginning to get free of their morning's work – grinding, drawing water, cooking and making bread. In many houses my coming is a signal for the women to gather quietly and listen to God's word being read and explained. In a few houses children are allowed to make a noise and women begin to shout to each other and chatter, but in many houses they are attentive because the reverence for God's word is so strong that they wish to hear. One anxious, worried-looking widow said, 'What you say is full of comfort; it gives me courage and brings peace into my heart, but after you are gone I forget. Do come often.' Some have said, 'This is truth.' Once when I had just read a portion of the Gospel, and before I could explain it, one woman said joyfully, 'Why, I understand all that; it is easy to understand.'[23]

"Another worker who visited Jhirak found the people very glad to be taught and visited again. The relatives of one girl were especially friendly and even asked if they might come to the workers in Karachi. Several sweepers also begged for teaching ... Although 30 villages were reached and 129 zenanas were under visitation the missionaries felt that the work of visiting was terribly neglected because of a lack of workers. The Indian worker who took up visiting among the Sindhis had to give it up owing to the need for teachers in the schools and the exacting claims of the educational work left little time for this.

"As one missionary writes: 'The morning in the city passes like a flash with 23 widows to superintend, college classes to take, practical teaching to supervise in two or three schools and Bible lessons to give; and day after day the inexorable 2:30 p.m. – time to go home to tiffin – arrives without a single house having been visited.'"[23]

Whilst undertaking their Zenana visits and their trips to the villages the missionaries would often encounter strong opposition from the Hindus and Muslims but despite this the local families were still sending an increasing number of children to their schools which must have been a real encouragement to the mission staff.[24]

By 1919 there was considerable opposition from Sindhis, Jews and Parsis because of the Bible teaching at the schools, but the missionaries continued to ensure the girls had their scripture lessons.

New School Building

The foundation stone for the long-awaited new school building was laid in 1919 and the following year, in an article entitled 'Walls Rising', Blanche looked back on how it had come about: "'Our landlord has sold the house and we have to leave this School on the 1st!' This was unwelcome news to greet a busy missionary as she entered a large day school in Karachi one morning about fifteen years ago. An interview with the landlord brought no comfort. The house was sold and the purchaser was coming to live in it on the 1st of the month. So a hasty and very tiring search had to be made daily in the city, only resulting in the School furniture being moved into a house much too small to receive it - very dark and gloomy, with only just room into which to squeeze the children, whilst drill and games were altogether impossible. The missionary stood at a breezy corner near the former school and looked up at an old tumble-down building. 'If the owner would only pull that down and build for us here!' she thought, 'Or if we could buy this house and build! Is the Lord's work always to be hindered by need of money? Must Mission Schools always be dreary and airless? He who loves the little ones must want them to have bright and cheery rooms and space for exercise,' and from her heart a prayer went up to the children's Friend, asking for a cool and airy school on that spot if it was in accordance with His will and plan.

"Time passed - like so many of our prayers, this prayer faded from the memory of her who had offered it; but not from the heart of the Hearer and Answerer of prayer. In time a rather more suitable schoolroom was found; educational work went ahead; a trained educationist was sent out from home and in spite of its still inadequate quarters the Teachers' Training Class was registered as a 'Training College', and obtained excellent reports, and a Widows' Industrial and Educational class was opened on the roof. By that time an urgent appeal to the municipality had obtained the promise of a free grant of land on which to build a new 'Teachers' Training College, Practicing School and Widows' Institute.' But a sudden blow came - a Hindu school stepped in; they wanted the land; they wanted the site which had been promised to the Mission - and they got it! But another plot was offered for the CEZ School, and after due consideration, it was pronounced as good, if not better, than the first; and this one was just across the road from the spot on which the all - but - forgotten prayer had been sent up so long ago. Here was a sign indeed that the Hand of the Answerer of Prayer was at work!

"After long waiting the lease was signed and sealed under the condition that the School should be erected in three years. But the money for the School Building Fund was still scanty. Time after time Jumble Sales brought in some welcome rupees; day after day school children dropped their 'mitai' (sweets) money into the collecting box; a friend left a sum which was added to the Bank account; and many larger or smaller gifts came in 'For the Building Fund,' each one causing joy and thanksgiving. Then the war broke out - and the cost of material and labour went up by leaps and bounds. Three years passed away without any work having been done, except the drawing up of plans, the filling up of forms, and the writing of numberless official letters. The difficulty of getting plans passed by the various departments to which they had to be submitted, and the correspondence involved, can only be realised by reference to a large file headed 'Correspondence regarding new building for Teachers' Training College and Widows' Institute.' One day a letter came from the Municipality stating that as the time allowed for the building to be finished was up the missionary in charge was requested to show cause why the site should not be reclaimed! More prayer and another appeal brought a concession-another three years might be given, but the building must be erected within that time, and this was only passed with difficulty. What was to be done? The Home Committee were only able to grant a small sum towards the building; prices went up, the value of rupees went down and the hearts of the missionaries went down with the rupee. But God had His own plan and raised up helpers in wonderful ways, and at last, after more than 10 years of filling in forms, and writing official letters, and getting up jumble sales and collecting funds, the 17th of December 1919, saw the foundation stone of the new building 'well and truly laid' by the hands of Mrs. Rieu, wife of the Commissioner in Sindh, who had herself been most kind in raising a large part of the money needed. And so the walls are rising, but owing to loss through exchange on three or four sums sent out from England, Rs. 2,000 are still needed ere the work can be completed ...

"About two hundred Hindu girls of good caste are being educated and will move into this School. About twenty-five widows (and some day we hope to house fifty) are learning to gain their own livelihood and to look upon the world with new hope; about fourteen students are being trained to teach by modern methods when they will be passed on to our other Schools; and, above and beyond all this, the Gospel of the grace of God is being proclaimed to each and all. May we not then commend this need to the prayers of the friends of INDIA's WOMEN, that it may be well and strongly built to the glory of God and for the truest welfare of the women and children of Sindh?"[25]

Itinerant Work

In 1911 Blanche and her colleagues conducted a short tour of thirty villages, some of which they had not previously visited. Again they were warmly greeted especially in the Muslim villages - in fact some of the Mullahs bought gospels and promised to read them to their fellow villagers.

Blanche did not want the readers of *India's Women* to romanticise about her tours to the villages outside Karachi, and was at pains to point out the strain of tearing herself away from the duties in the city, the work left undone and tasks left for others to do, who were already stretched. Added to this pressure and guilt were the 'troubles and difficulties' of camel travel, and the trials of 'temper and patience' as Blanche puts it.

Blanche writes, "A night's journey in the train brought Miss Vacher and myself to Meting station. There we obtained a cart and camel and after three or four hours further travelling we were safely landed at Jhirak in our little tent which was pitched close to our school and dispensary. Miss Roy, our Indian lady doctor, and one of the trained teachers from our girls' home are established in the bungalow and both medical and school-work are going on. The school chiefly reaches Hindus but the medical work brings us in touch with all classes. While we were there a woman was brought from a distant village on a donkey, and went away with a week's medicine. Then a boy with a fearful abscess was brought down the Indus in a boat from his village. The brave little fellow had a hard task to bear the lancing and daily probing; sometimes he had to cry out, but often he would smile again and say, 'Tomorrow I shall come jumping and running,' to try and cheer himself."[26]

Blanche's report continues, "But it was not an easy matter to start. We needed camels. In a few days, with some difficulty and a great deal of talking, riding camels were found, but baggage camels were nowhere. ... at last we heard that if we could get our baggage over the river a man with five camels would take it on to Banu, where we wished to go. In some fear lest this promised help should fail, we took down our tents and found carts to take them to the riverside ferry, and we waited until we thought the baggage had got a good start before mounting the quicker riding camels on which we were to follow. ... after having been kept waiting at least an hour in the burning sun while the boatman ate his dinner, and we enjoyed the sight and scent of a man washing a goat skin close to where we sat on our camel saddles. Truly we were having a change, whether pleasant or otherwise! As there was no trace of baggage or servants on the further side, we felt that they must have gone on to Banu, and that there was a hope of our having a roof over us for the night. The ride of twelve miles was a pleasant one, and we arrived in time to see the finishing touches being put to the tent, and to hear that dinner would soon be ready." On the Sunday the chief man of the village visited them and brought about fifty seven boys and nineteen men with him. He asked if the missionaries would preach to them, which they were happy to do.

The following day those who were ill started to arrive, and some came to them from a village several miles away. Blanche sat with Miss Roy while the patients came to her tent to be examined. There were thirty-six patients in total with ailments consisting of bad eyes, deafness, sores, skin diseases, and fever. It took Miss Roy about five and a half hours to see all the patients and to concoct the medications for them. The next day they rode out to a village nearby which they hadn't visited before called Rath. They saw a sad case of a Hindu boy who was suffering with pneumonia, and then they went from house to house to call on the people who were sick. There seemed so many.

As well as visiting the sick the missionaries were able to visit the villagers' houses to share the gospel: "In one Mohammedan house we had a large congregation of men, women and children and we sold a copy of St. John's gospel. A man who I think was the mullah, began to argue a little, but he believed the Gospel was true, so I kept to the last few verses of St. Matthew, and read how Christ said, 'All power is given unto Me in heaven and in earth.'

"Then we went to the Hindu part of the village, and had two large noisy congregations. A boy came to call us to a Mohammedan house ... there were two young women, sisters, one married and one unmarried, who could read. One of them said that she had heard us speak at the Gazi's house when she was a little girl. She was most attentive as I read St. John 19 and 20, and explained it; her face lighted up and she said, 'A lakh [large number] of thanks to God for His great salvation!' I think she really took in the truth as far as one could tell it her in one lesson. She bought a Gospel of St. Luke, so that she will be able to read it for herself.

"We met a woman to whom I spoke. She said, 'You came before, and sat in my mother's house.' Then she told me that the mother was dead, but she let us go into her house, and I found that she kept a sort of temple. We went into a large room in which she lived, all hung round with Hindu pictures. There were two small rooms opening into one big one, one was a temple to Shiv, and the other to Granth. We looked into the Shiv temple and saw a big stone, over which was a large figure of a cobra, and there were little lamps, and other things for puja [worship] (Hindu), and shells for making the noise to call worshippers. I had never seen it all so close before, and she did not seem to mind ... I said that it was very odd to be both Sikhs and Hindus and that Guru Nanak would not have liked the other worship. ... At last we got a good number of women only, and I began to tell them of a man who walked through a great city and saw many temples to different gods, and then came upon one to 'an unknown god,' and from that we got on to the Gospel. The women were very attentive and pleased to hear that we believed that the true Incarnation was coming again, having been once to give His life for them. It was the best Hindu congregation we have had, and no noise. We sold a Gurmukhi Gospel and several books ...

"One Mohammedan man we met on this tour was looking at the Gospel of St. Matthew, wondering if he should buy it. He opened it at Chapter 1, and I tried to get him to go on, fearing that the list of names might prevent his taking the book, but he said, quietly, 'It has the names of all our prophets in it,' and then handed me the price. How little one can tell what will be the best!"[27]

Georgina Vacher reported on the itinerant work at Jhirak in the winter of 1915: "I have been asked these questions in a letter from England: 'Do you find that the sadness of the War makes any difference to the women of India? Are they easier to reach since it began?' My answer is Yes, it has made a difference: I find all hearts now seem somewhat softened, and one has a great opportunity for pointing out how prophecies are being literally fulfilled. I may safely say we never enter into a house, or even the poorest hut, without being asked in earnest and hushed tones, 'What about the great war? Will the English win?'

"We have done some medical work chiefly in Jhirak where the Government dispensary was closed for fifteen days, and the people left entirely without help. One day a poor little baby of about two years old or less was brought to me with a hole quite half an inch wide in his forehead; his sister who carried him told me he had been poked by a cow in the street. I dressed this wound for several days and it got much better. Every day men, women and children come to us for medicine, and I find a stock of simple remedies most useful."[28]

Teacher Training College

The building where the Widows' Industrial Class was based was shared with the Teacher Training College known as the Kalij (college), which took place in another small room. Some of the Christian girls from the CEZMS home came to study and train to become teachers. Many of the teachers from the CEZMS schools also joined in the training sessions, so that they could learn new and better methods of teaching and management, which would help them advance and enable them to sit government recognised teacher examinations. Some of the widows with aptitude and a willingness to learn to teach also joined the College following their time being educated in the Widows' Class. The College and Widows' Class later moved into a new building where the facilities to learn and develop were much better, and there was room to expand. The foundation stone of this building was laid in 1919.[29]

The Teacher Training College had twenty-eight students including some day students. In the year 1914-15 ten girls passed their government teachers' examinations and the class received a very good report. As there were many languages spoken in Karachi, the training college taught in three languages which meant there were various classes and lots of coaching. To Blanche's delight, "The Teachers' Training Class has been registered and we received a grant-in-aid this year and a satisfactory report from the Inspectress."[30]

By 1919 Catherine Davidson was able to give this report on the Teacher Training College and student examination success: "The College proudly boasts a record percentage of passes viz., Marathi students ... one third year and one second year passed; ... Three students took the Bombay School of Art drawing examination first year (of whom only one passed); and the latest excitement is a new Sewing Mistresses code, entailing most interesting work, and giving still further scope for women whose talents lie in their fingers. The College Grant has been increased by the Government and the Widows' Industrial Grant largely so; for which, in these days of straitness, we cannot be too thankful ...

"With the practical work - which, of course, must be done in schools of the right language Miss Carey and Miss Bose lend a helping hand; and the rest Miss Ghose and I divide between ourselves. Coming out to preach the Gospel, one is, as a matter of fact, largely taken up with Nature study, Froebel [Froebel was an educator who believed children come to understand the world in play] and games, drawing and needlework, unearthing long-buried rudiments of geography, or learning up new tales of Indian history. But all this has a bearing on the Gospel too; and our prayer is that minds now waking up from the sleep of generations of ignorance, may awaken first of all to the knowledge and love of God.

"I do not know whether the effect of training is most apparent in the women, or the children whom they teach. A specimen of the former is a most amusing little Hindu widow of about 24 years of age. She came to us at 17; and I can see her now sat on a bench, cross legged, for her first interview. She looked then like a dull old woman, without a smile in her; chewed betel-nut*3 continually, and took no interest in anything, and would hardly take the trouble to answer questions. Now she is an alert, bright little person in shining spectacles, working up for her third and last teacher's examination ... Her forte is drill, which she shows off regularly to visitors ...

"During the last year's plague epidemic, she made all the arrangements for, and practically ran, our school out in the segregation camp; and during the influenza epidemic, she put her knowledge of hygiene to such practical use as to systematically nurse her mother and sister- both ill at once in different houses- and probably, human speaking, saved their lives ...

"Now, as we enter a new financial year, difficulties loom large and ponderous before us ... After-war conditions make an increase in salaries imperative, while the state of our finances make such an increase impossible without closing some other branch of the work. Workers are always few, have thinned out to a most distressing extent, till the few remaining feel like so many Atlases, with the burden of the world on their shoulders ... Sometimes we reproach ourselves for the multitude of duties left undone; sometimes we reproach ourselves still more for the haste which spoils the few we do; and always we live in the perplexity of deciding which of the many most necessary works must be given up for the day ..."31

Finance

The financial constraints faced by Blanche and the mission station would

---

*3 Betel nut chewing was a common practice amongst the Indian women; a small piece of lime was rolled into a ball, and in turn was rolled into a betel leaf adding a bit of areca nut for flavour. This was then chewed not swallowed.

not go away, even after the end of the First World War. The Home Committee was looking to cut costs rather than expand, causing Blanche to write passionately as an advocate for the work in Karachi, "'Curtail where possible' was the message sent out by our Parent Committee at the beginning of the war. This sounds like 'Don't let your child grow as we cannot afford him a new coat.' And I know mothers will sympathize when I tell them that the Zenana Mission child simply will grow in spite of all efforts to stop it. What will the Parent Committee think of me when I say that this year we are strongly feeling the need of yet another institution! A letter is handed in – a young convert is coming out – the anxious missionary writes that she knows we have no room, but she must beg us to help her, as she has, 'tried all other possible stations in vain.' What would you have done? ... So the convert comes, learns more, receives baptism, joins the industrial class, and proves to be just the one needed to teach crochet work there, and sets an earnest quiet, consistent example. Were we right to take her?"

The above example was just one of the many requests the mission station received to save women who were in personal danger, and some of these requests came from government officials asking them to take in women and their children who were in desperate straits. Another example was a girl whom they had met in Jhirak who was malformed, still looking like a child, but with a drawn and strained woman's face. She had been taught in Jhirak and they prayed earnestly for her. The girl had obtained her uncle's permission to come to the Teachers' College so that she might study and sit for the teacher's examination. The mission was able to take her in to be cared for and influenced by the gospel. However due to the shortage of funds opportunities were becoming more difficult, to the sadness of the missionaries. As it was these rescued ladies had to live amongst the children for lack of room. But as the requests for help came in the missionaries couldn't help but think, "God is sending us so many women, surely He must be leading us to start a women's hostel. We shall not, of course, do this unless He shows us that it is His plan by sending money specially for this purpose." Instead of reducing their expenses Blanche and her team wanted the work to grow further to help more women in distress.[32]

Undaunted by the financial situation Blanche pleaded with the Committee for another worker in 1916, an educationalist: "Think of the difficulties that there are in Karachi. There are eight primary schools, with eight hundred pupils, and three languages beside English. There is a Teachers' Training College with twenty-four students having to be taught in three languages. There is an Anglo-Vernacular School with sixty girls of good family, a school which has the whole field to itself at the present time, and which ought to become the Girls' High School of Karachi. There is nothing in the way of it becoming so, except that there are not enough workers. Miss Carey is not pleading for herself; she is pleading because the youngest member of that Mission staff (Miss Catherine Davidson) is working herself to death. She has all this work under her charge, and, in addition the Widows' Industrial work. Miss Carey says she is working from early morn till late at night, only stopping for her meals and this cannot go on.

"What they want is a second educationalist to enable Miss Davidson to continue living and working, and to enable the work to expand, as it would by God's blessing, if there were sufficient workers."[33]

Blanche assured her supporters that every effort was being made to keep costs down: "With retrenchment in view, we go carefully through the expenditure of each of our ten institutions and schools, only to find that the rupees spent yearly upon different schools are just the sums in every case which cannot be given up. Liari School? It is uphill work, and the girls are constantly being taken away to earn money, but on the other hand it is a little lamp burning ... No, it cannot be cut off. The Sindhi schools, then, and the Training College … shall we close them? But here lies the future hope for much of the education in Sindh ... Friends in England, must we close any of our work? The answer lies mostly with you."[34]

One way to reduce costs would have been to join together the CMS with the CEZMS. In April 1919 seven of the CEZMS missionaries gathered to discuss a proposed amalgamation of CEZMS with CMS. However, the CMS work in the area was predominantly amongst Christian communities whereas the CEZMS mission in Sindh had a primarily evangelistic focus in all its forms. Blanche's Schools had produced fruit in bringing in converts and introducing Christian thought to a couple of generations of girls and women. There were also the itinerant visits to villages which had no other opportunity of hearing the message of the gospel. Blanche believed that if the CEZMS remained true to its original vision of evangelistic work, it would be possible to raise the funds needed for the hospitals and schools, and reduce liabilities in the field.

The CEZMS Sindh missionaries strongly felt they could not join the CMS unless it changed its organisation. They thought that the CMS constitution had been created from a male perspective and that women had the same position like 'parish workers' in Britain. In India, they believed, it was essential that the work amongst women should be controlled by women, and they did not want to submit to having their work transferred to a District Mission Council in which women were not elected.

Plague

The year 1917 saw more plague in Karachi, and Catherine Davidson described the awful toll it took on the inhabitants and the workers, "A boy asking leave to go home, feverish, in the middle of his school examination one day - the next day, his dead body carried away to the burning. A little school girl taken out to burial in the morning; her little brother following her a few hours later; and the stricken mother left at home nursing her third and last child, already unconscious in the grip of plague.

"The authorities then beat a drum, and advise everyone to leave the city; which remark is treated with scorn, as being a futile attempt to disguise, under the cloak of plague, the fact that the Germans are at the doors, and forcing Karachi to be evacuated! But when some weeks go by, and bring no Germans, but only many deaths in house after house, the headmen reconsider the matter, and begin to emigrate. So now we exchange foul-smelling streets and alleys for dry, healthy, sandy spaces, where only the pure sky above, and a raging wind and burning sun combine to make things uncomfortable for any kind of germ or microbe; vermin-infested houses are replace by hastily erected matting-huts; and young women and girls cooped up for months at a time in the dark rooms in the city, are now allowed comparative freedom to stroll about in the long, cool afternoons. They all grumble - all but the children - and do their best to make this new abode homelike with the old familiar dirt and smells; but their faces grow rounder and less careworn and all agree that it is better at least than having the plague."

The workers tried really hard to carry on with their tasks within the camps, "... The Training Class dissolves itself into a first year and a preparatory student away in the western camp, a second year and two preparatories (sic) in the camp to the north-east, one second and two first years left lamenting in the city, two first years and one preparatory stranded high and dry at the bungalow. The Widows' Class is in an equal dilemma - a zari worker [intricate art of weaving fine gold or silver threads] here, another there, and a third out in a village which can only be reached by train and camel ... and when orders come in for several different things at once, it passes all one's powers of organization to know how to get them done!

"The schools sound easier to manage, as teachers are also among these scattered widows; and, even without supervision, they can be trusted to go on with their work faithfully and collect all possible children - our own, or belonging to other schools - but even here, difficulties crop up. In one camp the opposition is so keen that not only will no hut be given for the use of our school-children, but when the women collect a few in their houses, this is also strictly forbidden. In another friendly camp, every mother begs us to take away her tiresome children, and let her have some chance of a mid-day rest; and for school-house, our only difficulty is to choose between the many huts offered; but those of our widows, who happen to be here, can only rise to teaching infants and Standard I, so teachers have to be sent out daily for the elder classes. The senior teaching, by the law of contraries, have mostly remained behind in the city, where there is the minimum of children left, and it is quite a business to arrange to give them any work at all."[35]

Annual Conference Address 1913

Whilst on furlough at the CEZMS Annual Conference Blanche gave the following address at the Farewell meeting at Church House, Westminster, England, on the importance of children's work. "Many years ago a clergyman in Devonshire was called to the death-bed of a young woman. He found her peacefully resting in Christ and was told, 'I was converted when four years old, through the instrumentality of my Sunday School teacher'. How little is sometimes thought of the importance of teaching very young children, but surely it is as true now as in the days of old that 'of such is the Kingdom of Heaven.'

"I stand here today to represent India, and to voice its needs for all my fellow-missionaries in that country. I would gladly interest you in the work of preaching the Gospel in the villages; in the efforts made to reach the lonely widows, or the weary dwellers in zenanas. ...

"But I have chosen instead to speak to you on behalf of the young in their short period of childhood, because the subject is one which is not only occupying the thoughts of mission workers, but also of all those who are interested in the welfare of India.

"The time has gone by when it was thought right to offer learning alone and to disregard the training of moral character. The evil of such a course has been demonstrated, and now the cry is 'We must have moral teaching in schools.' But what form is it to take? Great interest was aroused last winter in Karachi when all the managers and teachers of schools were invited to listen to one who had come out to show how moral teaching might be given apart from any religious instruction. The lessons were carefully prepared and well given. Christians listened and said, 'yes that is good and true, but by what power does the demonstrator purpose to raise fallen human nature and enable it to walk in this path of righteousness?'

"They also wondered why he exalted the second of the great laws of God to the utter exclusion of the first. Perhaps some such thought passed through the mind of a non-Christian present for he rose and asked respectfully: 'Sir, do you believe in a God?' No answer was given to this important question, and parents were left to remark, 'We do not wish our children to be made atheists!'

"God's holy book abounds with references to young children, and not the least touching of these is the description given of their sufferings in famine: 'Her young children ask bread and no man breaketh it to them.' May we not take it spiritually, side by side with the other homely picture of a son asking bread of his father who would surely not respond by giving him a stone. Bread or a stone? Which is to be offered to the little ones of India? ...

"Shall it be the life giving bread of God's word which will produce the living faith that works by love and brings forth the fruit of love, joy, peace, longsuffering, gentleness, goodness, faith, meekness, temperance? Or shall it be the stone of a cold, lifeless morality, which shows a law of right doing but is powerless to render any aid to those who feel the impossibility of obedience."[36]

Obituary of Miss Condon

With great sadness in 1919 Blanche's fellow missionary pioneer Miss M T Condon died and Blanche wrote this obituary.

"When a young missionary first goes to the Foreign Field, she cannot be too grateful to find herself under a competent and wholehearted Head, under whom she will get a good start in the missionary life. It was my lot, thirty-three years ago, to be sent to Karachi, where Miss M T Condon was re-starting the work of the CEZ Mission. We arrived in Karachi in 1885, to find one small school with fifteen children, and we were told that not a single Christian teacher was to be had. When Miss Condon handed over charge to me seven years later the number of schools had risen to six, with about five hundred pupils, and we had a good staff of Christians at work. Prayer and faith with earnest effort, had caused this change. I well remember Miss Condon's words when told of the impossibility of finding fellow workers: 'if the Lord wants us to do the work, He will send the helpers.' God honoured faith, as He always does and the numbers steadily grew.

"Miss Condon was greatly loved by all her fellow workers, and her hearty, cheerful friendliness is still spoken of by the few English friends in Karachi who remember her. She read the Karachi Report year by year, and one of our schools in which Miss Condon was best known was given the name of 'The Condon School,' after its founder had left for the less-trying climate of Abbottabad, and we are glad that her memory is thus kept alive among us. She retired from Mission work after nearly twenty five years' service. Our dear true-hearted friend seems to have been called suddenly to the presence of her Lord, just as she would have wished. May grace be given to us who remain to follow in the steps of her child-like faith and earnest missionary spirit."[37]

View of the Indus river near Jhirak published in 1913.[38]

Itinerate travel on camel published in 1913.[39]

Itinerate camp published in 1913.[39]

A Plague Camp published in 1919. [40]

The Widows' Industrial School. [41]

Catherine Davidson published in 1909.[42]

Trials and Honour

Blanche, now aged sixty five, faced a number of major trials during the decade 1921-1930 but she also had the honour of receiving official recognition for her services to the women and girls of Karachi. The trials were doctrinal, practical and personal. She continued to work in these most difficult circumstances and kept her sense of humour. This was all done because of her dependence on Jesus Christ and her undiminished desire for the people of Karachi to hear the good news of her Lord and Saviour.

Doctrinal Trial - The Story through Letters
One of the first trials Blanche had to contend with concerned one of her most able and long serving missionaries and the one looked upon as her successor, Catherine Davidson. In 1921 Catherine revealed to Blanche that she was leaning towards the high church views of Anglo-Catholicism, and believed that she did not comply with the evangelical CEZMS Articles. These Articles were the Protestant and Evangelical teaching of the Articles of the Church of England. The particular Articles at the heart of the controversy were:

Article 2 - The Word made Man - the atonement
Article 27 - Baptism
Article 28 - The Lord's Supper

Blanche herself remained resolutely faithful to the Articles. The following excerpts from the letters at the time disclose the nature of the problem and the distress this caused to Blanche, to Catherine, to the CEZMS Committee, to colleagues and friends. Despite the difference of opinion all parties displayed grace in their correspondence throughout the dispute.

Catherine wrote to Rev. C M Gough, the Corresponding Secretary for the Punjab and Sindh region in Lahore, about the problems that had arisen in Karachi because of her views:

30 August 1921

... I told the society at home this time that I am not at all orthodox CEZ (i.e. Protestant) and it seemed to me it might be in some ways better to leave CEZ and to offer to SPG [Society for the Propagation of the Gospel], but Mr Sargent interviewed me and passed me to return; so I did so with joy.

However the fact remains that Miss Carey – very naturally – feels herself responsible that everyone here shall be brought up in the "Protestant" interpretation of the faith; and since I cannot teach other than or less than I hold myself (which is the "Anglo Catholic" interpretation of the same) things are rather at a deadlock. She says I am alright for the non Christians; but my great longing is to work among the few Christians we have ...

Miss Carey has not herself broached the subject of my living with the students, but she has decided she cannot let me prepare the Confirmation candidates this year ... So I feel the matter must be faced.

Yours sincerely
C I Davidson

Rev. C M Gough, after visiting Karachi, in turn wrote to Rev. Douglas H. G. Sargent, the CEZMS Clerical Secretary (General Secretary 1919-1929). Mr Gough agreed with the views of Blanche and shared her distress about the situation. Catherine had been seen as a likely successor to Blanche but now her views might mean she had to leave:

15 September 1921

..It is a matter which has very greatly perplexed and distressed both Miss Carey and myself. When I reached Karachi on August 30 I found awaiting me a letter from Miss Davidson, of which I enclose a copy. I talked the matter over with Miss Carey and also with Miss Davidson.

It will be a great trouble to Miss Davidson if she has to leave the CEZMS work at Karachi, and it will be a terrible blow to Miss Carey if she loses Miss Davidson. There is no kind of personal friction between them, though apart from views on religious matters they have different ideas to some extent as to methods of work ...

Miss Carey values Miss Davidson most highly as a colleague, and Miss Davidson in every way shows the greatest consideration towards Miss Carey and is most anxious to help and support her in every possible way.

Miss Carey is 65 years of age, but has no wish to retire, and is still so vigorous that there is no reason why the question of her retirement should come up ...

The natural thing would be for Miss Davidson to eventually succeed Miss Carey as the head of the Mission. But what are we to do in view of this change in Miss Davidson's religious views.

... Miss Davidson had reached a stage when she says that she must either be disloyal to what she regards as the truth by avoiding teaching it, or she must be disloyal to Miss Carey and to the CEZMS by teaching truths which they do not hold.

... I have the greatest esteem for Miss Davidson as one of our very best missionaries, and yet I should not be true to my own convictions if I did not say that our first duty is to be faithful to what we believe to be the truth.

... It is obvious that the present situation must be a great strain on both Miss Carey and Miss Davidson ...[2]

The Clerical Secretary, Douglas Sargent wrote to Catherine asking her for an explicit statement of her beliefs in writing.

5 October 1921

I need scarcely tell you how distressed I am, for I was quite satisfied after our interview when you were at home that doctrinally your views were not really or fundamentally different from those of which CEZ stands. However both Miss

Millner and I were completely satisfied that you could and would be loyal to the CEZ position.

My conviction was that while you were quite sound as far as essentials of the faith were concerned, you differed from us only in your preference for a more elaborate ritual than is generally associated with Evangelical Churchmanship. It seems now, however, from the correspondence before me, that things are of a more serious character.

... What would help us more than anything else would be an explicit statement as to what you do believe, and wherein your views differ from those of Miss Carey, for instance.[3]

Rev. Douglas Sargent also wrote to the Rev. C M Gough in Lahore outlining the Society's dilemma; they wanted to retain Catherine but they were finding it hard to find a solution:

6 October 1921

... Miss Davidson is such a valuable missionary that we feel we ought to keep her if we can. If however she is really out of sympathy with the churchmanship, etc for which we stand, we shall be obliged to transfer her to SPG (if she is willing), or in any case disconnect her. I sincerely hope it will not be necessary to do this.[4]

In response to Rev. Douglas Sargent's earlier letter, Catherine wrote down her beliefs in a letter to him (see selected extracts below):

11 November 1921

... The nine points I have raised are all that I can think of on which my views probably "differ from those of Miss Carey"...

1. Our Blessed Lord

I firmly hold the doctrine concerning our Lord's person set forth in Article 2. I hold to the fact that "two whole and perfect natures - were joined together in one person, never to be divided", but am of opinion that according to Phil 2.7 & Heb 2.17, 4.15 our Lord must have, to a certain extent, emptied himself of his Godhead while working out our Redemption - which he did, if I understand rightly, by virtue, not of His Deity, but of his perfect humanity.

2. The Atonement

I do not hold with Art.2, that our Lord suffered to reconcile His Father to us. Equally I do not hold the Atonement to be vicarious ...

I hold that Christ ... when he made the sacrifice of a perfect life, he potentially involved in that perfection of sacrifice the whole of the human race; though the actuality is only realised as each individual unit comes into living union with the Head. (Rom.6)

[Catherine continued in her letter to list her views on the sacraments, a key area of difference. She clearly believed in baptismal regeneration and the 'real presence' of Christ in the Communion service, two tenets rejected by Protestant evangelicals like Blanche as unbiblical.]

4. Holy Baptism

... [I] hold that the human being baptised - whether infant or convert - undergoes an actual spiritual change by means of the sacramental grace received in baptism ...

... I would urge baptism on would-be converts, not as a sign that they have become Christians, but as a means to their so becoming; counting it as the entrance into life, not as a mark of having already entered ...

5. Holy Communion

a) ... I hold the Sacred Elements to be the means whereby our Blessed Lord imparts Himself to His own. i.e. I take it that our Lord's presence - Real, Objective, Spiritual (not Material),- takes possession of the sacred elements after the prayer of Consecration.

b) The Offering of Christ once made is certainly that

perfect redemption, propitiation and satisfaction for all the sins of the whole world; yet it seems to me that the fresh sins of every age need a constant showing forth re-presenting of that Sacrifice ...[5]

When the Society's Clerical Secretary received Catherine's letter setting out her beliefs, he responded to her explaining the CEZMS position on the matter:

9 January 1922

Dear Miss Davidson,

I have to thank you for your letter of November 11th with the clear statement of what you believe and what you teach ...

Frankly some of the points you mention with regard to your teaching are not in accord with the evangelical principles of the Society, and therefore should not be taught by our missionaries. They are as follows ...

(4) Could not be countenanced, as it is contrary to the teaching of the Bible and Prayer Book and the practice of the primitive church. The Catechism makes this abundantly clear – "Q. What is required of persons to be baptised? A. Repentance ... Faith ..." Until there is clear evidence of repentance and faith in the adult, we are not justified in admitting them to Baptism.

(5) A Missionary who advocates fasting Communion or non-communicating attendance – even in the restricted sense which you indicate – cannot be said to be acting in accordance with the evangelical views for which the Society stands. To advocate such practices might open the door to superstition and error, and could scarcely fail to lead to some kind of belief in trans substantiation ...

Will you give careful reconsideration to these various points, and having done so, write to me again. I most sincerely hope that on further thought and after further study, your

95

views will be so modified that you will feel you can continue to work loyally in connection with CEZMS. We are praying for you that GOD may guide you and lead you into all truth, as He has promised to do, by His Holy Spirit.

With kindest regards,

Yours very sincerely

DHGS

Clerical Secretary[6]

Catherine replied to the Rev. D. Sargent with her resignation:

1 February 1922

... I can see no other course than to very regretfully send in my resignation; and this course I had already decided upon some weeks before your letter arrived. I am extremely sorry to leave Miss Brenton Carey and the work, when there is no one else to take my place; but I think we all agree that the present position is impossible, with its inevitable choice between being untrue to CEZ or to my own convictions.

Up until 1919 I taught and worked in absolute loyalty ... to Miss Brenton Carey as my senior Missionary. During my furlough in 1920 I decided that I could no longer bind myself to the beliefs of others ...

I believe the Society expects six months notice of resignation which from the date of this letter's arrival will expire by about the end of August. That will be a very inconvenient time for me to leave, however; as Miss Carey is bound to take her holiday in September. So I shall be glad to stay on, if I may, for her sake, till her holiday is over in October.

... I also thank the society for the privilege of twelve years of very happy work out here.

Yours sincerely,

C I Davidson[7]

Something of the mood of the missionaries at this time, in particular Blanche's and Miss Ghose's personal feelings can be seen in this excerpt from a letter that Blanche wrote to friends. Blanche though was still able to find some humour in the tragedy:

2 February 1922

My dear Mr & Mrs Ireland Jones,

... It really seems as if Sindh, both CMS and CEZ were going through a great time of trial and testing.

... Catherine Davidson's affair is much worse. She feels she must go ... I much trust that time will see her safely through this phase as it did Miss Hewlett, and also three relations of my own, who came back to their early evangelical views after getting very "high" ...

... It makes matters most difficult. I cannot think how we can carry on the work. God may have other plans. We shall be shown, but it is most strange ... Poor Miss Ghose is down in the depths about Miss Davidson & I feel so anxious about her (CID) & her health, for she could never get all the loving thought and care she does here about food etc. It is a most terrible upset and Catherine is amused that I say I would much rather she were going to be married!!

Yours affectionately,

Blanche Brenton Carey[8]

Blanche, who seemed to be unaware Catherine had already resigned, writes a letter in the same month to Rev. Douglas Sargent. Blanche was desperately trying to find a way whereby Catherine could stay, but remains steadfast in her own evangelical position:

9 February 1922

I feel I ought to write something to you about Miss Davidson but hardly know what to say after having read her "views" ... I am very distressed about them. They are worse than I thought and I quite understand that it is not surprising if you feel she should not remain in CEZ. ... I hope that, as is often the case with others, she has such a good foundation of evangelical truth, that these below the surface views do not really come to the front in actual work. You could not of course allow them to be taught.

At the same time I feel that for Miss Davidson to leave Sindh is a very serious step. She knows the language so well. She loves the people and her one desire is to lead them to Christ. Would it be possible to ask her to stay on for the present but not teach anything which she knows to be contrary to CEZ principles. She might be asked to keep to the College, Widows and school, but not teach Christians. There is plenty of work in the city. Of course she could not live with the Christian students around her, as she so much wished but she does not seem so anxious about that as formerly.

I quite know you must act as you feel led by God and I am afraid even to suggest anything in case it may not be according to his plan but I just send these thoughts for what they may be worth.

... I have a strong hope that Miss Davidson will grow up out of these views ...

... I would much rather that she was separated from us than that one of God's little ones should be turned away from the pure truth of the Gospel; and if after a trial she feels the position suggested impossible, I shall feel that separation is the only cause.

... I know he (Mr Gough) would say that Miss Davidson will not and cannot accept the position, but sometimes a woman's instinct goes further than a man's reasoning power! and her love to the widows and others will make it hard to leave them.[9]

Four months later, Rev. C M Gough wrote to Rev. Douglas Sargent confirming Catherine's resignation:

21 June 1922

I note the resignation of Miss Davidson... I am very sorry

98

indeed that Miss Davidson has felt obliged to take this step. I hope that someday she will come to see things differently.[10]

So for the time being Catherine moved away from the work in Karachi, and left a big hole to fill. The story which had dragged on through 1921-1922 didn't end there however as Catherine did later change her opinion on a number of issues and was able to accept all the Articles of the Creed. After leaving Karachi Catherine went to Southern India to Dohnavur where Amy Carmichael was working. Catherine, still understandably troubled and wearied by the whole experience, shared with Amy the letter which detailed her views. Once Amy Carmichael had spoken to Catherine she felt that the latter's views did not align with her written statement. Accordingly Amy Carmichael wrote a letter to Douglas Sargent expressing her thoughts on Catherine. On Catherine's beliefs which she had articulated in her letter, Amy put, "I don't think she ever was there. I think she over stated her views in her fear of understating them."[11] Rev. Sargent was greatly encouraged by Amy Carmichael's letter, agreeing with her that he thought Miss Davidson was "not where she thought she was"[11] but "her mind was all over the place."[11] He confirmed to Amy that it would be a joy to have her back working with the CEZMS.

During Catherine's time in Dohnavur, Amy Carmichael had helped and supported her rather than directly trying to change her views. She had brought Catherine to a place of "quietness where the Great teacher could teach her". Amy delighted in working with Catherine and never came across anything divisive. Interestingly, not long after this episode with Catherine, Amy Carmichael faced her own doctrinal trial in the form of the liberalism of a new co-worker, Stephen Neill. Like Blanche, Amy stood firm on the trustworthiness of Scripture.

So Catherine rejoined the CEZMS in 1923 and was located in Asrapur - Atari.

Practical Trial - Accommodation Crisis

Another major trial for Blanche occurred in 1921 when their living quarters collapsed. This affected all the missionaries and workers for the next seven years. Hilda Corke, one of the missionaries who joined in 1919 wrote, "the Mission House that was and is not, for a few weeks ago it began crashing down and now not a brick remains! However, we have all managed to find sleeping accommodation in the compound, and we have our meals in a large tent."[12] What were they to do? They started to discuss their situation and the future, which now seemed uncertain after losing their accommodation. The imminent loss of a key member of the team in Catherine Davidson exacerbated this sense of uncertainty. All seemed to be literally falling about Blanche's ears.

The first priority for Blanche was to find accommodation for the workers. They set up home in the four-roomed Guest House and ate their meals under canvas, whether through the heat of the sun or through the rain. There was no place from which to manage the large workforce and all the other duties needed to run such a sizeable organisation. In 1921 the workforce consisted of five missionaries, three assistant missionaries, twenty three Christian teachers, nineteen non-Christian teachers and seven pupil teachers.

To add to their physical discomfort in their new living conditions was the mental anxiety of doubt over the future of the mission. There were questions over the tenure of the land, and the cost of rebuilding at a time when general funds were insufficient for such a project in addition to the bad exchange rate.

Due to retrenchment the CMS had sent out the order to close their mission in Sindh: they felt it was 'a barren field' and 'yields little fruit'. In 1923 Blanche records the impact of this decision on the CEZMS in Karachi: "In Sindh, the uncertainty as to what Society - if any - will carry on the work among men and boys has somewhat affected the CEZ work also. It causes an unsettled feeling among such of our teachers as are related to CMS agents; our building has been partly delayed on this account perhaps, as it was thought that, if the CMS houses should be left vacant, they ought to be secured by us. Perhaps the Home Committee too has felt the uncertainty and thought it hardly worthwhile to make any great effort to supply missionaries to occupy the gaps left in our ranks."[31]

Blanche faced the real possibility of the Mission being closed by the Home Committee. It took all of Blanche's resolve and persuasive reasoning, assisted by enthusiastic appeals from high officials in Karachi, to prevent this disaster.

The following correspondence details the exchange of views about whether to build or not and the possible options available. Those who have been involved in a building project will understand some of the tensions that are created by those who wish to go ahead as quickly as possible working alongside those who want to take a more cautious approach. Added to this, the mission team were living in a world where communication was predominately by letter or by short telegrams, and therefore experiencing the frustration of inevitable delays in receiving replies and decisions.

Catherine Davidson, still in Karachi during the early months after the bungalow collapsed, helped Blanche by writing a review of the work for Mary Millner (CEZMS Foreign and Candidates Secretary 1916-1923).

11 July 1921

The bungalow having fallen down, and so landed us all as it were at a parting of the ways, we are spending a great deal of our time these days in discussing the future of the Karachi Mission ... Miss Carey has asked me to write to you officially from an educational standpoint ...

... The training class (registered about six years ago as a College). The number of students is small – on an average only eleven or twelve; but we have to train students in three different languages, for three different codes, and send them in for their examinations at three different times of year, according to the Government Colleges in conjunction with whom we work.

... The staff ... consists of Miss Ghose and myself with odd help ... besides that I have the entire burden (with the help of one teacher and a girl in training) of the Widows' Industrial Class. This is a matter of some 30 widows to be kept in work: but the more serious part of it is that it also is a Training school, where we train women for Industrial examinations, also up to the third year. (Mercifully needlework has no language.) In drawing and needlework theory alone can they be at all worked in with the school students; otherwise all their training is separate ...

... Miss Ghose and I have between us the Sindhi Practising school of about 200 children, with a small feeding school in the city. We have no head teacher, and only 3 in the whole school who are at all trained, and that school in itself would make enough work for one person. (Miss Ghose ... has the orphanage of 33 children on her hands ...) ...[13]

The Home Committee, under increasing pressure to cut costs, was feeling uncertain about the work in Karachi in the light of which they considered whether or not it was right to build a new Mission House. In 1924 the Committee suggested reducing the costs of the work in Karachi which had a current working balance of four thousand Rupees by one thousand Rupees a year. They questioned whether the Karachi missionary staff was satisfied that the Training College and Widows Industrial Class were effective mission agencies. They also thought transportation costs were excessive and suggested the workers could live nearer to their place of employment; perhaps they could use the existing CMS compound. Blanche was not present at the time this was discussed at the meeting but on the minutes there is a handwritten scribbled note which simply says "Miss Brenton Carey thinks this ridiculous."

Eventually in November 1924 Blanche arrived in England to plead her case. She did not want to see forty years of work end, she wanted to see more people coming to know her Lord. She was confident that God would raise up the people, money and resources to rebuild the Mission House and to carry on His work in Sindh. The Lord had provided for the Mission Station before and Blanche did not see this problem as insurmountable.

On arrival, Blanche had many interviews and committee meetings. The CEZMS Committee was not unsympathetic to her case and there was a will for the work to carry on but there was not the financial resources available. How could they help? Blanche aged sixty eight was given permission to travel the country and gather support to raise the necessary funds herself so that the work in Karachi could continue and lost souls could still be reached with the gospel. By means of meetings, appeals in newspapers and to individuals she was able to raise £850 before her return to India. Blanche sought to raise the remaining funds back in India with the help of Mr Aston, Honorary Treasurer of the Building Fund and Mr Hudson, Commissioner in Sindh, and his wife. This was a long and drawn out trial for the missionaries which made living and working conditions extremely inconvenient, but the Lord provided through the help of many friends.[14, 15]

Rev. C M Gough wrote to Rev. Douglas Sargent in May 1924 suggesting a possible solution to the financial problem; a takeover of the Sindh mission by the Bible Churchmen's Missionary Society (BCMS). A number of CMS missionaries and supporters had formed the BCMS which continued with the CMS' original theological and missionary principles. The founders of the BCMS felt that the CMS had moved away from their original theological position.

Upon hearing of a possible takeover, Blanche wrote to Rev. Douglas Sargent, expressing her concerns for her fellow workers, but also her commitment to the spread of the gospel above everything:

18 June 1924

Your letter of May 22nd 1924 has come as a great shock to us all. I should be very, very sorry to be disconnected from CEZ after 38½ years of happy work in it. At the same time the good of Sindh and the furtherance of the Gospel must come before any private feelings and I am in full agreement with the views and beliefs of BCMS and would have welcomed them gladly as fellow workers. Nevertheless I shall feel most keenly being cut off from the life of CEZ and our Punjab missionaries ...

This is my personal feeling. Now for a wider outlook. P.C. [Parent Committee] must realise that they cannot cast off a Mission of many years standing as they would an old garment. Our Indian fellow-workers are entitled to some consideration. They are mostly women who have been in this Mission— (I will not say have <u>served</u> this Mission, as I trust they have served the Lord Christ) for 20, 30 & 36 years or thereabouts and some have steadily refused Municipal posts in which they could have obtained far larger salaries and pensions. They have lately been led to expect some help when they shall become past work. They cannot look to a new Society for this. It is futile to tell them they may move to some other CEZ Mission. Does P.C. know of any other CEZ station where Sindhi, Gujerati and Marathi are the languages used? The visiting and the village work? If these points could be solved I believe all would be willing to subscribe to the doctrines of BCMS as they are those which we, as members of CEZMS have always held most firmly.

When you think the matter over, you will I am sure understand that it is one thing to sit round an Office table and vote to "hand over Sindh to some other Mission" and quite another to face the difficulties of carrying this out. We have local funds in trust for a certain orphan and for the Orphanage Building which can be spent on nothing else, and lately a lady asked me how she should word her Will so as to leave money to <u>Karachi work</u> done by CEZM I must now tell her to wait until we know what is going to happen and which Society will be working in Karachi.

The whole business of handing over, if this is to be done, will take so long that I hope you will in the meantime, let us get on with the Orphanage alterations and repairs, and clean up the Compound by using up the old stones, wood etc. I am in a most uncomfortable place between two fires. I get letters from the Military authorities asking me to build and so clean up this most unsightly Compound and on the other hand I am held up by P.C. who will not give consent, although local friends have given me the money which can be used for <u>nothing else</u>.

If they cannot give us a house just now, we could – by getting the Orphanage work done – reclaim one room, for a while, and that would help somewhat until brighter days come or BCMS takes over. But <u>please</u> do not keep us longer in this state of dirt and untidiness than is absolutely necessary. I am daily expecting an ultimatum from the Cantoonment Authorities to build or quit and should greatly value a cable from Home with the word "Build"!

I hope I have not written this in a "hot weather" mood, but I have written strongly because I want to make an impression. I am quite sure that the Committee members do not mean to be unkind or thoughtless about us and it is only the old saying proving true "out of sight out of mind". Could the Committee take a walk through this compound from end to end and compare it with the tidy gardens on each side I believe the word "Build" would fly over the cable without any more pleading on my part!

With very kind regards,
Yours sincerely,
B Brenton Carey[16]

Rev. Douglas Sargent replied to Blanche on behalf of the Committee:

17 July (1924)

Thank you for your letter of June 18th, 1924. Negotiations in regards to CMS and BCMS have fallen through, and we are now taking another line which you will hear of from Canon Force Jones in due course. You will understand when you hear what this new line is that we could not send you the cable for which you ask.

Please accept the Committee's assurance and mine that nothing is further from the actual facts than "out of sight out of mind."

The holding up of the question of rebuilding has been quite unavoidable, and the fact that no decision has yet been arrived at is due not to want of full and sympathetic consideration, but to want of money. You are at liberty however to use the funds you have for the orphanage for cleaning up and repairs – if you and Canon Force Jones agree as to the advisability of doing so, after he has received the joint letter which Mr. Wigram and I are sending him. But you must only use your funds in such a way as not to commit us to any building scheme requiring to be financed from home.

It has been most cheering to us all to find how deeply attached to CEZMS all our Sindh missionaries are.

Things are working out all right according to GOD's plan, I am sure. May He bless you all.

Yours very sincerely,

DHGS[17]

Rev. Douglas Sargent also informed Rev. C M Gough that the CMS did not accept the proposal:

July 17

After very careful consideration the CMS has not accepted our proposal for a joint approach to BCMS ...

Wigram and I are sending Force Jones a joint letter asking him to confer with our Karachi missionaries to see if they can evolve a plan of concentration for the work of both Societies in and around the CMS compound, and so reduce expenditure and save the great expense of rebuilding our bungalow (£4,000) or at least part of it.

Our Committee were led to feel that they could not and must not try to shed any of the responsibilities GOD has entrusted to them, and that therefore we must make greater efforts to increase our needs. It seems evident at present that He means us to carry on the work in Sindh ...

Kindest regards,

Yours very sincerely

DHGS[18]

But by 1925, four years after its collapse, rebuilding the Mission House still seemed to be touch and go. Mr. Joseph Redman, a former missionary in Hyderabad, wrote to Rev. Canon Roland Force Jones (Corresponding Secretary for the Punjab and Sindh Mission) urging the necessity for the continuance of the work in Karachi:

16.1.1925

My dear Force Jones,

We hear from Miss Oldfield that the CEZ Home Committee are seriously considering the advisability of closing their work at Karachi.

Mrs. Redman and myself would consider such action to be a very great calamity. You know how keenly interested we both are in Sindh, and that for more than 20 years we worked in the Province. Having visited it frequently in recent years we have a quite up to date knowledge of the present circumstances. Sindh and its needs have constant remembrance in our prayers.

We understand that the reasons which weigh with the Committee are two-fold. First the financial straitness and housing conditions. Second, lack of results.

Now if any one of the three CEZ stations in Sindh have to be closed through lack of funds the Committee should carefully consider which could best be abandoned with least loss to the work in general.

My own opinion very distinctly is that if one station must be sacrificed that one should not be Karachi, but Hyderabad. To close the work in the latter place would be pain and grief to both my wife and myself. For 19 years we worked there, and yet I am convinced that if one place must go that is the one that can be best be spared. Of recent years missionary influence has not been strong there. The work there, useful and valuable as it is from the philanthropic and humanitarian stand point is not of great power from the missionary point of view. The Sindhis, specially the Amils of Hyderabad have had great opportunities for many years past, and much effort has been expended amongst them; the response has been very disappointing. From this point of view the loss would not be great were the station closed.

At Hyderabad the CEZ possess a very valuable property in the Mission House. This property might be sold, and the proceeds would go along way (possibly the entire way) to meet the financial needs in Karachi.

The value from the missionary point of view of the Karachi work is very high indeed. There is great spiritual power behind the work that Miss Carey and her fellow-workers are carrying on.

Whether one considers the number of non-Christian women and girls reached, and the clear earnest message constantly brought before them, or the widespread net work and scope of influence, work being carried on in at least five different languages in the Karachi Mission, or whether one takes account of the training of the Christian teachers and workers, and the upbringing of the girls in the Orphanage, the loss entailed by the closing of the work there would be deplorable and irreparable. The CEZ work carried on in Karachi, is by far the greatest power for Christ exerted in the whole Province.

The high regard in which Miss Carey's work is held by both Government officials, and members of the Mercantile community in Karachi is testified to by the large amounts contributed by them to the upkeep of the work. I am sure the closing of this invaluable Christianising and civilising agency would be looked upon them as nothing less than lamentable.

When the matter is carefully reconsidered in all its bearings I cannot but think that the Home Committee will feel that they absolutely dare not shut down work, upon which God's blessing has so markedly rested in the past, which has been such a great power for Christ for so many years, and which has in it the promise of so much blessing for the future.

I have not drawn attention to the fact that though the work no doubt is costly to maintain, yet it has won to itself the service of many honorary workers. There are at least two ladies on the staff at present, who are working without any remuneration.

With kind regards,

I remain,

Yours most sincerely,

(Sd.) Joseph Redman. [19]

This powerful testimony to the value of the work of the mission station in Karachi may have carried some weight. Whatever the case, eventually the Committee granted permission to build. In September 1925 it was announced that, "The question of reconstructing the Orphanage and building a new bungalow at Karachi was considered and it was decided to authorise Miss

108

Brenton Carey to proceed with the reconstruction of the Orphanage at her own discretion, using the funds locally available."[20] Although permission to build was given, by 1926 they were still eating their meals under the tent which was now worn and full of holes. But the spirits of the workers at least seemed cheerful.[21]

After many uncertainties and much making do with their living conditions, in *India's Women* (November 1927 issue) we read, "Miss Gough of Karachi told with great thankfulness how the foundation stone of the new Mission House at Karachi had actually been laid in July. On it was engraved the words: 'This was wrought of our God.'" This was a great encouragement to the ladies who had been putting up with less than ideal conditions.[22]

Some extracts from the Karachi *Daily Gazette* were published in *India's Women*: "Before a large assembly of European and Indian ladies and gentlemen the foundation stone of the new Church of England Zenana Mission House was laid by Mrs W. F. Hudson (the wife of the Commissioner in Sind), on July 29th. The guests were received at the entrance of the compound by Miss Brenton Carey, Miss Fox Grant, and Miss Oldfield of the CEZ Mission in Karachi."[22]

The Rev S Hinde, a missionary for the CMS in Karachi, gave a brief address acknowledging God's hand in all the work, "It was God Who by His sovereign hold on the hearts of men, by the beauty of His holiness and by the constraining power of His love in Christ, brought the CEZMS into existence, and it was God Who called together these workers, some from different parts of this land and some from across the sea, to build up this work in Karachi. God was in its beginning, God had been its daily strength, and to God everything in it shall turn when its work shall be complete. First and foremost, therefore, with glad hearts we acknowledge God."

Following a song sung in English by the Indian girls based on Psalm 121, Blanche spoke about her meetings in London to find ways of gaining the necessary funds to continue the work in Karachi. She thanked all those who had supported them with words of encouragement and for their most kind gifts. Echoing the earlier words of Rev. Hinde and the hymn by Adelaide Proctor, Blanche ended by saying, "Above all we are thankful to God Whose 'good Hand upon us' has brought all this to pass and moved hearts to come so willingly and kindly to our aid. We look up to Him and say: 'We thank Thee, Lord, that Thou hast made Joy to abound; So many gentle thoughts and deeds Circling us round.'"

Mr. W. F. Hudson C.I.E., I.C.S., Commissioner in Sindh and a firm supporter of the mission station's work, remarked, "It is now six years since the larger one collapsed, and ever since then the Mission with all its inhabitants have lived under conditions which any of the rest of us would, I make bold to say have considered intolerable ... But the Mission went steadily and uncomplainingly on with its work – its wonderfully useful and unselfish work- to the admiration of us all."[22]

The Mission still required the necessary funds to complete the building, and issued a plea for continuing financial support: "The Committee wish, however, to make the urgency and importance of the need widely known. Part of the building is already complete and the opening of a portion of the Missionaries' bungalow was a matter of rejoicing. The remaining work is urgent and the Local Committee are anxious to push on with it in accordance with approved plans as soon as funds are available."[23]

Finally after seven years in 1928 the house and a large hall for Guide Rallies, meetings, and family prayers was near completion. With a full heart Blanche thanked the generosity of local friends.

Queen Alexandra School Opens 1921

At least there was some good news as the new Queen Alexandra School and College had been completed, Blanche reports on the opening, "'So the wall was finished.' How quietly Nehemiah states the fact! One seems to forget the opposition; the hard fights; the letters, for and against; the Babylon officials; the temptations to give it up as too difficult; the half-heartedness of even those who wrought in the work. All this was past, the good hand of his God had been on Nehemiah all through, and so 'the wall was finished.' How well we CEZs of Karachi understood Nehemiah's feelings as we stood in the Drill shed one afternoon of late, facing the kind friends who had come to see the new workroom for the widows, the new study room for the Training College, and the bright classrooms full of Sindhi girls and their teachers which were to be opened that day."

With humour Blanche remarks about the new site, "The air here is delightfully fresh from the sea and the teachers and children will be nearly blown out of the drill shed on a windy day!"

But the opening of the school was tinged with sadness as Blanche records, "our kind friend Mrs. Rieu, wife of the Commissioner in Sindhi, who had collected over Rs. 11,000 of the cost of the building, and who had been gladly looking forward to being present to perform the opening ceremony, had been laid to rest three days before in the presence of a crowd of Indian and English mourners."

Blanche concludes the piece on the new building by saying, "Years have passed while we have been writing of 'Waiting Walls' or 'Walls Rising,' and now we gladly report, 'Walls Finished.' Pray that within these walls the Name which is above every name may always be glorified and that His presence may be felt there every day."[24]

Hilda Corke, one of the Karachi mission staff, describes the new facilities, "It is a substantial stone building - all our own, surrounded by a spacious playground in which is a large drill shed. On the ground floor, in the airy classrooms and verandahs are seated little and big Sindhi children."

Upstairs was the location for the Widows' Institute in a long airy room, and Hilda Corke continued, "Seated on the floor, with their backs against the walls are thirty widows of all ages, from the little twelve-year-old to the white haired toothless granny ...

"we must pass on through the breezy verandahs as to the Training College room. What a diversity of students, languages and codes! Some have to be prepared for their first exam, others for second year, others for third year. Some are Marathi students, some Sindhi, some Gujerati. With so many languages and codes you look around for the corresponding lecturers, where are they? There are only Miss Davidson and Miss Ghose to do it all -training work, widows, the day school, and the visiting in that quarter!"[24]

The Annual Report for year ending March 31st 1923 details the scale of the work which Blanche was overseeing. [25]

The number of primary school children on the rolls:		People group:	
Sindhi 'Queen Alexandra School'	259	Christian	46
Lyari (now closed)	28	Beni-Israel	15
Gujarati 'Condon'	171	Muslim	44
Gujarati 'Joria Bazaar'	76	Hindu	552
Gujarati 'Sudder Bazaar'	64	Brahmin	46
Marathi School I with AV	113	Low Caste	12
Marathi School II	11	Parsee	7
Total	**722**	**Total**	**722**

The missionaries in Karachi were:
Miss Brenton Carey - General Work and Supervision of Schools
Miss Roberts - Visiting
Miss Ghose - Children's Home and Queen Alexandra School
Miss Zöe Bose - Visiting and Condon School
Miss D Keshav Christie - Training College
Mrs Mansukhani - Widows' Class

Miss Sundrabai Vishwasrao - Zenana Visitor

The work among women was as follows:

Instructed in weekly or daily classes(teachers and others)	45
Houses visited in Karachi	279
Taught to read at home or English	34
Students in Training College	10
Widows' Industrial Class	32

There were no visits that year to the villages. This was almost certainly due to a lack of workers in Karachi as pointed out in the annual report for 1923.

Blanche provided an update in 1923, "With great regret we have closed our Makrani School in the Lyari Quarter. For some years we have not been able to get any number of pupils to stay beyond the Preparatory Class, and as the teaching had to be in Sindhi we felt that the children were not getting much benefit from Scripture lessons either. We are far too short handed for anyone to learn Makrani, and so decided that the time of both Christian Teacher and Superintendent could be spent elsewhere. The children are very lovable and it was hard to give them up. We handed back the "Kachha" School Room to the Karachi Municipality; and the Rs.800, given as compensation, has been returned to the Building Fund account, from whence it came. Our other Schools go on satisfactorily in spite of new ones springing up all round, which announce themselves as "National" and "Ghandi" Schools with more regard to attraction than to truth. These draw away our girls for a time, but mostly, in the end, the Sindhi proverb holds good 'the ship of truth may roll and pitch, but it is never engulfed.' Many girls return better satisfied to be with their own teachers and new ones fill up the gaps. It is most important that the highest Christian standard should be maintained and that the teaching should be the very best.

"Our Sale of work last July was a wonderful success. This was due to most kind efforts on the parts of friends, as the days are past and gone in which we could say 'all the work comes out prepared for us from home and we only ask you to sell it and buy it.' The great exodus from Karachi of many faithful friends this Spring might make us tremble for the future, but we are sure others will step into the gap and help us to make the coming Sale even more successful. It is I think remarkable that in the old days when the CEZ Sale was the only one in Karachi, we did not make as much as we do now, when the large YW Sale is also claiming support. Is it that 'the heart grows rich in giving' and those who give much are inspired still to give more?"

Blanche's faithful concern for the spread of the gospel was undiminished: "But what are the spiritual results from this year of work? Results of work among women are not easily tabulated. Many seeds may be growing in the dark which shall suddenly spring up to cheer us, but some results we do see. A more earnest spirit among our young teachers this year is apparent. It is a joy to find those, whom we have brought up almost from baby-hood so keen about the spiritual work in their classes and earnest in seeking to win younger girls of our Home for Christ. How much of this must be due to the prayers of those who support, and pray for, individual children and girls! Then continue in prayer, for the reaping time will surely come, even in this barren land, for indeed "we dare not doubt that Sindh needs Christ and that Christ wants Sindh."[25]

Ellinor Roberts, responsible for home visitation work, reported in 1923: "Sundrabai, our Zenana teacher, partially supported by the B & F Bible Society, is welcomed as gladly as ever in numbers of homes, she delights in her work and her whole hearted service and ever ready sympathy win her many friends.

"Had you come with me the other day to a small ram-shackled old house, and climbed the steep- ladder like staircase and entered a small room you would have seen a poor Hindu woman lying on a charpoy [light bedstead] dying slowly, going for months with the dread disease consumption. Listen to what she is saying to her friends gathered round - summoning all her little remaining strength to say it - 'I am very happy, I am going to Jesus, He is holding me, keeping me, I am not afraid, always listen to His Words for they are true Words.' Later when unable to speak, a radiant smile and finger pointing upwards showed where her heart was, till a few hours later her spirit flew from that little room to the 'Many Mansions' prepared by her Saviour."[26]

Minna Ghose described in 1923 some of the human conditions in Karachi, "You see children - some running wild, ill clad and neglected, learning to gamble and quarrel and use bad words. Others cared for, clothed and fed, but with no one who wants to teach them to pray to God or to tell them sweet stories of Him who said 'Suffer little children to come unto Me' and some learning much that will do them harm from the example of ignorant uneducated mothers.

"Then there are care-worn women - sad women - sorrowing women - young women who have lost their bread winner early in life - who have never enjoyed childhood or youth on account of their early marriage. Women who should still be happy school girls getting spiritual, mental and physical training, but who, before they are out of their teens, are sitting with bowed head mourning the loss of husband and sons and looking forward to a desolate future.

"There are about 300 children in our Queen Alexandra Practising School where our teachers are trying to improve and educate our pupils and teach them of the love of God in Christ. How sad we feel when year by year some of these children are taken away from school to be married often at the age of 10 or 12 or even younger. We know what lies before them when we see them so happy with their fine clothes and jewels, but what do they know?

Zöe Bose, engaged in visitation and school work, wrote in the same year, "As I go about the city looking up old friends I sometimes meet the answer 'she is dead or gone away,' thus reminding us of how fleeting opportunities are. The women are very affectionate and welcome you to their houses like a personal friend. Even when the town was most obsessed by non-co-operation not a single house was closed against us.

"The Gujeratis are very religious race; as they see us in the street or in the houses, they themselves will invite us to sing or read.

"The other day a woman, worn with toil and a hard life, she had been a widow for fourteen years with a young family to support, came and sat in the house where I was, and listened to the story of Christ's Atonement with undivided attention; as I finished she said 'This is a true word,' and we know there are others who think so too, but dare not confess Christ openly."[27]

Miss D E Gough in 1927 provided updated numbers, there were now "six schools holding over 700 children, mostly Hindu, where day by day the Gospel story is taught, and where twenty Christian teachers daily witnessed by life and work.

"In the Widows' Industrial Class there were some thirty women meet day by day to work and learn about Christ, and much visiting is carried on in the city.

"The Children's Home shelters a family of over thirty, from a baby of two upwards ... Some seven in the last three or four years had married Christian young men, and now have happy homes of their own."[28]

In 1925-26 there were further difficulties with two of the schools. For twenty-eight years the Condon School had been housed in a building especially adapted by a friendly landlord. This sympathetic friend died, and ownership of the building changed hands, leading to a jump in the rent. As a result new premises had to be found and unfortunately the only available place was a four storey house entailing significant work. Another new landlord acted in much the same way towards the Marathi school and they moved into a temporary resting place in an unused CMS bungalow. They were still in need of an educationalist for all the schools.[29]

It was also reported that due to: "unavoidable retrenchment, we regret to say, involved the retirement of Miss E. B. Roberts after 21 year's devoted service."[29]

An extract of a letter from Blanche in 1926 to a friend Mrs. Ross Lowis of Wimbledon, gives an insight into her personal thoughts on her heavy workload and the stress she was feeling at this time as she was getting older:

> Now that I have no one to help with the schools it is very difficult. Then the girls take a lot of time – I mean the Home. So much has to be talked over and also they need being talked to. I cannot feel too thankful that God continues to give me health and strength needed to carry on. At the same time, having passed the 70th milestone I feel that the Committee should seriously think of sending an Educationist for our schools and training college. The Municipal Normal School has been done away with and the training, as far as Karachi is concerned, is all in our hands, and should be the very best. Miss Christie, and of course Miss Ghose and Miss Bose, are very good and careful, but we all feel that we need some one younger and more up to date to take the lead in this work. At the same time we would rather have nobody than one who does not come as a missionary first and with a true faith in the Bible <u>as a whole</u> and a real heart knowledge of Christ. I know you understand this.
>
> Here I had to leave my letter for two hours in one of our Gujerati schools. Inspections are drawing near and the Teachers beg me to come and criticize their drill, etc. while there is time to put things right.[30]

Along with the joyful opening of the new Mission House in 1928 came the long-needed additions to the staff. Three missionaries joined the team: Agnes Fox Grant, to revive the Marathi work, taking Bible classes, visiting the Zenanas and superintending the work of the Biblewomen; Dorothy Langdale-Smith, a trained educationalist and former missionary of CMS in South India; and Miss K M Treloar a new recruit coming out for the first time. The Karachi mission embarked upon a new phase of life; extra workers and the new dwelling after seven years of struggle in circumstances of great discomfort.

Teacher Training College

There was good progress in 1921 with all the first and third year Training College students passing their May exams.

Minna Ghose provides an example of one of the students in the Teacher Training Class: "She was one of our happy bright school girls; she was married at ten years old; an unhappy mother of five daughters at twenty; a sad impoverish widow at twenty one! Now she has come back again to us to learn; and is struggling on with the hope of being trained as a teacher. Just before her husband died he arranged a marriage for the eldest of the five daughters, then 10 years old. A few years after the widow managed to marry off two more, aged 10 and 8, but had to run in debt to do so. And then a terrible blow fell, the eldest daughter became a widow with a little baby girl of her own to care for and support, and was turned out of her husband's home to be once again on her mother's hands, who was still supporting the two unmarried girls as well as an old mother-in-law. Other cases are nearly as sad. A widow of about 20 asks to be taught to teach who comes from a household full of widows, who are all dependent on one young delicate brother-in-law who keeps a small shop.

"About ten of such women have been trained and are teaching in my school earning their own living and happy in their work. Their sad lives are made brighter by the knowledge of the love of God which is taught to them daily."[32]

Article: *Story of the Year* **1924**

In response to a question "Tell us if it is necessary to carry on this or that branch of your work." Blanche wrote the following article in 1924: "Let us start with the Children's Home. What is being done? Needy children without parents, or needier ones with unworthy parents, are fed, clothed, taught and cared for. A few others are boarders whose relations pay all expenses in order that their children may have the benefit of the Home and its training. All live and work together ...

"Where is home? It is in the CEZ Mission compound. No wonder this question is asked, as we have no large building fit to house thirty-two girls. But, like most of our work, it arose from a small beginning. The girls did not come in when the building had been carefully thought out and prepared for them; the first one or two were put to sleep in unused servant's houses; then- a kind friend having given £100 - a dormitory was built, and now the verandahs are full of sleepers. With perpetual fine weather and an open verandah this is uncomfortable but not unhealthy. But the old servants' rooms have become damp and are dark; winter winds sometimes demand the shutting of doors and windows, so an effort has to be made to improve matters ...

"By whom is the work of the Home being done? Now, in spite of all the wisdom of the Montessori System, we find that thirty-two girls from two years old to twenty will not get up, cook, dress neatly, clean the house, and be ready for prayers at nine o'clock unless they have a busy, bustling Head! Priti Bai, one of our old girls, formerly of Katni Marwara, has grown up to be a valued fellow worker as Matron of our Home, under Miss Ghose, who also spends much time among the children.

"Is it necessary to ask why this work is being done? Is the child-life precious? Is it worth saving? We think it is. Really valuable Christian teachers have been produced by this effort ..."

Then Blanche highlights the school work, "Our schools ... We have seven, in which the languages being used are Sindhi, Gujerati, Marathi, Urdu, and English. In some we have the children of the rich and influential parents; in others those of good caste artisans, and in one we have a bright set of little 'untouchables,' who look as clean and tidy as the pupils of high castes and are just as clever.

"The Gujerati Sudder School and the school for the Depressed classes are about five minutes' walk from this house. The Marathi and English ones are about twenty minutes walk away and the Condon School about a quarter of an hour's drive in another direction. The Joria Bazaar School is in the midst of a busy part of the city still further away, and the Queen Alexandra School- a very large one- is about three miles distant. To this is attached our Training Class and a large number of children from our Home attend that school daily. It is on the upper storey of this school that Miss Oldfield has her Widows' Class."[33]

Kaisar-i-Hind medal

In the 1928 Royal Birthday Honours List, Blanche was awarded the Kaisar-i-Hind (Silver) medal. The Kaiser-i-Hind Medal for public service in India had been instituted by Queen Victoria in 1900 to recognise any person who had distinguished themselves by 'important and useful service in the advancement of the public interest in India'. Agnes Fox Grant wrote, "All her friends were much charmed ... when Miss Brenton Carey was honoured by the bestowal of the Kaiser-i-Hind Medal in recognition of her service to the good of the women of Sindh. She is touchingly modest about this medal, leaving it to her fellow missionaries and friends in Karachi to express their delight at her having been chosen for the honour."[34]

The Clerical Secretary of the CEZMS, Rev. Douglas Sargent conveyed the congratulations of the Society:

5th July 1928

Dear Miss Brenton Carey,

The Committee desire me to send a few lines of congratulations on the well-deserved honour that has been conferred upon you by the award of the Kaiser-i-Hind Medal.

We are glad that your work should be recognised in this way – glad for your sake, and also because it brings credit to the Society and still more, I believe, to the cause of missionary enterprise.

All best wishes,

Your very sincerely,

DHGS[35]

Blanche was glad if the award was helpful for the credit of the Society, but wanted no glory for herself:

31st July 1928

Dear Mr Sargent,

Will you please thank the Committee of the CEZMS very much for their kind congratulations on my having received the Kaiser-i-Hind medal – I am very glad if it can be of any help to the Society, and the missionary cause. Will the Committee pray that it may be so and that for myself I may, like St Paul consider it "a very small matter" only wanting to be "a workman approved unto God", that is what really matters ...

Yours very sincerely

Blanche Brenton Carey[36]

For Blanche there was still work to be done: this was not the time to rest on her laurels. Sindh was always considered to be rocky soil, a "dry and thirsty land where there is no water", but despite this Blanche believed that even Sindh had "its little oasis". Her unquenchable desire was to keep on speaking to the men and women of Sindh about Christ while there was still time. She felt her "weakness but dare not ask to be excused, as the opportunity is priceless." The Word of God was alive and able to change the hearts of the people of Sindh and she asked for prayer that this might be accomplished.[37]

Personal Trial

Following the problems with finance, lack of workers, and building needs which had occurred in the 1920s, Blanche now faced a personal trial which threatened not only her mission service but her life itself. Up to this point, she had enjoyed excellent health and seemed to have a robust constitution. But in 1930, at the start of the new decade, Blanche became seriously ill with symptoms which were at first misdiagnosed as malaria. However, she did not recover and her friends were very concerned that she seemed to be getting worse. They insisted that she should get further medical opinions: then after many consultations and examinations she was found to be in need of an urgent operation. The following correspondence unfolds the story of Blanche's illness and recovery, and reveals just how important she was to the missionary society.

Rev. Canon Roland Force Jones in Lahore wrote to the Rev. A J Mortimore (CEZMS Clerical Secretary) informing him that Blanche was unwell and in bed, which was unusual for the normally energetic Blanche:

13 February 1930

Miss Brenton Carey has been in bed for ten days or so with what looks like malaria. She has practically never been ill and it seems strange to think of Miss Carey having to stay in bed and let others do the work. She is better than she was and I trust that she will be quite well again in a short time.[38]

Rev. Canon Force Jones updated Rev. Mortimore on Blanche's lack of progress:

10 July 1930

I am still rather worried about Miss Brenton Carey. I wrote last Thursday to Mrs Snee wife of the CMS Missionary and asked her to ask the Doctor Major Brooks, to call in someone else for a consultation ... the doctors seem quite sure that Miss Carey has Malaria, but this has been going on for weeks. She has a slight temperature every day.

Miss Davidson of Quetta went to Karachi last Saturday and I hope that she will be able to suggest something which will be effective. Her very presence, I am sure, will be a help to Miss Carey. Mrs Snee writes, "She looks dreadfully tired and worn and old." The difficulty is that we cannot get her away from Karachi at present. The desert journey would be much too risky.[39]

Rev. Canon Force Jones wrote again to Rev. Mortimore to explain the seriousness of Blanche's decline in health:

17 July 1930

We are still very worried about Miss Carey ... Miss Davidson writes to say, "we are very much distressed and do not know what to do. She is steadily going down the hill but does not seem to realise it in anyway." She insists that she has the right to manage the doctor etc herself, but Miss Davidson adds that we feel that eventually we shall be held responsible for her to the Society and to her relations.

They are calling in the Civil Surgeon and Miss Davidson has also suggested that they send for Dr Holland from Quetta and she promises to write again as soon as she can. Miss Carey is of course distinctly old and apparently she has been suffering from what is described as digestive trouble for about a year ... We are doing all we can.[40]

A week after that letter, Rev. Canon Force Jones lets Rev. Mortimore know the latest news he has about Blanche:

24 July 1930

I have not heard from Karachi since the 19th, that is five days ago. Miss Davidson then wrote to say that the Civil Surgeon had been called in and his verdict is that there is nothing serious the matter with Miss Carey. She is on new treatment and is to rest more than hitherto. I am hoping that with the new treatment she will soon be much better ...

(later) I have just heard again from Karachi. The Doctor has decided Miss Carey must go to Quetta. It is not a good time

to travel, but he feels it is best for her to go. The fever continues & she is getting weaker daily. Holland will look after her at Quetta. [41]

A few weeks later, Rev. Canon Force Jones had more serious information about Blanche to convey to Rev. Mortimore:

27 August 1930

We got her away to Quetta and now the doctors have diagnosed her complaint. A few days ago I had a telegram from Holland the CMS Doctor there "Miss Carey has cancer uteras immediate operation necessary can doctor Lamb come." This arrived on Friday and I sent Dr. Lamb on Saturday. I hear however that the line is broken and Dr. Lamb only got as far as Lahore on Saturday. I hope she has got through ere this.

It appears that Miss Carey herself very much wished Dr. Lamb to be present and although it is a long way to send a Doctor and also Dr. Lamb was on holiday, I felt we must accede to Miss Carey's wish. I trust this will meet with the P.C. approval. I need scarcely say that the matter is serious especially for a woman of Miss Carey's age. It may be that Dr. Lamb will decide not to operate and will say that Miss Carey must go home. In that case I think we shall have to send some one with her. [42]

Rev. Canon Force Jones let Rev. Mortimore know the outcome of the operation:

3 September 1930

Dear Mortimore,

I have just heard from Dr. Holland that Dr. Lamb operated on Miss Carey on Saturday last and that she had stood the operation very well, but he says she must go home as soon as possible to have radium treatment as owing to the extent of the disease they were not able to remove all that was necessary.

I expect this will be in a month's time. Some one must go with her. I am trying to arrange for Sister Simmonds to accompany her ...

Yours sincerely,

R. Force Jones[43]

Blanche was loved and esteemed by so many people, in India and in Britain, that the news of her cancer must have come as a great shock. Rev. Mortimore wrote to Blanche sending the Committee's sympathy and prayers:

25 September

Dear Miss Brenton Carey,

We have all been very distressed to hear of your serious illness and operation. The Committee have asked me to send you the assurance of their real sympathy and prayers. We are all so glad to know that the operation has been successful, and we hope that you may soon be regaining health and strength ...

With every good wish,

Yours very sincerely,

ajm[44]

The following month, Blanche was on her way back to England, accompanied by Miss A Simmonds (CMS nursing Sister). Prior to Blanche's voyage, Rev. Canon Force Jones had visited in her in India, and was able to give a report to Rev. Mortimore:

22 October 1930

Dear Mortimore,

... I saw Miss Brenton Carey at Karachi when I was there, and considering what she has gone through she was looking remarkably well. This does not mean that she is well, but she looked much better than I expected. Dr Lamb has written to Dr Hamilton (I think) about Miss Carey. Dr Holland of Quetta felt that there should be no delay in arranging for further treatment for her. I do not know in what condition Miss Carey will reach England. She was able to sit up in a chair when she left but was not able to walk. The "City of Valencia" goes to Plymouth and Liverpool and I presume that Miss Carey and Miss Simmonds will disembark at Plymouth and come straight to London. Could you arrange if necessary for Miss Carey's arrival ...

Yours sincerely,

R. Force Jones[45]

During Blanche's period of convalescence in north London, at the Manor House, Highbury, the Clerical Secretary wrote to her on behalf of the Society:

20 November 1930

Dear Miss Brenton Carey,

I was asked by our General Committee yesterday to convey to you a sense of their very real sympathy in your recent illness. They were glad to know that the operation had been successful, and they very much hope that your time at home may help to build you up, and that you may be spared for even longer service for the Kingdom of God. We cannot think of Karachi without remembering you.

With kind regards,

Yours sincerely

ajm[46]

A month later, the CEZMS wrote officially to Miss Bose, who seemed to be holding the fort in Karachi in Blanche's absence and anxiously waiting for news:

12 December 1930

My Dear Miss Bose,

We have heard now from the specialist about Miss Carey, & it is not recommended that she should have radium treatment. Her general health is reported on as improving and it is advised that she has as much fresh air and as good *conditions as possible. She has been out for tiny walks and is very cheerful, and hopes to be at the Manor house for Christmas ...*

I will write again when there is any further news, for I realise how much you are all wanting to know about Miss Carey.[47]

Miss Bose was not the only one concerned to know how Blanche was faring, and the Clerical Secretary's pen was busy. Rev. Canon Force Jones in India needed an update.

4 December

Dear Force Jones,

... You will be glad to know that <u>Miss Brenton Carey</u> is going on very well, and we were told that she was proposing to walk to church last evening, so that she must be feeling better as well as getting better ...

Yours very sincerely,

ajm[48]

Nine months later, the Clerical Secretary wrote to Rev. Canon Force Jones about Blanche's situation:

25 September 1931

... she has seen Dr Hamilton, our Medical Officer, who reports that Miss Carey is wonderfully better, and she thinks it probable that the Medical Board may pass her return. The opinion expressed verbally is that she has apparently made a complete recovery, but that her health can be considered as probably precarious ... Miss Carey is eager to return ...[49]

Rev. Canon Force Jones was delighted to receive the news, as he told the Rev. Mortimore:

8 October 1931

It was very gratifying to hear such a wonderful report of Miss Brenton Carey. One lady at the Standing Committee ... read us a little from someone else's letter who mentioned that

Dr Hamilton thought that either Miss Carey did not have the growth originally or her cure was a miracle. I think that she would have to acknowledge it was the latter. I do not see how half a dozen doctors and a Bacteriologist could possibly be mistaken when an operation was being performed.[50]

Although happily Blanche recovered from such a major operation in a seemingly miraculous way and was able to return to the work in Karachi, this story is tinged with sadness: within a year or so, Rev. Canon Roland Force Jones and Dr Jessie Lamb who, in their different ways, had laboured so hard to keep Blanche alive, both died.

The Karachi Mission before the bungalow collapsed.[51]

All that remained following the collapse.[52]

Blanche sitting on the ruins.[53]

The widows at work published in 1925.[54]

Financial Pressures and Jubilee

In the decade between 1931 and 1940, the missionaries in Karachi had to contend with several global and local events of historical significance: the Great Depression, growing anti-British feeling in India, an earthquake in Quetta, and the beginning of another tragic world war, which would put India under the threat of Japanese invasion. The significant milestone for the mission and Blanche was the joyful celebration of Blanche's fifty-year Jubilee.

Meanwhile the CEZMS Committee needed someone to provide leadership to the Karachi mission during Blanche's recovery from her operation in England. Agnes Fox Grant offered to help and she returned to Karachi to take over the mission work.

Finance

The Great Depression, a severe worldwide economic depression which started in 1929 and ran on into the 1930s, had a devastating effect across the world, including Britain and India. For the CEZMS where finance was already a matter of concern, the impact was considerable. On 4th June 1931 Blanche requested that a special day of prayer should be held in India, for bringing the financial needs of the Society before the Throne of Grace, so that no further cuts in the work might prove necessary.

In 1932 Karachi, as well as other CEZMS mission stations, experienced a year of reductions. The grants from the Municipal school board had been in arrears and the teachers had to take half pay for a while. Eventually the money arrived, which was sufficient for the salaries and rent. One school had to close though. The mission also had to reduce the equipment used in its teaching, but they hoped no further reduction would be necessary.

The Widows' class was not immune from the economic pressure but also recorded answers to prayer, as we read in *India's Women* of June 1932: "The Widows' Industrial Class has felt the financial stress and five widows had to leave while three were put on half time. Only 32 are now on the roll. When 'cuts' became necessary the widows were asked to pray that money might come

127

in. They all did so, and the following morning a letter arrived with an unexpected donation, enabling one especially needy widow, a hunchback to remain full time, though it has been found necessary to reduce the pay of all widows receiving over Rs10."[1]

Lillie Oldfield in 1932 reported: "This last winter we have had to reduce all pay, even so, several times there has not been enough in hand to pay the women at the beginning of the month and they have had to wait until nearly the middle - but we thankfully acknowledge that money has come in to meet this need.

"During the last 12 months we have had rather a hand to mouth existence financially, but one or two large orders - for tablecloths for Dak Bungalows in Baluchistan - from an old helper of the Widows' work, and for guest towels, from the Quetta Club, have been a great help, not to mention initialling done for the Sind Club, Karachi."[2]

The District Local Board gave a much needed grant to the widows' work and individual members of the Board gave donations. They were also helped through a sale of work in Ziarat and this coupled with the Sale at Government House enabled them to continue the work until further grants came in.

The schools were also an object of focus when it came to reducing costs. In an article from the October 1932 edition of *India's Women* Agnes Fox Grant argues that they should not withdraw from educational work because of its evangelistic value but she makes suggestions for how they can reduce expenses which would allow them to continue. She writes, "In these days many of us are feeling that should we be obliged to withdraw or close schools, education would be carried on by the people themselves.

"But here the missionary side of the question comes to mind. That the schools are centres of Evangelisation is a fact which cannot be gainsaid especially when we realise that a large proportion of the Christians of our community are the results of the very schools which many of our friends the other side of the Indus [river] wish to see closed.

"And so I ask: 'Do reductions necessarily mean retreat? Why not close one school here – double two into one there – concentrate on the amalgamated and reduced number of centres? And charge moderate fees; for why, in these days of progressive views on education, should we give free education to those who know it is well worth paying for?'

"In my opinion we can in these ways continue to reduce expenses at least, here in Karachi ... and so, by preventing our workers from being hampered in their work, help to bear them up in their eager wish to spread throughout this Province the knowledge of the living Saviour, even our Lord Jesus Christ."[3]

Agnes Fox Grant gave several reasons for joyfully praising God despite their difficulties in the 1932 report:

"That we have arrived at the end of our financial year without a Deficit is a cause for a jubilate.

"Another is the return of Miss Carey wonderfully better.

"Another is that during a very lean time during this past year when some of our Teachers had to wait for the money to come in before they received the balance of their pay, they took these delays so cheerfully.

"Another thing about which we did not feel joyful at the time was the closing down of one of our oldest day Schools - an act rendered necessary through the uncertainty and irregularity of the income to support it with. There were other directions in which it was possible to reduce expenses without seriously curtailing the work [the school was the Joria Bazaar where Emily Prance worked].

"... And a special surprise pleasure came in the shape of a generous offer, through a friend, by an Anonymous giver, of sufficient money to build and equip a Sick Room for the Children's Home. It was given as a thank offering for Miss Brenton Carey's recovery; and it was finished in time for her to be present at the opening on her arrival from home.

"I close with a reminder of one of the last commands of Our Lord and Saviour Jesus Christ while on earth: 'Go ye into all the world, and preach the Gospel to every creature ...' As this is our warrant for being out here in His NAME, this our right for believing His great Message of deliverances from the burden of past sin, and daily salvation from the power of it in our lives, is rightly called 'Good news,' and is meant for East as well as West- for every race, and peoples of this Earth."[4]

As if to compound the financial difficulties there was disappointment in 1932 that the mission was unable to hold its usual Sale of Work, normally a source of valuable income. However God stirred up some kind friends to collect for an "Imaginary" bazaar which raised as much money as the previous year's real Sale of Work, and donations continued to come in. Blanche commented, "We are indeed grateful for this wonderful help and 'thank God and take courage.'"[4]

Despite the financial hardships supporters in Britain encouraged the missionaries by sending presents to the girls as we read in *India's Women*. In 1935 Blanche reported: "When I arrived from the lovely views and fresh air after a time spent at Khyber House, I was glad to find the welcome 'tea chest' standing in my office. It was some little time before we were able to find time to open and unpack the gifts. It was a pleasure to do so, and we said to one another: 'I think there are specially nice things this year, people are kind to send them.' ... We are warmly grateful for all those nice gifts, and wish our friends could look in on Christmas morning to see our large family seated on the floor in our school room. One and all exclaim with delight as they open their Christmas presents for it is 'give and take' all round, and the children love to present the 'Miss Sahibs' with sweets or some other gift at the same time as they are receiving their own. Pray that one and all may take the gift of the Great Giver and also give themselves to be His own."[5]

After many years of advocating the use of education for evangelism, Blanche was faced with a change in direction for school mission work on the part of the Society's Home Committee. Certainly during the 1930s, if not before, missions were starting to adopt the practice of educating children from native Christian families in order to enable the local church to become self-propagating, rather than taking in children from other faith backgrounds. Blanche was faced with arguments to reduce the number of schools because the majority of pupils in the mission schools in Karachi were non-Christians and so did not fit in with these new aims. In addition, reducing the spend on schools which were used to teach non-Christians would help the mission society to balance their books.

Political Unrest

With the rise in nationalism and increasing demands for independence from Britain, India felt the full force of the campaign of civil disobedience. During the disturbances, there was picketing at the mission schools. The police sometimes had to be called upon to help move the picketers, usually when small boys were carrying stones. In the face of all this, the local staff remained very loyal to the missionaries. And despite the anti-British movement, at the Queen Alexandra School the parents continued to send their children and many had to be refused owing to the lack of space. The women who had been visited in their homes listened very willingly and continued to welcome the missionaries. Initially at this time of national unrest, whilst Blanche was absent, much needed cover and leadership for the mission in Karachi was provided by the experienced Agnes Fox Grant.[6]

In 1935 a riot took place in Karachi. The *Sydney Morning Herald* of March 23 1935 reported that a Muslim 'mob' rioted in Karachi, and that government troops opened fire, killing thirty-three and injuring more than a hundred people. In a subsequent edition these figures were increased.

The newspaper report stated that the attack on the government was incited by Muslim members of the Legislative Assembly at New Delhi. A mob had gathered during the burial of a Muslim man who had been executed for murdering a "man who written offensively about the prophet Mohammed." It was alleged that the soldiers fired 'indiscriminately' into the crowd. The report goes on: "Sir Henry Craik Home member declared that the troops had fired entirely in self defence as they had been attacked by 10,000 some of whom attempted to seize their rifles. If they had broken through there would have been widespread looting and attacks on the Hindus". The total force of troops and police totalled one hundred and were completely outnumbered.[7]

The following month, the *Sydney Morning Herald* of April 11th 1935 reported that there had been an investigation into the incident and the soldiers had been exonerated. Lord Brabourne, Governor of Bombay and Viceroy Lord Willington thought that a public enquiry, demanded by the Legislative and the nationalist press, would "serve no useful purpose." Further they believed it would cause more feelings of bitterness between the Hindu and Muslim people.

These reports highlight the tension there was at this time in Karachi between the different religious communities. It also suggests the mounting difficulties the government had in managing political unrest without resorting to the use of armed forces. These deaths and the subsequent internal investigation would only serve to heighten those tensions. Amongst all this political unrest and its associated dangers the single women missionaries attempted to share the peace of the Lord Jesus Christ.

Blanche welcomed back

Blanche returned to Karachi following her convalescence in England and was able to provide an update on the work in 1932 which reflected her complete dependence upon the Lord: "'Wait thou only upon God for my expectation is from Him, He only is my Rock.' This seems to be the motto for Karachi CEZM for this year, as in all by-gone years. 'He only' has helped and will help. It is a great joy to be back once more, and to be of some help in the work. Miss Fox Grant had carried on all most splendidly in spite of being in very low water with regards to funds."[8]

Blanche received a loving welcome back from everyone at the mission station, including the children in the Children's Home. Minna Ghose wrote, "Last year we were trusting and this year we are rejoicing as well in Miss Carey's return to us. There was great rejoicing in the school where she is loved, not only by the present girls but by their mothers and grandmothers also. There was great rejoicing in the Children's Home, on the safe return of the children's Man-ji for whom they had prayed day and night. And we older ones rejoiced also when our wise Head and friend returned, though we have been very thankful to have had Miss Fox Grant in her place. One of our little ones, six years old, has great childlike faith in her Heavenly Father; when her Man-ji was very ill and some of the children were crying, she said 'Why do they cry? God can make her well.' Now we are praying for funds and she says 'God gives when we ask.'"[9]

Zöe Bose wrote, "This year opened with the grateful thought in our hearts, 'The Lord hath done great things for us, whereof we are glad', for our beloved Bari Miss Sahiba had came back to us. This joy sent golden gleams through the leaden clouds which hang over the future of our work. We still wait and wonder what the future will bring. Are these institutions to close, which have lasted so many years that they are like landmarks in the place? Long ago by the Galilean lake the Master gave the commission, 'Feed my lambs.' He would not be on earth any more to draw them to Himself by loving word and work, and so down the ages He has come to us, His servants to do it for Him. In our schools there are scores, all together they number hundreds, of little ones, who gather together every day to hear the old old story which they might never hear otherwise and we feel it cannot be His will 'that one of these little ones should perish.'

"'Who is Jesus Christ?' I asked my class of small infants, a little voice answered 'Our God,' and as day-by-day she knows more of the love and tenderness of the One she thinks of as her God, who can tell what influence that thought may have in changing her heart.

"It is the practice in our school to begin the day's work with prayer and reading the portion from 'Daily Light.' My head-teacher or I used to read, but at her wish we now let the others have their turns, one of them is so eager to do so that she will scarcely let the others have their turns. During the Civil Disobedience movement a woman outside the school was speaking against Christianity, our Mahommedan teacher went to her in great indignation, it might have been zeal without discretion, but at least it shows the influence of Christ is breaking down the barriers of caste and bigotry. These teachers have been with us since their childhood and have had all or nearly all their education in the school.

"But even in the houses where they think it is part of nationalism to oppose Christianity, there is not much bigotry. ... the Condon Mission School is doing a useful work in educating the Gujerati Christian girls. Last year in the highest class out of eleven pupils nine were Christians, this year also the greater number are Christians and we may get more later on. If they are successful in the examination of this class, called the Vernacular Final, they get a Government certificate and can be trained as teachers. With us they get Christian teaching and training, as well as an education which will enable them to earn a livelihood.

"The Day of Opportunity is with us still and though we can scarcely pick up a paper without reading of financial and economic depression, which are making prospects all over the world so dark and gloomy, we will lift up our eyes unto the hills from whence cometh our help."[10]

Blanche lamented that they were not able to do any District work in Jhirak in 1932; they still had the houses there but they lacked the resources. However she highlighted the encouragement from the Bible of God's great provision in times of need and man's responsibility to continue to work: "Those who read the daily chapter of 'The Bible and Prayer Union' ... will have come lately to 2 Kings. They will have had their attention drawn to wonderful instances of the power of the living God. The case of a poor widow with 'nothing in the house.' A city without bread. A child who was 'not awaked.' A host longing for water. Instances of God's ready help in time of need. To us in Karachi all these stories bring words of cheer, and seem as though written for these times and for the different departments of our work! In all the cases mentioned, Our God was the supplier of the need. But the needy ones and their helpers had also their work to do. Vessels had to be brought for the widow: the child had to be awakened from the sleep of death by prayer and close contact; the bread had to be brought into the city by those who believed the word of God, no 'windows in Heaven' were necessary; and ditches had to be dug before the water was sent to fill them.

"The spade work of our Mission! How much there is of it. The valley must be full of ditches and then, though we 'see neither wind or rain,' we know that water will 'fill the pools,' because the promise has gone forth.

"... We Mission workers earnestly ask that our spades may be left to us, by your kind help, that we may continue to dig our ditches in schools and house and villages, feeling sure that the Water of Life shall come at last to be greeted with greater joy by the inhabitants of Sindh. 'For he who drinketh of that water shall never thirst, but it shall be in him a river of living water springing up unto eternal life.' Let us continue to dig and to pray!"[11]

Schools

The schools continued to be well attended despite the political uncertainty. In the report from March 1932 the following number of pupils were recorded.

Sindhi 'Queen Alexandra'	268	English Classes	24
Gujarati 'Condon'	148	Urdu School	32
Gujarati 'Sudder Bazaar'	123	Jhirak Village School (Closed)	
Marathi School I	131	Training College	12
Marathi School II	64		
		Total	**802** [12]

By 1935 the total number of pupils had increased to 888. However the number of Muslim students had dropped to only fourteen; the vast majority of the girls were from a Hindu background. This demographic of pupils in the mission schools would have a significant consequence in the next decade, when Partition occurred in India and Karachi became part of Pakistan with its majority Muslim population.

Article: *Sailing On* 1935

In 1935 Blanche reported: "We have 'Sailed on' during 1934-35. As we look back we have no great events to record, but the chart of faith, by which we sail, assures us that progress has been made. We have much for which to thank Our Faithful God.

"'Was Abel right to offer his sacrifice?' I asked a class who were learning by heart Hebrews 11 the other day. 'Yes' came the answer at once. 'Then why do we not offer sacrifices now?' This was a puzzler - no answer for a moment - and then a little girl of about 10 years old, after thinking for a while, stood up and said clearly, 'The Lord Jesus gave Himself as a sacrifice for our sins and now there is no need for us to offer any other.' How good to hear this truth, 'which sages would have died to learn,' coming from the lips of an Indian child!

"A few days ago Miss Ghose met one of our old school girls who has been married for some years and living in a far away part of the town, beyond the reach of many visits. She heard from this young woman that she was in the habit of calling the girls of her quarter together and reading the Word of God to them! Miss Bose was passing a house a short time ago and was called in 'Come and tell me about the death of Prabu Jisu.' 'What do you know about Him?' she asked. 'Oh, my little girl came and told me how He was nailed to a cross and that it was for us. Do tell me more' was the reply.

"Our Children's Home has 'Sailed on'. A good many fresh passengers have been taken aboard! Some new girls whose parents are able to pay for them, and a small boy, also two who cannot pay anything! They have just lost their father who has left a widow and five children, he was a Christian man drawing good pay in the Railway. We are trying to make a teacher of the poor little mother and should be very grateful for help towards the support of the girls. Whooping

134

cough has been one of our 'storms' but we found the isolation room a great comfort at that time. All the children are now well again and full of life ...

"The Finance which often causes us missionaries to pause and think. That too has not run short, or only long enough to make us conscious that our needs are being supplied by Him Whose we are and Whom we serve.

"So we start a new year of 'Sailing on' and this the 50th since Miss Condon and I arrived in November 1885 and re-started the work in Karachi, it does not seem a long time as one looks back and it is good to know that in spite of storms, or fogs, or even mutiny; troubles that arise within, or without, our Pilot will guide aright as He has done in the past and the Breath of Heaven will fill our sails if we faithfully carry out the part assigned to our care. May this 'Year of Jubilee' be used indeed to proclaim 'liberty throughout the land unto all the inhabitants thereof' and may any who, through carelessness or wilfulness, have 'sold for naught' themselves and their inheritance, be called back to know the joy of returning to The Father's house-hold and rest and peace."[13]

Quetta Earthquake

In 1935 there was a devastating earthquake in the city of Quetta which killed an estimated thirty to sixty thousand people and destroyed many CEZMS mission buildings located there. Catherine Davidson, who was working in Quetta at the time, was evacuated and housed in Karachi. Blanche wrote, "Quetta Earthquake has been a terrible shock to the whole Mission of Baluchistan and Sindh. We thank God for the saved, and we 'humbly praise His Holy Name for all those who have departed this life in His faith and fear.' Our Senior Christian Teachers very gladly obeyed an S.O.S. from a Mohammedan Rest Camp to help to nurse the injured Refugees and spent a week of their short summer holiday in this work until trained nurses were available from other towns."[14]

Dorothy Langdale Smith wrote, "the devastating Quetta earthquake has taken place and hundreds of the refugees and injured have been evacuated to Karachi. I have been visiting many of the latter in the hospitals and they were listening to the Gospel message of consolation and healing with such desire that I was forbidden entrance into two of the temporary Hospitals, for they said I was 'making converts!' There are still numbers elsewhere whom I am free to visit, thank God! and when I go to them they nearly always beg me to pray and when I explain that I can do so only through the name of our Lord they raise no objection. I feel convinced that through this great catastrophe many will be led to know and accept Jesus Christ as their Saviour."[15]

Jubilee

The year 1935 marked fifty years of Blanche's service in Karachi and in September the General Committee of the CEZMS sent a letter expressing warm congratulations to Blanche on the occasion of her forthcoming Jubilee as a missionary of the society:

26th September 1935

Dear Miss Carey,

I am asked by our General Committee ... to send you a message of congratulations on your forth coming jubilee. The latest reports about you are that you are as vigorous and active as ever, and we are so glad to think that your recovery after landing has been so thorough. We shall always look upon it as a miracle of Divine Grace, and to you it must have seemed a prolongation of life because God still needed you in the corner of His vineyard where you have laboured so assiduously for so many years.

We do trust and pray that if it be His will you may be spared for years to come to further the extension of His Kingdom in and around Karachi.

Yours very sincerely,

ajm[16]

In recognition of her Jubilee of fifty years of service Blanche asked the Committee if there could be a day of prayer held for the people of Sindh. Friends abroad could join with the missionaries and workers in Karachi in prayer for the gospel to be proclaimed and accepted. And so November 21st (the anniversary of the actual date when Blanche arrived in India) was put aside for a day of prayer. This formed an appropriate preliminary to the Jubilee celebrations in Karachi which followed, when tokens of appreciation were received from friends in many walks of life, both Indian and European.[17]

Blanche reflected on her years of service in Karachi, "Have fifty years really passed away since our C.E.Z.M.S. party for Punjab and Sindh sailed from Liverpool in S.S. Belgravia?

"Is it 50 years since the 'Willows' days when 'the foreigners,' as those were called who were destined for foreign lands, used to meet in little groups and pray so earnestly: 'If Thy Presence go not with us carry us not up hence'?

"Some of that group have had to retire after longer or shorter service for their Master, and some have reached a better Country where they see His face. A few of us- by the wonderful grace of God- still remain 'to preach among the nations the unsearchable riches of Christ'- a privilege for which we cannot be too thankful.

"Someone has truly said: 'No greater reward can be given to the servant of Christ than the wages of going on.' To be permitted to continue in the work to which He has appointed us, is in itself our highest reward.

"The arrival in Karachi fifty years ago, on November 21st 1885, is still a fresh memory. Dear, brave, out-and-out Miss Condon was there as leader. Her faithful words are well remembered, when the utter impossibility of getting Indian Christian fellow workers was put before her 'If the Lord has sent us to do the work,' she said, 'He will give us the workers.'

"How true those words proved! One by one the Lord of the Harvest sent them to us: and it is to those faithful and God sent fellow-workers that any success that may have attended CEZMS work in Karachi is due. What is a colonel without his regiment?

"Looking back over fifty years, the words, 'left undone the things which we ought to have done and done those things we ought not to have done,' come home to one personally with a new meaning. And yet how kindly the Master's Hand has put in the lines left out, and smoothed away the little tangles! Truly goodness and mercy have followed all the way.

"Surely the names of those who have helped to bear the burden and heat of the day in the past fifty years should be remembered:

Miss Dawson, much loved by the Sindhis for her cheerful manner;
Miss Prance, now Mrs. Day, who for thirteen years 'laboured much in the Lord' among the Gujeratis, and was also a sympathetic companion and fellow camel-rider among the Sindhi villages in Karachi District;
Miss Vacher, one of our most earnest district evangelists,
Miss Currie, who worked for a time among Marathis;
Miss Edith Carey (afterwards Mrs. Sinker), whose memory still lives in some Sindhi hearts, and whose knowledge of nursing came in so usefully in the great plague epidemic, when we had the privilege of helping in the Civil Hospital;
Miss Roberts, who spent many years working among Gujeratis and whose Parsee friends still enquire after her;
Miss C I Davidson, the pioneer of our Teachers' Training College and Widows' Industrial Class; not to mention others whose short stay among us also left its mark on our school work:

Miss Pope, Miss Clark (now Mrs. Seymour), Miss Morrison (now Mrs. Harper) and Miss Corke (now Mrs. Fieldhouse). Those who are still with us need no mention, but are not the less a source of joy and thanksgiving.

"For all these 'fellow helpers in Christ Jesus,' and also for those belonging to this country, who have worked so earnestly among their own sisters, I thank God.

"If we have not seen all the results for which we hoped as the fruit of our labours, we grieve over any want of faith which has made our wonder-working Master unable to show His mighty works, but we trust that it may be that the seed is growing in the dark and may yet spring forth suddenly. We are looking to God very specially in this Jubilee year to give an abundant harvest that sower and reaper may rejoice together, for surely 'the fields are ripe unto harvest.'

"As a child, when walking through the 'pathfields' of Devon, how often I have seen women at work gathering out the stones before the seed could be grown in that plot. So, if much time in this fifty years has been spent in the necessary work of 'gathering out the stones' and preparing the ground, surely it has been time well spent.

"We believe that many friends in the Homeland who desire to see Christ glorified in Sindh joined us in prayer on November the 21st this year, and we hope that they will not fail to continue in prayer for us. More Sindhis have been baptized lately than ever before, and we believe that God will do exceeding abundantly above all that we can ask or think."[18]

The Jubilee celebrations continued the next day for Blanche. Zöe Bose wrote: "Miss Ghose, the teachers and I had long been thinking and planning for the 50th anniversary of Miss Brenton Carey first landing in Karachi, unknown to Miss Carey as we wanted it to be a surprise for her.

"At her special request the actual day was set aside as a day of prayer so that many in her homeland might join with her and with us in prayer for the extension of Christ's Kingdom in Sindh.

"From 6 am till 8:30 when it was time to prepare for the special morning service in the CMS church, there was a chain of prayer, one and another taking it up every half hour. There was a good attendance at the service and also at Holy Communion, which was celebrated twice that day to suit the different members of the congregation, once at 10 am and again in the evening after another service where there were special requests for prayer. After the morning service we had a prayer meeting in the CEZMS House, conducted by Miss Carey.

"This day of prayer was a fitting prelude to the Jubilee celebrations of one whose whole career of successful work has been begun and carried on with prayer.

"On the 22nd our special celebrations began. Six or seven buses were chartered for the use of the schools which were too far away for the children to walk. The children from the nearer schools walked to the CEZMS compound, where a merry go round and a swing were put up for their enjoyment! The children were wildly excited as one school after another, by classes, took their share in the fun. At 4:30 in the afternoon they left their beloved swings and assembled in their hundreds, with many other friends and sympathisers to do honour to Miss Carey.

"After Miss Carey's reply to the address read by Miss Ghose, we led her to a specially prepared spot where she planted a tree in memory of the day. After the planting the Rev. C Haskell made a beautiful speech comparing Miss Carey's wonderful life to a great spreading tree, firm in its adherence to truth and principle and yet sheltering and restful for tired, perplexed souls. Each of the 8 CEZMS schools had their own special Jubilee song, and Miss Carey was nearly hidden behind the mass of flowers as one school after another garlanded her and gave their little gifts.

"After dark the Compound was brightly illuminated and we sent the children home happy and contented each with her own packet of sweets to keep we hope the memory of a joyful day. We Hope too that in the years to come the grateful remembrance of one who spent 50 yrs in obeying the Master's command 'Feed my lambs' may bring with it also thoughts of a Saviour, who loved and called little children to Himself.

"On the following Sunday we had a thanksgiving service, and the week after the celebrations were still being kept up as Miss Carey's other friends, both English and Indian, wanted their own occasions for congratulating her.

"I cannot close this account better than by quoting from the local newspaper, and also from the address we presented to her:-

'The whole evening's ceremony was a remarkable testimony to the keen appreciation by masses of Indian girls and women of the value of the help given to them by the CEZMS under Miss Brenton Carey's guiding hand ...

"'Wherever there is the uplifted hand of human need in this weary, sin sick province, there you are willing to be found, following in the steps of the Master, who we thank for lives like yours.'"[19]

Queen Alexandra, the Queen Mother

In the year of Blanche's Jubilee the mission station sent a gift of "handsome Sindhi gold and silver embroidery" made by the Widows' Industrial Class to the Queen Mother with the following letter:

139

'The members of the Church of England Zenana Mission Widows Industrial class very humbly ask your Majesty's acceptance of a specimen of their Sindhi needlework. They are deeply grateful that you have allowed Your Majesty's name to be given to their Institution and trust that the new building may be a great blessing to many widows in Sindh. They will look at the photograph which your Majesty has so graciously sent, and remember with affection and gratitude the kindness and love of their far away Queen Mother.'

The Widows' Class later received a letter of sincere thanks for the gift from Queen Alexandra's equerry.[20]

Growing old together

By this stage, some of the missionaries who had worked with Blanche or were still working with her were getting much older and some had left this life. Blanche herself was 79 in 1935. In 1938 Blanche reported the death of Georgina Vacher, looking back affectionately at her friend's service: "She was a member of the CEZ Mission for 20 years, and will be remembered for 2 special pieces of work.

"One was a school for Makrani girls, which she carried on for a time with great zeal, but which had later to be given up.

"The other was that of village itineration. As the cold weather drew nigh she was always anxious to be off into Karachi District, and did not need such incentive as was contained in the letter of a small schoolboy who wrote to me once from the village of Gharo "Is it not time for you to stir up and come out to teach us again?"

"Miss Vacher had taken some hospital training and greatly loved to treat any simple cases which came in her way. She had a wonderful way of dealing with the dreadful sores that are so plentiful in the villages, and I still remember one poor baby whose little head was in a shocking state, but which soon yielded to her treatment. The grateful mother was willing to listen to the Gospel Message and kept repeating 'these are people like ourselves', a compliment in which we rejoiced, but we heard our old chokidar [gatekeeper] exclaim indignantly, 'people like ourselves indeed! Oh these djat manhon! (ignorant peasants).'

"We hoped these words of scorn were not heard by the small patient's mother and that she realised how glad we were to be looked upon as real sisters.

"The wordless book was our most used text book and we had a simple little chorus which Miss Vacher would sing over and over again. I am sure that some must still remember the Word spoken and sung though we have not been able to have a real tour for many years.

"Miss Vacher remembered Karachi constantly in prayer and during her illness last year insisted on packing her usual parcel of little gifts, collected at the Empty stall at the Worthing CEZMS sale and sending them out as usual. She worked hard for the CEZMS Worthing but was also busy with the Children's Special Service Mission [CSSM now Scripture Union]. The work naturally claimed her interest as it was at meetings of the CSSM in Southshields that Georgie Vacher, when a child, first gave her life to Christ, since which time her one desire was to serve Him, Who has now called her to higher service."[21]

Agnes Fox Grant passed away in Dublin after a short illness in March 1938 and was greatly mourned in Karachi. When Agnes left her colleagues in Karachi to go home following months of illness she had said to them, "To those who love in Christ Jesus there is no real farewell. We are bound to meet sooner or later in His Presence." Since the Society had accepted her as a Missionary in 1898, she had served nearly all her time in Karachi. Blanche wrote, "'Faithful and devoted service' are the words used by the Committee of the Society to describe her work for the women and children of Karachi ... We thank God for all that He has enabled her to do, and pray that He may water the seed so prayerfully and faithfully sown."[22]

War and the need for change

Tensions between the aims of a home-based committee, responsible for overall policy and finance, and overseas missionaries working in the field, acutely aware of local needs, were not a new thing. In the early nineteenth-century, the pioneer missionary in India, William Carey, had experienced such tensions as his old friends in England died and were replaced by new committee members. Besides, change is usually stressful, and becomes increasingly difficult to contemplate as people get older and more entrenched in set ways of doing things. Blanche and her senior associates in the Karachi mission had served so long and faithfully in particular avenues of work which had borne so much fruit that they could not bear to relinquish them.

In July's edition of *India's Women* in 1939 a brief article written by Canon Hyde, Home Secretary of the Missionary Council highlighted the volume of work undertaken by a small band of long-serving staff:

"The CEZMS is facing the most urgent and vital problems of the women in

India. The work as I saw it can be summarised: loving care of homeless, friendless women and girls, especially the widows, education, medical work and evangelism. These women need and gladly accept Christ and they make faithful disciples.

"The vast amount of work undertaken by missionaries is out of proportion to the size of staff."[23]

War was approaching and Britain was re-arming. By the time that Britain was engaged in the Second World War severe financial pressure again was felt by all missions including Karachi. Changes were needed at the mission station but as the senior missionaries were now elderly it would be difficult for this to be implemented. A new retirement age of sixty-five was brought in by the CEZMS, which meant a number of the missionaries in Karachi who were already past this age were required to retire. At first it was thought that when they retired they would leave their mission homes, and changes could be made more easily. Ultimately however change was forced upon the mission by external world events and the partition of India.

The following correspondence gives us an insight into how the dilemma was viewed by the Home Committee and those on the mission field itself. Nobody wanted to upset Blanche but change was needed. Olive Cocks the Secretary in Lahore wrote to Rev. Mortimore about the problem they faced:

26th January 1940

... Having now seen for myself the situation in Karachi I do realise afresh how difficult it is going to be to ask Miss Carey to leave the house. She is very frail and was bothered with sciatica. A good deal was said in Women's committee that was not put in the minutes as we did not wish to embarrass further an already difficult situation.

We felt that we should have to locate one of the strongest women missionaries from the Punjab to see the change of regime through ... I would suggest that if Miss Carey were allowed to stay on it should be in her office and not the rooms that she now occupies ...

Yours sincerely.

O C Cocks [24]

Minna Ghose was due to retire from CEZMS in June 1940 but she wanted to stay and continue to work at the mission station. Minna wrote to Rev. Mortimore:

8th February 1940

I hear I am going to be retired from June 1940. But I should consider it a great favour if I may be allowed to stay on here and carry on my work on ½ pay or whatever the society may see fit to give me. I have no Provident fund. I am very fond of the Christian children of this our CEZ children's home of which I have been in charge since its foundation.

There are children of those girls who have been married and sent out onto the world from this home, now under my care and it would be a great wrench to leave them. I am well and strong and quite fit to carry on the work some time longer! I have also work in the city. I am in charge of a large Sindhi school. When I first took charge of it there were only about 30 children in it, and now there are 300 or more and they are sent to us mostly by mothers who once were in this school as children and pupils. I also visit these mothers and others in their houses and preach the gospel to them.

with best wishes
yrs sincerely
M Ghose [25]

Blanche hoped that Catherine Davidson would come to help them navigate the change that was required to reduce expenditure. Blanche wrote to Rev. Mortimore:

9th March 1940

I am afraid our affairs are giving a good deal of trouble at home. We will do all we can to help in cutting down expense so as to injure the work as little as possible.

It is a lovely idea that Miss Davidson should come to help me in this matter. She loves the work which she helped to build up and all the workers love and respect her and would trust her knowing that she loves them all as i do. I wrote at once to beg her to say "yes" to your letter ...

I think you do not understand that the Christians of

Karachi are Gujerati as well as Urdu speaking people as well also a few Marathis. Our Marathi school has as well a good number of very interested Beni Israels or Jews. Miss Zoe Bose very nobly suggested that the closing of her big school which she greatly loves, would much help to reduce expenses, but this I trust we may avoid. I propose that she should be in charge of all the Gujerati and Marathi work - schools and Bible women. She would do it well, with the help of Janie Begun our office helper who is now well able to do accounts and returns and to write official letters.

If you will leave it to us on the spot we will work out the whole scheme and send it to you and will not ask for more than the RS 5000 which you suggest. We hear that school grants may be going up and I feel that if is God's will that our schools should still give a true witness to one thousand girls and their parents in six different parts of this large city "the Lord is able to give us much more than this".

We have good Christian Head teachers who will carry on well if backed up by Miss Bose, so we should not need to ask for more missionaries or money. When Miss Laugesen is named we hope Miss Turner will be sent back to us - you may be sure we will do all with definite prayer for God's guidance and will not run the Society into more expense.

With kindest regards
Yours sincerely
Blanche Brenton Carey [26]

Catherine Davidson did not share the same enthusiasm as Blanche, but she did not wish to cause her pain. In correspondence in March1940, Catherine writes: "The closing of the schools which would be like the amputation of Miss Carey's limbs from her body, would in my hands be a case of Et tu Brute."[27] Personally Catherine had thought there was an opportunity fifteen years prior to this when it might have been possible to restructure the work but that opportunity had now been lost.

The Rev. Mortimore replied to Blanche letting her know that Catherine would not be coming:

4th April 1940

Dear Miss Brenton Carey,

... We are so glad you are prepared to do everything possible to cut down expenses at Karachi, of course with as little injury to the work as possible.

I am afraid Miss C I Davidson, from whom I have heard, feels it would be a very difficult matter for her to re-organise, with your help, the educational work, as it would mean dismissing teachers who are old personal friends and with whom she has had close personal relationships in their early days. ... you may have heard that she has received a tentative request from the government superintendent of education to initiate the post of inspectress of schools in the Baluchistan province ...

Having regard to this rather unusual offer, and also her own feelings as to settling in Karachi for the time being, the Committee have agreed that she should accept the Government offer, which means that she will of course not be able to accept responsibility for the educational work in Karachi, as at first suggested.

The Committee feel that there should be only one junior missionary definitely located to Karachi, which would mean either Miss Turner would not return to Karachi, or that on Miss Turner's return Miss Laugesen should be located elsewhere.

In regard to your request that Miss Ghose, on her retirement, should be allowed to remain in her present quarters, the committee have sanctioned this, subject to annual reconsideration

With kindest regards,
Yours very sincerely,
ajm[28]

Olive Cocks was increasingly concerned with the situation in Karachi and informed Rev. Mortimore that a "senior missionary with a strong personality" was needed there to implement change:

145

23 May 1940

Dear Mr Mortimore [London],

I feel I should share with you in a frank and confidential manner some of the difficulties concerning the Karachi work. Unless you send a senior missionary of strong personality, it does not seem likely as if any change whatever will be made by Miss Carey in the CEZ work there. I do not think she has any intention of closing a single school and she is insisting on admitting a fresh batch of students to the Urdu training class. You may remember that the following minutes have been passed: ... Urdu training of teachers of Karachi shall not be started at present ...

There is only one Christian girl in this class, and by admitting a new batch of students now, we are pledged to carry them on for another 2 years. It would still be possible to stop the admission by cable if that is the mind of the committee in England which is dealing with Karachi affairs. Again no improvement in the living conditions for orphans and teachers in the main mission compound will be possible, as long as Miss Ghose remains there. Is it quite out of the question that when Miss Gibson returns she be located to Karachi?

I think it requires someone of her strength of character to get changes through. I had a talk with Miss Davidson about the matter when I was in Quetta and she said one reason why she refused to go to Karachi, was that she had tried in the past to institute changes and had found the barriers to change insuperable. I feel uncertain as to what the position of Women Standing Committee is now with regards to Karachi, as the matter is being dealt with direct by committees in London. Hence I feel I must bother you with my anxieties about Karachi. I think Miss Carey will strain every nerve to keep existing work going within the budget of Rs 5000 suggested.

    Yours Sincerely

      Miss O C Cocks

      Hon. Secretary[29]

During the War years there were difficulties in receiving correspondence, resulting in delays in the arrival of finance and anxiety for the missionaries who felt cut off from their loved ones in Britain. Olive Cocks wrote to Rev. Mortimore expressing their feelings:

17th June 1940

… We feel very cut off with no air mail and sea mail being so very delayed but we must not grumble nor do anything to make more difficult the terrible burden that is resting upon you all. The news grows more and more grave and we are anxiously watching the situation. We are as much in touch with things as you are at home as we get full news bulletins several times a day over the air. Mrs. Hinde here has a very good radio which is much appreciated in these days.

    I am in difficulties over finance as no news has yet reached us about the grant we are to draw from July onwards. I shall pay out as little as I possibly can and hope for the best …

    … <u>Karachi.</u> It is difficult to know what to do with this situation. It would not matter so much if we did not gather that the great need of the church there is people for district evangelistic work. It may be so wrong for us to tie our people up into this institution work when there is more vital work crying to be done but as long as Miss Carey is there no change is possible. She is gently firm and immoveable in her point of view.

    At the same time I fully agree that we must not do anything to hurt her at this period of her career. She is such a saint and has done such a wonderful work. It may be that *the war situation here will intervene to make changes of a kind that we do not wish for. Karachi naturally is one of points that would be open to attack should an enemy ever get as far as the coast of India ...*

Yours sincerely,

O.C. Cocks [30]

As mentioned above Marian Laugesen came to help in Karachi in c1939 and it was Marian who was to take the lead in Karachi following Blanche's death. At this time the new missionaries had to serve a time of probation and a report was produced by the senior missionary about the probationers suitability for missionary work. Blanche wrote the report for Marian in January 1940: "Good, very bright, kind and helpful, and is carrying on the Urdu branch of the Teachers' Training Class very well indeed during Miss Turner's absence.

"She works very hard and keeps well as a rule, sometimes I feel she may be over doing it, but I think she is wise.

"She is most earnest about the Evangelistic side of her work, and has a real belief in the Whole Bible and desire to win souls. A very true missionary."[31]

Retirement

In 1940 Blanche's official CEZMS retirement neared at the age of 84. Blanche loved the Sindh people so much and had lived among them for so long that she wanted to stay on and continue to work in Karachi alongside the missionaries.

There were concerns over the health of the missionaries during the War years, particularly that of Blanche. Olive Cocks wrote to the Rev. Mortimore:

9th July 1940

Miss Brenton Carey has been ill with a septic throat and her blood pressure is dangerously high. She was in hospital for a time but is now at home but able to do very little.

I am urging everyone to take special care of health just now when there is no possibility of travel. [32]

The Rev. Mortimore wrote to Blanche on her retirement, confirming that Blanche could continue to live at the Mission House and would in fact still be leading the work:

11th July 1940

Dear Miss Brenton Carey,

I am afraid the time has come as you will be aware, when we have had reluctantly to include your name on our General Committee agenda as one of those about to retire under the new retiring age rule, and I am sending you a resolution which was passed unanimously by our Committee yesterday.

While you are no longer on our roll of Missionaries as such, we realise that it is only the official connection which is being broken, and that in fact you will still be continuing to lead the work of the CEZMS in Karachi, and continuing to live in the Mission House. We very much hope and pray that you may be given health and strength sufficient for the needs of each new day, especially in the difficult times through which we are passing.

With every good wish,

Yours very sincerely,

ajm[33]

The resolution passed by the Committee on Blanche's retirement reflects the enormous esteem in which she was held:

"The Committee much regret that, under the recently adopted rule as to a retiring age, it has become necessary to record the retirement of Miss Brenton Carey as a missionary of the society.

"Miss Brenton Carey was accepted as a missionary of the society in 1885, and located to Karachi in the Punjab and Sindh mission, and at this station the whole of her missionary career, extending over nearly 55 years.

"On returning from her furlough in 1924, Miss Brenton Carey set about collecting the sum of £2,000 to meet the cost of rebuilding the Mission House, which had collapsed some four years previously and by her faith and enthusiastic appeals had the satisfaction of seeing the required amount raised.

"In 1928 her services to India were recognised by the government in the award of the Kaisar-i-Hind silver medal.

"The 21st November 1935 - the day on which Miss Brenton Carey completed 50 years of service in the Mission Field - was spent at her own request as a day of prayer at home and in the Field for the work at Karachi. This formed an appropriate preliminary to the Jubilee celebrations in Karachi which followed, when tokens of appreciation were received from friends in many walks of life, both Indian and European.

"The committee take this opportunity of placing on record their grateful appreciation of Miss Brenton Carey's many years of devoted service and particularly in the education carried on in varied tongues of her Indian sisters, and including a class for the training of teachers. Indeed she has taken a sympathetic interest in her own district in the forward movement among the women of India.

"... the Committee are glad to think that after her retirement Miss Carey is continuing to reside at the Mission House and to carry on the work so far as health and strength permit, her knowledge, experience, and spiritual influence will still find means of expression. They wish her God's richest blessing in the days to come."[34]

In her letter thanking the Rev. Mortimore for allowing her to stay at the mission station in Karachi even though she had officially retired, Blanche took the opportunity to restate her desire that none of the primary schools would close. She was still able to put her case forward eloquently:

29th July 1940

Mr Mortimore

I am very thankful to CEZ for their kind arrangements for me and for letting me go on at present with the work ...

I very much trust that we may not be forced to close any of these primary schools as I feel they are doing such an important work – of course I know CEZ cannot give what they have not got but we are all praying that the God who loves children may help us to keep schools for them where they hear and love the gospel story.

So many now in Sindh say "we love Christ" and I feel our prayers alone can bring them to the most difficult point of a confession of their faith in front of others – the lower castes are coming in good numbers and some are really true Christians who I trust may help the below class Hindus to see that the religion of Christ is a real thing.

... It is good to know that we are constantly remembered in prayer as we also remember you. What we need in Sindh is the mighty power of the Holy Ghost to bring out those who "tremble on the brink".

Mr Bakht Singh Charbra wishes to have a special effort here in October. He has been greatly used in other places and we trust those will use him here also.

With kindest regards

Yours very sincerely

Blanche Brenton Carey[35]

When Blanche received the letter of the 11th July from the CEZMS regarding her retirement she replied with her usual self-deprecation:

3rd September 1940

Dear Mr Mortimore,

Thank you very much for your letter of July 11th which reached me last night. I am rather over whelmed by the most kind– I am afraid too kind – resolution of the Committee.

It reminds me of a story told by our Presbyterian Chaplain a year or two ago when he had been receiving a farewell speech from one of the elders – he told of a minister in Scotland who was preaching the funeral sermon of some man and when it was over a relation came up saying " Aye Minister – your words were just wonderful – but it was no our John you were describing!" That is how I feel. However I am most grateful for the "wonderful words" and kind thoughts. Please thank the Committee members very much indeed and *also for the most generous allowance made for me.*

We are thinking so much of you all in England at this trying time and constant prayer is going up from our schools as well as united prayer in all the protestant churches week by week on ... Some of our Indian Padris pray in Urdu at these meetings. We are sure that prayer is being answered but long to hear of the enemy being altogether driven back.

With kindest regards to all members of the Committee and yourself

Yours very Sincerely

Blanche Brenton Carey [36]

Writing in *Looking East* in 1940 for her last official report, Blanche reflected over a year when the schools were full and many more pupils wanted to enrol in them, "As we look back over the year 1939-1940 we may certainly 'call the name of this place Ebenezer'". Ebenezer meaning stone of help: - a remembrance of the Lord's power and protection; the Lord has helped us.[37]

The Queen Alexandra School Karachi published in 1935.[38]

Some of the children at Karachi[39]

Zöe Bose and Minna Ghose during Minna's Jubilee year published 1939[40]

Journey's End

The decade 1940 - 1950 saw the continuation of the Second World War, the Partition of India and the creation of Pakistan. Partition would change forever the work of the CEZMS Karachi Mission which Blanche had worked so hard in the Lord to establish and expand. Most of their pupils were from Hindu families and the majority of these would leave Karachi, as the Hindus migrated to the new state of India and the Muslims moved to the new state of Pakistan. It would prove an enormous disruption to the mission, indeed to all the missions in this area. Many of the missionary ladies were now very old, and their service was ending; big changes would be required if the work was to continue.

War Years 1941 - 1945

In an *India's Women* article from December 1939 Gustaf Lindberg, a Swedish university lecturer who specialised in Christian missions, drew lessons from what had taken place in the First World War to highlight the problems that missionary societies were likely to face during the Second World War. These difficulties included disruption to necessary communication between the home countries and those on the mission fields. Funding for mission work would fall from Western nations - Lindberg noted that this had already started to happen in Germany. In addition the national movements abroad, who were not friendly to the foreign missions were likely to take the opportunity to further hinder the work of missions. All of Lindberg's forecasts came to pass for the CEZMS in India.[1]

Once again discussions were taking place regarding how British mission organisations could help the German missionaries and their mission stations if and when they were interned by allied powers

Amongst all that was going on the missionaries in Karachi managed to get news out to their supporters in Britain. Blanche provided a "business as usual" update in 1941: "The elder girls of the Children's Home, Karachi ... are just now going up for their teachers' examinations, and after coming to me for prayer, start off morning by morning very hopefully. A successful student last year was happily married a few months ago, and now helps us from her own home ...

"In spite of our stern resolve that until we get an upper storey we must not take more children, we have just had to receive two charming little motherless creatures, Golden and Virginia. They and their father, a very poor Christian cobbler, who works daily by the roadside, were locked out of their house because the rent was in arrears, and they had all been sleeping in the street. Could we do less than rescue them from such a life, even if their father can never support them? Could we do less? Can we not from now on do more?"[2]

Blanche continues, "There have not been quite as many students in the Queen Alexandra Training College this year. One of the reasons given for this is rather interesting. We are told that Sindhi girls living one-and-a-half-miles from the city are afraid to pass through it to attend our classes as they fear war-time unrest and the Mohammedan population! Those who 'carry on' in London in spite of raiders and bombs will hardly credit this! All four branches, Marathi, Gujerati, Urdu, and Sindhi have done well and we rejoice in the large number of Christian trained teachers." Perhaps this was a sign of the changing times in India and what was to happen post-war.[3]

As the Japanese army advanced into Burma, the fear and reality of war drew ever nearer to those in India. This put even further strain on the missionaries. In some parts of India the mission stations were preparing for air raids, sand was gathered and placed around the buildings in readiness for the fall of incendiary bombs. First aid lectures were given and medical equipment collected to provide first aid posts in case of aerial attack.[4]

The Punjab was considered to be the "backbone"[5] of the Indian war effort, it contributed nearly as many soldiers as the rest of India combined. However rumours abounded because of the uncertainty of the war. In Quetta which was about 370 miles away, Catherine Davidson often heard the rumour that every Cantonment was to be forcibly evacuated. Such was the panic at times caused by the rumours that when Japan's army was at the border of Burma some people left Quetta on aeroplanes which were travelling hundreds of miles nearer to Burma.[6]

Catherine also pointed out that, "The political situation in general creates endless difficulties which we used never to meet in our relations both with Christians and non Christians".[6]

Marian Laugesen, a missionary from New Zealand recently come to Karachi writing in *Looking East* February 1943 reports on the recent evangelistic meetings:

"Before we closed for Christmas we had an evangelistic meeting in each school, to which we invited the mothers and their friends and relations. Much prayer preceded these meetings. In both Gujerati schools, where the pupils are mostly Hindus, the women came in crowds, and we had not even seating room on the floor ... and in both these schools we sold over six dozen gospels and had people asking for more.

"In the Marathi schools, where the women are mostly Hindus and Bani-Israel -Jew it was much the same. Not so many came to the big Sindhi school in the city, partly because the women were busy cooking in preparation for a Hindu festival the next day. But several old students and girls from other schools came and listened most attentively. They did not buy many books but the teachers sold many the next week, showing that interest had been aroused.

"The pupils in the Urdu school are Christians and Mohammedans and as purdah women do not go out very much, we were pleased that quite a number came. During the whole of the meeting I felt sure that the Spirit was working powerfully, but Satan, too, was aroused, and at the end, before the last prayer, a woman stood up and told us of the beauties of Islam and of Mohammed, and the other women began to get quite roused in their enthusiasm for their prophet. Miss Carey whispered to me to pray and so we closed the meeting in the Name that is above every name. I realised then more than ever before that our warfare is 'not against flesh and blood but against principalities and powers, against the rulers of the darkness of this world.' We were not able to sell a single book afterwards, nor would they accept free portions. My heart goes out to these Mohammedan women ... such lovable dear women they are.

"On the last Friday of the month the Government Gardens in Karachi are closed to men and hundreds of purdah women remove their long white burkas and wander about the lawns and gardens in gaily coloured costumes. I have often had the privilege of going with a teacher to sell books, or sitting on the lawn talking quietly of the Saviour to little groups. At times we get crowds longing to hear, and at other times we find sullen looks, angry words and real opposition. But we know His promise, 'My Word shall not return unto Me void.' So even if it is only a gospel to a friendly shop assistant or to a little boy riding along-side one on his bicycle, we rejoice greatly."[7]

Blanche wrote to Winifred M. Chapman (Foreign and Candidates Secretary 1938-1957) commending Marian Laugesen's work:

2nd August 1943

... She is a wonderful worker! Splendid in the schools and leading the teachers upward and on ward in spiritual things – very good also in all the many business matters that come before her from time to time, flying off on her bicycle to interview officials, builders, and others or to talk over school and training college codes.

She is very 'all round' and I call her 'Dame Hubbard's dog' – you are too young to remember the pictures? 'feeding the cat' 'Reading the news' 'playing the flute' etc etc. I wrote a parody which I sent to her mother in New Zealand and this caused her great delight! She really is a very dear little thing and a missionary well worth having – I tell you all this as you are not likely to meet her and I know you like to be able to picture your missionaries!

Miss Langdale Smith and I shall be left alone when these two go, but I hope that will not prevent Miss LS from getting out freely into the district where she is doing a great work. I shall have Miss Bose who looks after my health and comfort in every possible way! Our rooms are side by side ...

... Mr Chandu Ray was a great help and we feel very thankful he has come here. We trust he may be the means of blessing to his own people. Sindh has had much teaching but very little real result. So many admire Our Lord but only as <u>one</u> of many leaders and one of the roads that lead to God. Pray that they may know Him as <u>The</u> Way <u>The</u> Truth and <u>The</u> Life ...

All the schools have had their inspections and seem to have done well. It is a great joy to hear non Christians speak of the work being good and thorough as it is a way in which our Christians can speak louder even than when giving a

Bible lesson to the children. How much India needs prayer at this time. ...

     With love

     Yours affectionately

     Blanche Brenton Carey[8]

Dorothy Langdale Smith continued to visit the villages near Karachi: in 1943 she travelled with an Indian colleague Dora Christie and camped for three weeks. There they taught a small number of converts and went out to the villages. Dorothy reported opposition: "Arya Samajists from Karachi and Hyderabad had gathered to oppose us. They tried to threaten and bribe our people and succeeded in taking away some who were living some little distance away ... The converts in the village of Chinisia, near Karachi have remained true although they also have been much troubled by Arya Samajists."[9]

Dorothy started to take some of the CEZMS school teachers out to the villages in the hope that this might lead to a desire amongst some of them to undertake village visitation in the future.[9] In 1944 she reported encouraging news from another visit, "One of the Christian men in a certain village, whom we prepared for baptism about three years ago, and who has since been working as a manad, [honorary/preacher] has brought about thirty of another caste to Christ in a faraway village. I was not able to go to the baptism, but just before I left Karachi he brought about ten of the village leaders to see us, and Miss Christie and I had the joy of teaching them more. They seem so keen and steadfast."[10]

In the May-June edition of *Looking East* in 1944, Marian Laugesen reported on local opposition due to the rise of Indian nationalism: "The Sindhi School and College at Karachi had a very difficult time for a year or so. Hardly had the children returned from the districts after the war scare than Congress trouble began. One day boys and girls came in crowds to the school demanding we should close for Ghandi's birthday and hoist the Congress flag. This we did not do, so for three months they did all they could to prevent the Hindu children from attending school. They stoned the school bus, broke windows in the school, and waited in groups in the streets to catch the children. Then they would sometimes beat them and sometimes shut them up for the day. Our numbers for a day or two were down to ten, and for a long time not more than twenty faithful ones managed in various ways to get to school. The roll had been nearly 200."[11]

However, Marian was also able to record her sense of thankfulness to God for His faithfulness even in these trying times: "But we kept open and tried to show the love of the Lord Jesus through it all, and we praised Him, when at length our numbers went steadily up. We have been able to have our usual Evangelistic Meeting in the Sindhi school before Christmas both these last years, to which many of the old girls come. There is much prayer for this Meeting because the teachers are afraid no one will come but there have been more each year, and this time such a spirit of friendliness and a desire to hear the Gospel that we realised afresh that, 'He doeth all things well.'

"We have also a gathering of old girls and students from all the schools, and it is a joy to have the opportunity to tell the Good News. Talks are given in Hindi, Gujerati and Marathi and we sing hymns, translations of which were to be found in all these languages. It was rather strange to hear 'Rock of Ages' sung in four languages at one and the same time!

"The death of a Hindu girl from one of our schools has made us realize that many in their hearts believe and are witnessing quietly in their homes. She asked for prayer and a favourite hymn, while her Hindu relatives and friends standing round were unable to help her soul, and almost the last words she spoke, loud enough for all to hear were 'everlasting life' and 'living water.' We visit many old pupils who like us to read and pray and sing with them. Many Bani-Israel families welcome us and read with us from their own copies of the Word of Life.

"I do thank God for calling me back to Karachi to permanent work here. It has been a wonderful time of proving Him to be the faithful and wonderful Saviour that He is. When I look back over the two years, the first thing that comes to my mind is just praise and thanksgiving to Him for what He has taught me of Himself, of His holiness, and of His infinite loving kindness. It has been a learning of the deeper meaning of 'Not I, but Christ be honoured, loved and adored.'"[11]

Integration with the local church

As the twentieth century progressed, local Christians in many parts of the world began increasingly to take over leadership responsibility for their own churches from overseas mission agencies. Christians in India came to "think in terms of church rather than mission",[12] and even more so as they became more nationalistic in their outlook. The reduction in grants from England added to their desire for indigenous oversight. Members of local congregations took more of a role and representation on the councils of the Diocese. This change of emphasis precipitated a move to merge the Mission and its organisation into that of the Diocese. The Rev. C A Bender, former Corresponding Secretary for the Punjab and Sindh Mission wrote in 1943, "the Anglicans in North-west

India may be responsible for managing their own affairs and the missionary societies may give them such help, material and spiritual, as they be able to.

"There is still great need for our help if given in a spirit of love and service, so let us pray for our missionaries that they may be full of the spirit of Him Who came not to be ministered unto but to minister; and for Indian leaders that they may consecrate and develop their power of leadership for His sake and His Kingdom."[12]

In 1943 the CEZMS was working closely with the CMS missionaries, and the Women's joint conference (CEZMS and CMS) controlled the women's work for both societies. The work in Sindh was now organised separately to the work in Punjab. Within the diocese of Lahore a church and mission council for Sindh was set up in Karachi and the missionaries cooperated with the new council. The CMS work in the province was taken over by the New Zealand CMS.[13]

One by one, the faithful band of ladies who had served together with Blanche in the work in Karachi for so many years began to pass on to glory.

Minna Ghose

Blanche and Eleanor Pegg wrote an article in *Homes of the East* (November - December 1942) remembering Minna Ghose under the title "God's Messenger in Sindh".

"In February (1942) this year there passed away one who for 53 yrs had been one of God's messengers in Sindh. Long after Miss Minna Ghose had reached the age limit and had officially retired from the CEZMS she carried on her work keenly, only taking extra rest when obliged to do so. Five days before she was suddenly taken ill she was at the Sindhi school taking a Bible class for the elder girls and for the widows in the Industrial Class.

"'God's Messenger in Sindh' described the Indian Christian whose story follows; that at least was the description of her given by an English friend and fellow worker who had known her through long years of service.

"Sindh is a large province of India to the south of the Punjab, and watered by one of its great rivers.

"A new pastor Rev. Bholanath Ghose had just been appointed to Karachi. His home was in Calcutta but he had been turned out by his parents when he became a Christian, and had gone with his own young family to live and work in the Punjab.

"His daughter Minna and her sisters were pupils at the Alexandra school in Amritsar, but they spent their holidays at home in Karachi and so became acquainted with the 2 CEZMS missionaries who were attracted to the clever young student.

"Minna was then working hard for the Calcutta Entrance Exam and the young English missionary studied some of Milton's poems with the Indian girl, and they rejoiced together when the exam was passed.

"The missionaries were cheered by the thought that Minna might join them once her exams were passed, so they were sadly disappointed to find that she has planned to take up work in a Government school, where she would have little opportunity of witnessing for Christ. Somehow the fact of their disappointment reached Minna's ears and it came to her as a real call from God. Again and again she pondered the question and found that she did really and truly wish to give her whole life and service to her Saviour, Jesus Christ. And so the little school now increased to 30 children came into her charge, and the heartfelt prayers of her missionary friends were answered.

"Minna was a young girl of 20 then, keen on her work and very bright and jolly and helpful. Marriage passed her by, but hundreds of little girls shared in her love, and as the years went on their children and grandchildren crowded into her school, and looked upon her as a family friend. In the inner courtyards where the women live they would gather round her to hear again the "old, old story" and to sing the well-loved hymns she had taught them at school.

"Later on an orphanage was opened in connection with the Mission, and quite naturally Minna Ghose was put in charge of it. The babies became her own! She carried them about in her arms and they loved her dearly. One should be very respectful to babies, for who knows to what wonderful heights they may attain! Of Miss Ghose's past babies, one is now the very capable head teacher in her old school; and several are teachers in Mission schools or are efficient hospital nurses; others of course married and became the mothers of the next generation, and in their turn passed on to their children some of the influence of Miss Ghose's Christian character and teaching.

"In 1941, 50 years from the time she joined CEZMS, loving friends kept Miss Ghose's jubilee. She was so much loved and respected that the wife of the Governor of Sindh Lady Graham and many other European and Indian friends came to the happy gathering to wish well to the dignified but still cheerful old Indian lady whose life had made so great a difference to their own.

"Teachers and children sang, Indian fashion, a song they had composed in her honour with quaint choruses 3 times repeated. They sang of the young girl now grown old in their midst, of the school increasing from 30 to 300, of orphan babies grown into teachers and prayed that her heart might be filled with joy as she looked over "this field well-tilled" and saw the "full-grown trees springing up." A large circle of happy little girls, singing of a length of time which surely they could not grasp, ended up with loving enthusiasm.

"Bless, Lord (tis' our earnest plea),

Fifty years of work for thee."

"Very soon after her jubilee Minna Ghose took her last earthly farewell of her lifelong friends and fellow-workers, and entered triumphantly the Kingdom to the extension of which she had given her heart's service."[14]

Lillie Oldfield

Another old colleague, Lillie Oldfield, died in 1947. Her death was reported in *Looking East*: "... an unattached missionary of the society from 1922 built up the well known Widows' Industrial Class which gave employment over many years to some 35 needy widows. Miss Langdale Smith writes to say that at her beautiful triumphant funeral service all her widows were present. To the Mission staff at Karachi and especially to her old friend Miss Brenton Carey our thoughts and prayers go out." [15]

Catherine Davidson wrote: "Station people both in Quetta and Karachi thought no end of Lillie Oldfield; and her fellow workers, though perhaps rather taking her for granted, as one does the sun in heaven, loved, respected and leaned upon her. But she was never on committees (too deaf); never to the fore in any way; never allowed herself to take the lead, or advertise herself or her work.

"Granted no widows ever openly 'came out' but who can tell the influence of her 26 yrs service and devotion, carried on in patience and courage, in spite of physical frailty, advancing years, shortage of workers and financial difficulties. To all the people among whom she worked, her life was a tangible demonstration of the love and care of the Father."[16]

Lillie Oldfield's last report of the work came in 1946/47 – "The Government Inspectress gave us a good report on her last visit and seemed quite satisfied with what she found.

"The widows seem to be taking more interest in their daily Bible lesson and we pray for much result from years of faithful teaching. There has been a good deal of illness in Karachi this year and two widows have died. One of these was certainly trusting in our Lord and His love, and we have His promise that whoever cometh will in no wise be cast out.

"I hope to carry on this work as long as the Lord gives me strength but one ought to think ahead to the future. Is there anyone at home with a gift for work of this kind, who would be willing to take over from me?" [16]

Blanche the Veteran

Although officially retired and now 88 years-old in 1944 Blanche continued to lead Bible classes and prayer meetings, "As I have received a paper with the words 'A Report must be given by each missionary' so I am making bold to send a few words in spite of the fact that I am only a 'Retired'! ... I live in a Zenana mission house by the kindness of our Home Committee, and am in daily touch with all the good work carried on by the active missionaries. Very active they are! and I sometimes feel I must remind them that missionaries have bodies to be cared for, as well as souls! It is a great joy to join in prayer for all the many branches of the work, and to be allowed to take my turn in leading the weekly Prayer Meeting as well as daily Evening Prayers.

"Another privilege which I greatly value is a weekly visit to the large 'Queen Alexandra School' ... Here I take a Bible Class for Miss Oldfield's widows including two who years ago became school teachers ...

"The other day one of these greeted me with such a shining face and the words, 'How very good God is.' Then told me that her grandson for whom we have been praying, had ceased to give trouble and she trusted, was now seeking the Lord.

"Until a few months ago I had also the pleasure of a weekly visit to a blind school, about 1½ miles distant, where a party of about five or six blind men looked out eagerly for a Bible reading. Three of these were Christians, but the non-Christians were anxious to come, and asked for copies of books of the Bible in Braille type which they could read with their fingers as fast as I could read an ordinary copy with my eyes! For some time we were joined by a sailor who was not blind but whose leg was injured, and who gladly accepted a copy of the New Testament in Hindi as well. These men have all left Karachi now having finished their training and I miss them very much. I am hoping for another piece of work to fill up that spare afternoon. More might be done save for the war time difficulty of conveyance without which I am no use these days.

"Some of our long-ago friends may remember a missionary-in-local connection, Mrs. O'Connor, who did a good work among Gujerati-speaking people in school and homes. She now occupies one of the nice rooms in a Widows' Home quite close to us, in connection with Holy Trinity Church, so I am able to have the pleasure of a visit to her from time to time.

"I should like to send warm greeting (sic) to all old friends with the message: 'Let all the people praise Thee, O God, yea let all the people praise Thee ... God shall bless us and all the ends of the earth shall fear Him.'"[17]

Blanche reported in 1947, "In November, 1885, I arrived in Karachi, and have been here ever since, except for furloughs and holidays which are now no longer possible, as movement is difficult for me. I want to acknowledge the wonderful loving kindness of God, that He has still permitted me to do a little work in connection with our dear CEZMS after these sixty-and-a-half years.

"My tiny bit of regular work is this. Every Friday I go down to our large Sindhi school in the city, which I have seen grow from a class of fifteen children in a small room in the town to 250 girls working up to high standards, led by Christian teachers brought up in our own Children's Home, and holding certificates from our Teachers' Training Class. By the good hand of our God upon us we were able to build the present School in 1919, and our thanks are always given to many kind subscribers and to the Karachi authorities who granted us the land.

"In one of the rooms on the upper storey Miss Oldfield holds her 'Widows' Industrial Class', to whom I have the joy of giving the Bible lesson, or rather a gospel address weekly. For this class we are also joined by about thirty of the Training College students. Pray that the message given may be 'of God and not of man,' and may find good soil in the hearts of these women and girls.

"We have had encouragement lately. This is my 'outside' work but I also take my turn with Miss Laugesen and Miss Bose in conducting our Teachers' weekly Prayer Meeting. Other bits of work come in the form of writing and answering letters and visits paid to me as I sit in my armchair. I again thank most heartily the CEZMS for making it possible for me to do this much for Sind and to remain in Karachi, which has been my home for nearly sixty one years. Pray that these few seeds sown weekly may bear fruit to the glory of our Lord."[18]

Partition

In 1947 the Partition of India took place and this was to have a serious effect on the mission work at Karachi. Winifred Meredith the CMS Secretary in Lahore wrote to Rev. Campbell Milford Acting General Secretary CMS in London describing the tragic picture of what was happening, but also displaying great faith in God's sovereign care amidst all the uncertainty:

30 September 1947

Dear Mr Milford,

We have a shrewd suspicion that letters from here may be censored and if not approved of just not sent, so I have been fairly careful what I have written, but now Sister Pennington is going home so I am asking her to take this with her, so as to try to give you a picture of life out here, as far as I can. The one thing above all others that seems certain is that everything is uncertain! Everything is in such a fluid state that one cannot predict the future and I am afraid all thought of realignment had to be put off for a few months till we see what will happen.

It may be that there will be certain areas where it will be quite impossible to work, on the other hand there may be places which may be more important centres than they were before, but there are so many ifs that one cannot make any decisions at present ...

As far as I can see one of the biggest things we can contribute to the life of Pakistan and India at present is a sense of confidence in God the changeless One in the midst of a changing world where there is no sense of security. As we carry on our work quietly, open our schools and hospitals even in places where tension is very great they will have a steadying influence and help morale. I think perhaps God is teaching us the lesson He taught you all during the war along these lines.

Others have I imagine told you of the many happenings that just fill one with horror, refugees from both sides attacked with great savagery by the opposite party, even women and children not being spared, but being killed or shockingly mutilated. One's heart just aches and aches for so many one knows of who are in great trouble, and then, when one realises that these cases are repeated in thousands of thousands of instances one is just staggered, but I shall not say any more about that as you have doubtless read of many of the terrible happenings.

There is an almost complete stoppage of trains except refugee trains. ... as there are hundreds of thousands of refugees, travelling by many of the trains is almost impossible, then posts are very uncertain, especially from one dominion to the other ... Much of my time at present is spent trying to get school & hospital staffs helped on their way back to their stations. We can sometimes get seats in military trucks for some of them or for ourselves to collect them from their homes.

Finances are an <u>appalling</u> headache for everyone, for hospitals have not time to do surgery for which they get big fees, they just spend all their time dealing with the ailments of the thousands of refugees. Schools have in many cases had to remain closed for four months and have therefore had to pay the staffs when no income was coming in. ... In many centres hundreds have had to be fed and so much more than usual has been spent.

... in most of the country towns the banks are not functioning nor is the post safe, but it has been just wonderful the way God has raised up people going to different places who have been able to take the money here and there for us, so that there are very few places now where we are still unable to have it conveyed, and we know He who has planned for us in so many tiny details will not fail to meet these needs too. I wish we could have a book telling of everyone's journey down from the Hills, so many have told of God's guidance as to the exact day on which to come down and how that was the only day when they would have reached their journey's end without incident. ...

All I have said seems to me to be summed up as follows:- We know nothing! God knows all! Thank God!!!

Goodbye now, its a great life fraught with tremendous possibilities for the spread of the Kingdom.

Brethren pray for us.

W. Meredith [19]

The CEZMS review of the year 1947/48 reported that Karachi had witnessed much change and upheaval. Miss Oldfield's death in April necessitated the closing of the Widows' Industrial Class. In September thousands of Hindus - business men, sweepers, gardeners and washermen left the city which disorganised the city's life. The four CZEMS day schools were forced to close and the number of students at the Teachers' Training College fell from fifty two to two Muslim students. Miss Langdale Smith was able to continue her visits to the surrounding villages with Zöe Bose, finding 'stupendous opportunities'[20] in the work. Even amongst the chaos and discouragement, it seems that a door of opportunity for the gospel was still open.

Towards the end of her life Blanche was still supporting the missionaries, writing the following letter to Winifred Chapman (the Foreign and Candidates Secretary) communicating the situation in Karachi during the transition period:

12 January 1948

... I fancy neither Dorothy or Marian can have had time to write at this very busy season with its difficulties of curfew and all other troubles of which we hear so much, but mercifully do not share.

Our mission part of the troubles has been that a party of Mohammedan refugees have walked into our large Sindhi school "the Queen Alexandra" when it was closed for a few days holiday and taken up their abode there. Miss Laugesen went to some of the authorities about it and they do not seem able to drive the Refugees out at present, but will see that no harm is done to the building and school furniture, as very many of the girls are away at present. We can only hope that we may get the school free when they begin to come back, which they may do soon as the city is getting quieter.

The present curfews are very upsetting and troublesome, but we feel they are keeping the town from real troubles ...

I fear my writing is getting worse and worse. I hope you will be able to read this. I am getting very blind and deaf. Which is not wonderful. I shall be 91 on February 15th.

With best wishes to you and all the committee for new year.

Yours affect.

B Brenton Carey[21]

A few months later, the Venerable S N Spence wrote to the Clerical Secretary Rev. J Bates CEZMS about the possibility of the government taking over the Alexandra school in Karachi, and the strain on some of the missionaries:

May 1949

There is a move afoot in Karachi by Govt. to take over the Alexandra School of the CEZMS which has been occupied by refugees since shortly after the partition of this land. As the former Sindhi school had to close, they seem to have the right, in the terms of the lease of the land, to do so. I have urged them in Lahore to see that your interests or claims if any should not be forgotten, and I have offered to do what I can for them here. Miss Langdale Smith finds such matters rather more than she can manage ...[22]

Winifred Chapman was pleased to hear news from the mission station and replied to Blanche:

29 January 1948

... We are so glad of all the news you send as it helps us to pray intelligently for you all – and you may be sure that you are very often in our thoughts and prayers at Headquarters in our Prayer meetings and individually.

... It must have been hard to say goodbye to so many people you knew in all the uncertainty as to what further troubles they would encounter.

It is good to know that Miss Laugesen has been having encouragement in the villages in spite of everything. ...

With love to you all

Yours affectionately,

wnc[23]

Amidst all the change and uncertainty the work continued after Partition as the CEZMS review of the year 1949/50 records, "Miss Langdale Smith tells of a year of much blessing. Work has been concentrated in the villages. Work amongst the Mohammedan women and children is not only increasing, but many are giving a definite witness.

"In 1948 Miss C. I. Davidson, of the Hyderabad school stressed the urgent necessity for schools for Pakistan Christian girls, in view of the fact that the Minister for Education was foreshadowing a thorough Islamic Educational set up throughout the state. The year 1949 has seen both these points accentuated; the latter adding urgency to the former. The former Christian basis for education has been publicly repudiated and exchanged for a strong Islamic basis. Miss Davidson writes:

"The Methodist Communities are equally disturbed with us over the education of their girls. So a plan is on foot for us to join forces through the Church – we supplying our ready-made buildings and they helping financially and the children from both churches benefiting ..."[24]

Blanche's Homecall

Finally after so many years of active service in the Lord's work, Miss Blanche Brenton Carey's health deteriorated. The following correspondence traces Blanche's declining health and her joyful entrance into the Lord's presence.

The Venerable S. N. Spence reported to the Clerical Secretary Rev. J Bates on Blanche's physical and mental state.

May 1949

... Miss Brenton Carey is slowly becoming more and more infirm and now never leaves her room. She hardly remembers even her oldest friends ...[25]

Winifred Chapman informed Mary Brenton Coward (an ex-missionary in Karachi) in Otford, Kent, of her aunt's condition.

10 January 1950

Mrs Coward,

I have been asked by Miss Langdale Smith our missionary at Karachi to let you know of the serious condition of Miss Brenton Carey's health.

She is failing rapidly and is practically bed ridden and alas her faculties are deteriorating. One cannot hope that she will continue in this state for any length of time, and after the wonderful work that she had done for God amongst the women and girls of Sind, and knowing how ready she is to go to the Master whom she has so long loved and served, one can only hope that her home call will be a speedy one.

I know it will be a great comfort to you that she is being most lovingly cared for by Miss Langsdale Smith and her Indian colleagues, and that everything possible is being done for her comfort.

Yours sincerely,

Foreign and candidates secretary.[26]

Mary Brenton Coward replied to Winifred thanking her for telling her the sad news, but Mary was pleased that she was being cared for.

12th January 1950

Dear Miss Chapman,

Thank you so very much for writing to me about my Aunt Miss Brenton Carey.

I was beginning to feel that she was failing and am so thankful that she is in such kind hands.

I was out in Karachi during the first world war and so know some of missionaries out there but I expect Miss Bose is the only one left who would remember me. As you say my Aunt has done a wonderful work in Karachi and now that her condition is so serious one would not wish her to linger on.

It was most kind of Miss Langdale Smith to write and I am posting a letter of thanks to her today.

I am so glad that I can picture the mission house so

clearly and know what lovely care my Aunt is getting.

Thank you so much again for letting me have the latest news of her.

Yours sincerely,

Mary Brenton Coward[27]

Following her illness Blanche Louisa Mary Boleyn Brenton Carey aged 94 finished her race on earth and went to be with her Lord on the 25th May 1950. Winifred Chapman wrote to inform her niece Mary Brenton Coward:

26th May 1950

Dear Miss Coward,

We have just received a cable telling us that your Aunt, Miss Brenton Carey passed peacefully on yesterday morning. For her sake one can only rejoice, but there will be many who will mourn the passing of a dear friend. ...

With kind regards,

Yours sincerely,

Wnc[28]

Blanche's passing was simply reported to the CEZMS supporters in the September periodical *Looking East* with the following obituary:

In Memoriam

One of the outstanding pioneer missionaries of the society Miss Brenton Carey built up over nearly 60 yrs important evangelistic and educational work in and around Karachi. She retired officially in 1940, but remained to end in the country and among the people she had loved and served so well.

It would be impossible to over-estimate her influence on several generations of Indian women and girls or the value of her service in the cause of Christ's Kingdom. In the words of one of her Indian colleagues wherever the uplifted hand of human need was raised, there Miss Carey would hasten to give all the help and relief she could. Miss Carey's physical presence is no longer with us, but the influence of her wonderful, self-sacrificing life can never die.[29]

Appreciative letters were forwarded to Blanche's family from the 'girls' in Karachi. When she received the letters, Miss E. Brenton Carey replied to Miss

D A Cocksedge CEZMS.

18th August 1950

It was most kind of you to send me the translated copies of those truly lovely letters written about my dear Aunt by some of her "girls". It is very wonderful to hear of the love and devotion of these fellow workers in the mission – my aunt must have had great happiness in the work and she must have felt sometimes that even "down here" she had her reward – Hers was a beautiful life and I feel sure that her influence and teaching will live long after her name has been forgotten...[30]

The translated letters of Blanche's "girls", many of whom were teachers in Karachi or Hyderabad, recorded Blanche's last hours and her funeral service, conducted by Archdeacon Spence. It is very clear how much she was loved by the girls:

Letter 1.

"Praise and thanks to the Lord that He called our very very beloved "Maja" out of this world, which is full of trouble, to Himself at 10 o'clock today. Praise that she is now at rest in her heavenly home.

"But now there is no limit to the sorrow of our hearts - oh! so sweet was our "Maja" that to look at her was to forget everything else, because her love was wonderful. She looked to be in perfect rest and peace. Her funeral was at 6:30 this evening. Archdeacon Spence took the service in the big church and he spoke beautifully about her. There were lovely hymns.

"Miss Langsdale Smith a week before had gone on her holiday but there was a Salvation Army lady staying here, who served our "Maja" with wonderful love, and right to the end did all she could. How kind is the Lord who knows the needs of His servants. What a strange will of the Lord it was that none of you was here. Nearly all her old girls came - just as "Maja" would have liked. It is very difficult now to think that "Maja" is not here. May the Lord help us all and give us grace to walk according to the example of our saintly sweet Maja!"[31]

Letter 2.

"Our heart beloved Maja left us and went to her Heavenly Home on 25th May at 10 a.m. Thanks be to the Lord that He has given her deliverance from this painful flesh. Yes, now she surely is there in happiness and rest. What a great comfort to us Christians this knowledge is, when we are in sorrow.

"On Tuesday the Doctor said that if there was any relation in India, he should be informed, but even then we hoped our "Maja" might get well. On Thursday morning early she did not have any special trouble - she went suddenly.

"Archdeacon Spence made a good arrangement for her funeral. He gave the people a good message about her life and he remembered you people who had worked with her for so long. All Maja's girls came to the funeral, they brought their children and the church was full. Mrs. Walker, a Salvation Army lady who is staying here helped lovingly at the end and seeing everything, praised Maja very much. I told her with what wonderful love she brought us all up - and with what love she trained us. Yes, we can never forget this sweet memory and this love. May the Lord give us that same Spirit so that we also, with her, may receive everlasting rest."[31]

Letter 3.

"We are all very sad at Maja's going - none of us can ever forget her. Our hearts become very sad as we remember her words and the things she used to tell us, and often we weep, but now it is much better for her that she should be with Christ. Truly she was a true Mother to us - one who suffered for us. I often used to sit with her and sing hymns to her because as she could not go to church, I thought she would like it - "Into the heart of Jesus deeper and deeper I go" "How sweet the Name" "I know not why God's wondrous Grace" and others out of Golden Bells.

"We were all thankful that it was our holiday time, so we were able to be near her and serve her - and that was her wish too.

"On 25th morning both Jotmani and I felt sad and about 8 o'clock I went in to help her. When I saw her I felt doubtful, but still I did not think too much of this and at 9:30 a.m. I went to do my daily shopping. Soon after this when Chandrabbaga, Jotmani and Miss Bose were with her, she changed, opened her eyes and looked up as though seeing a heavenly vision. Jotmani sent someone for Mrs. Walker who is a very good spiritual nurse. Soon after she arrived Maja went! Mrs. Walker did everything very beautifully and with the help of all the teachers got her ready. At 10:15 I returned and all were weeping. I wept too. Archdeacon had come and prayed with us all.

"At 5:00 p.m. she was taken across to the church. We had 2 hymns in church, "Jesus lives" and then all the teachers who were her children sang "I know not why God's wondrous grace" - her favourite hymn. Archdeacon told something of her life. Many people put roses on her. I made a special wreath of double jasamine and Hira made a cross. There was a lovely wreath from all the teachers - everything was very beautiful. We all wore white saris. At the grave also we sang those hymns which she would have liked. The Lord did everything well for His servant ...

"... We have now much comfort from Miss Bose, praise that she is near us. Now may we who have been with her all the time, like her, in our separate places, shine for the Lord Jesus. Indeed we are very weak but something at least must be seen in the lives of each one of us."[31]

Letter 4.

"We have this comfort - that, after returning to Karachi for our holiday, we were able to serve our Maja for 8 days. Thanks to the Lord that we were with her at that time.

"When her last hour came we were near her - all the teachers had gone out to work. No one thought this was her last hour. When she was breathing her last, she opened her eyes widely and looked up - it seemed that there was something she was looking at very intently. But she did not say anything because she was so weak. By her going it seems to us that we have been left orphans. You know that she had a wonderful and true love for us. But thanks be that now she is in her everlasting rest ..."[31]

In March 1954 Zöe Bose touchingly remarked, "The Cemetery is not far off so we can go to Miss Carey's grave from time to time, and see that it is properly cared for. I have had a red bourgainvellea planted at the head. I thought it would look pretty against the white marble."[32]

Work Continues

After Blanche's death the work in Karachi, although very different, continued. Dorothy Langdale Smith continued to visit the villages until she left in 1951, at which point Marian Laugesen took charge of the mission work in Karachi. Zöe Bose started to visit the nearby villages by bus, which must have been energy sapping, in March 1954 she remarks, "God has blessed us with such exceptional good health, that I feel I ought to use it for Him, instead of wasting my time in useless pursuits".[32]

Recognising that the nature of the work had profoundly changed, Zöe Bose wrote in May 1952, "New Beginnings at Karachi. It was a sad time 3 yrs ago or more, when the work in Karachi which had gone on for more than 60 yrs built up by Miss Brenton Carey's faith and earnest prayers, had come to an end owing to Partition.

"There were flourishing schools where day by day hundreds of children were taught about Him who said suffer the little children to come unto me.

There was also evangelistic work in various parts of the city, where we were welcomed and the Gospel message given. Then came the great cataclysm and one after another the various branches of the work had to close down. Afterwards although things became more settled we felt that the work could never be the same as it had been."[33]

However, Zöe Bose trusted that the Sovereign God who had been working out His plans in past years would continue His work in future days. Blanche Carey's long service would not be forgotten in the new arrangements:

"God had new plans for Karachi. A school for Christian children was the great need of the moment. The former buildings were not available and would not have been suitable but the CEZMS house with its spacious compound and large airy rooms met the need. Also a feeder school was needed to take surplus children from our girls' boarding school at Hyderabad, which owing to Miss Davidson's effort and ability in raising it to a High School was full to overflowing. So it was planned to open a school in the Karachi CEZMS compound. There were many difficulties but at last we had the joy of being able to put up the notice, "The Brenton Carey Primary School.""

"On the morning of the day it was opened we all gathered for prayer to ask God's blessing on this new venture. A large photo of Miss Carey was on the wall and after the prayer was over the Headmistress, a highly educated and qualified Indian lady, stood before it and said that although she had never met Miss Carey, she wanted to carry on the work in such a way as to be worthy of her. Now the school is well established with trained teachers and an ever increasing number of pupils.

"But there was still need for an orphanage and boarding establishment for those who could not be day scholars. For this a resident missionary was necessary and to meet the need Miss Laugesen arrived from New Zealand in the middle of the Sind hot weather. A formidable task awaited her, for although all the requisite buildings were here, yet it was not easy work to open the boarding hostel after it had been closed for so long. With characteristic energy Miss Laugesen set about it and within 2 months everything had been renovated and was in working order. Now there is a happy band of children here well fed and clothed in spite of rising prices. We feel the Lord has set his seal upon this new venture by thus providing.

"A few of the children are just past the baby stage but they are not too young to understand the love and care of the Good Shepherd. One little boy was heard murmuring in his sleep, the lord is my shepherd.

"We who have been here for long years have seen the wonderful life and service of Miss Brenton Carey and Miss Piggott. They have passed on to their rich reward and received the Master's "Well done." And we who are left cannot but be grateful that God has chosen two such consecrated workers to fill their places."[33]

Marian Laugesen wrote in 1955: "It is five years this June since I returned from New Zealand to reopen the orphanage here. So I feel I want to witness to the wonderful loving kindness and faithfulness of the Lord through these happy years. 'He abideth faithful'. Once a dear friend said that as we grow older, we are more and more amazed at the mercy and loving kindness of our Lord. I have fallen so short of what He wanted me to be ... I have left undone so many pieces of work He wanted me to do, but in spite of all that, He has magnified His Name through this little piece of service and has brought the knowledge of His love and Salvation to some who would never have heard without this witness here. He has been a Refuge and a Strength to some who have come here and we all know the preciousness of His being a very present help in trouble ...

"The school has grown and we now teach more English. We have freedom to teach the Scripture because it is a private school without Govt. recognition, but of course the value of the Bible lesson period depends on how the teachers use it. So we need teachers who are truly born again and who can tell the children by a personal experience that the Lord Jesus can do for all who call upon Him. I take the Scripture examinations. We do not make it compulsory for the non-Christian girls to sit the exams, (though all attend the classes throughout the year) ... Mostly this exam is taken orally and this gives an opportunity to talk personally with every child. These are precious times, so will you please pray for me in March when the annual examinations begin. Ask the Lord to guide me to make the challenge to those He has prepared."[34]

Like Blanche before her Marian also undertook a building project to add a second storey to the Children's Home. The Rev. S N Spence forwarded to the Rev. Bates a photograph of the new storey in May 1957. In the accompanying letter the Rev S N Spence remarked, "The tradition and spirit of Miss Brenton Carey is being wonderfully carried on by her successors."[35]

Final Words

In 1929 Agnes Fox Grant wrote of Blanche, "Behind all the growth through these nigh fifty years ... stands the figure of a woman who inherited the mantle of 'a dauntless Irishwoman' [Miss M Condon], who believed that 'if God put us here to work he will give us the workers' – who has proved that 'Prayer changes things' – 'our Miss Brenton Carey.'"[36]

"She will tell you of a long line of faithful fellow country women - of the splendid work of Indian colleagues, giving more valuable witness because of their nationality, than any 'foreigner' can give – proving that Christ is indeed 'the Christ of the Indian Road.'

"And although Karachi to the unobservant eye would be classed with 'barren Sindh' for 'results' – so far as baptisms and a growing outward church are concerned – are disappointing, those who know Sindh, who live and love in its midst, who have kept a finger on its pulse, realise that a great change is taking place. Christ has become the acknowledged 'Friend' of many hundreds. He is known and honoured in secret even where no public acknowledgement is possible. His servants are loved and warmly welcomed in countless homes representing three or four generations of Sindhi Hindu girls who have passed through our schools, while many orphans have grown up in our orphanage and many have gone forth to build happy homes of their own, founded on Christian ideals or are still unmarried & working as the evangelists in the schools ...

"The growth, as Miss Carey herself pointed out recently - may be 'in secret' but it is there, and the Day shall reveal it."[36]

The life of Blanche Brenton Carey is a testimony to what God can do through Jesus Christ with a woman of "fair average ability" who had been assessed as a "second rather than a leader". This story of a humble, remarkable life devoted to the service of her Saviour the Lord Jesus Christ can be summed up by two newspaper articles which were written at the time of Blanche's Jubilee in November 1935. These reports, published in the local newspaper *The Daily Gazette,* capture a sense of the love her fellow workers had for Blanche and her love for the people of Sindh.

23 November 1935

"... Over a thousand women, girls and little children, brightly and newly dressed, some holding aloft crimson banners glittering inscribed with letters of gold, had assembled to pay tribute to a charming lady who had worked amongst them, and for their advancement since the middle eighties of last century. Procession followed procession, - mostly school girls - each with their gift of necklaces of flowers and other delights, - each singing its paean of praise and gratitude, - each returning to its position in the encircling thousands of devoted admirers who, quietly seated in masses as far as the background of shrubs and trees would permit, watched the proceedings with twinkling eyes and happy smiles. Miss Brenton Carey arrived in Karachi for the first time on 21st November 1885, to carry forward the work of the Church of England Zenana mission; so this was her Golden Jubilee, and the occasion of a wonderful outpouring of love and gratitude by the women of Sind ..."[37]

25 November 1935

Zöe Bose addressed these words to Blanche, "... it is usual in an address to touch upon work done and objects accomplished but neither time nor space will allow of our doing more than to touch upon these in your case ... The schools your faith and prayer have built up are appreciated & valued in this town of many schools & many sects. Hundreds, indeed we may say thousands of girls have gone out of them to face the world, its want & pain, with the comfort of Christ's Gospel in their heart ...

"Among the happy faces which surround you are many of those you have taken in and looked after in the children's home, a home in a real sense of the word. Your mother-heart has overleapt all differences of race & station and from infancy, childhood & girlhood, and as long as they have been under your care you have tended, planned, and cared for them guided by love & wisdom sought for from above.

"... a sorely perplexed soul comes to ask advice & however busy you may be, you listen patiently & give the needed word of counsel. Another wants your comfort and prayer and you give up your much needed rest to help and console.

"... we lift our hearts in deep, heartfelt gratitude to the Father of all good on this day of your Golden Jubilee."[38]

The final words are left to Blanche in her reply, "Have you ever wondered why I came out to Karachi and why I have no wish to leave this land in spite of my age? You who have read the gospel (or good news) of the Lord Jesus Christ will remember that when he left his disciples & ascended up to heaven he told them to go in to all the world and to give His 'Good News' to everybody. I believed that my Master wanted me to do this & so I very gladly came away to this far away land to give you - & especially women & children, this 'Good News'.

"Have you read the delightful parable - story written by John Bunyan in which he describes a man with a big load upon his back which he cannot get rid of? What does it mean? King David wrote in the Psalms 'My sins are a heavy burden too heavy for me to bear.' Have you ever felt the burden dear friends? Do you want to know that your sins are all forgiven and washed away?

"I know you believe I am your friend & that I love Sindh & its people otherwise why have I lived here so long & tried to help you & your children in any way I could. Although I know that I should have done much more to show you the extreme importance of accepting the good news."[38]

Blanche with Minna Ghose published 1942.[39]

Blanche at a reunion at the children's home published in 1946.[40]

Blanche Brenton Carey[41]

Epilogue

Opportunities for women were beginning to open up towards the end of the nineteenth century but it was still fairly uncommon for a single woman to have such control and management of a large organisation especially in a foreign land. Her service was sacrificial in personal terms, as she was prepared to give up hopes of marriage or children of her own, leaving behind family and friends at home to make Christ known to the people of Sindh. Blanche may have had the advantage of coming from a privileged background in terms of home life, family connections and her undoubted language skills, but nevertheless with her humility and self deprecation she was only able to start her life of ministry because the Lord called her and equipped her in a most remarkable way.

Blanche was undoubtedly a woman with courage, who had a sense of adventure, was resolute, persistent and able to win people over to her views whilst still being loved. Most importantly from a very early age she wanted to serve her Lord with all of her life. She entered a lifelong ministry with a deep desire for people to come to know the Lord Jesus Christ as their Saviour. Blanche had to overcome many setbacks, and personal hardships, but she was able to overcome these obstacles through her trust in her Saviour. Above all, she was a woman who knew the vital necessity of prayer, nothing could be done without bringing her petitions to Him.

She loved the people of Karachi through thick and thin. She cared deeply for the needs of the women and girls of Sindh, and took many risks in order to reach out to as many people as possible.

Blanche was one of hundreds of women who devoted their lives to the work of Christ, for the Gospel's sake. In the Apostle Paul's letter to the Philippians 2:25-30 Paul writes about a fellow-worker called Epaphroditus who was a great example to the believers. He risked his life and came close to death for the work of Christ. Paul says that Epaphroditus should be held in honour for his service to Christ and I think the same can be said about Blanche Louisa Mary Boleyn Brenton Carey.

Appendix A

The following is a translation of a letter written by Indian Christians appealing for missionaries to help them in 1891:

"'GREATLY RESPECTED."- Forasmuch as your humble servant for nearly four years has been occupied in the Lord's work in a place called Sultánwind, near Amritsar, very many visits have been paid to the people of the surrounding villages. The Lord's work is going on well, and my wife also very diligently works in Zenanas. The harvest is ready, but there is great need of labourers, therefore let the Lord of the Harvest be besought by means of prayers, that He may send a labourer. And to the Lord's people is this petition, that they fulfil their duty. Therefore the request of the people of Sultánwind and the aforesaid district, and my request is for a Miss Sahiba, who may do spiritual work in Zenanas, and that spiritual benefit may be obtained from her society. Let her live in the above Sultánwind and work in the surrounding villages, and let my wife be her fellow-helper. Let the Miss Sahiba also make use of a little practice in medicine, that by this more spiritual benefit may be obtained. Miss Wauton Sahiba with her own eyes has herself seen Sultánwind and the above-named villages, and often helps us, and is kind. In Sultánwind itself nearly 6000 people live. May God give a place for our request in the hearts of His servants!

ABDUL GANI
Inhabitant of Sultánwind "'*4

---

*4(CEZM Possible publications Web. 14/08/2021. http://www.ResearchSource. amdigital.co.uk/Documents/Details/CMS_1_Part5_Reel86_Vol6. Image 35 © [2021] Adam Matthew Digital Limited

References

Abbreviations

CEZMS   Church of England Zenana Missionary Society
CMS   Church Missionary Society
CRL   Cadbury Research Library, Birmingham
DoM   CEZMS: Correspondence re: deaths of missionaries, A-Z, 1930s-1950
IW   India's Women and China's Daughters. London: Church of England
        Zenana Missionary Society. Available through: Adam Matthew,
        Marlborough, Church Missionary Society Periodicals
LE   Looking East at India's Women. London: Church of England Zenana
        Missionary Society. Available through: Adam Matthew, Marlborough,
        Church Missionary Society Periodicals
RC   Records of the CEZMS at the Cadbury Research Library, University of
        Birmingham
UoB   University of Birmingham
Web   Date last accessed on the internet

Front cover
Outline map based on the drawing of CMS Mass Movement Areas in India. This Mission Hospital Volume 35 issue 405 1931 Copyright Church Mission Society CRL.

Formative Years
(1) Churchman's Monthly Review 1845 'Universities Oxford' Web. 12/09/2021 https://books.google.co.uk/books?id=rfIDAAAAQAAJ&printsec=frontcover&source=gbs _ge_summary_r&cad=0#v=onepage&q=carey&f=false
(2) In Memoriam Rev. A F Carey Vicar of Brixham leaflet - Re-printed from the "Brixham Western Guardian".
(3) The Elizabethan June 1900 Vol. 11 No.5 Elizabeth College Guernsey Digital Archives page 102 Obituary. Web. 12/09/2021 https://elizabethcollege-heritage.daisy.websds.net/Filename.ashx?tableName =ta_elizabethan&columnName=filename&recordId=105&page=2&end=5
(4) Life and Services of Vice-Admiral Sir Jahleel Brenton by Rev. Henry Raikes 1846, Published Hatchard and Son Piccadilly Page 648
(5) The Illustrated London News 1863 Volume 33 page 103
(6) The Graphic - Saturday 30 August 1879 Image pg 210 Web. 10/08/2021 https://www.britishnewspaperarchive.co.uk/viewer/bl/9000057/18790830/038/0018 © Illustrated London News Group. Image created courtesy of THE BRITISH LIBRARY BOARD. "MISCELLANEOUS." Mackay Mercury and South Kennedy Advertiser (Qld.:1867 - 1887) 29 October 1879:3. Web. 20/08/2021 http://nla.gov.au/nla.news-article169530956. National Library of Australia

(7) Encyclopaedia of Religious Groups in Latin America and the Caribbean: Religion in Mexico Second edition 2020 Prolades Web. 12/09/2021 http://www.prolades.com /encyclopedia/Second-Edition/rel-mexico-2nd-edition-august-2020.pdf page 48, 49

(8) CEZMS: Missionaries' blue packets, including name and address, arranged alphabetically: B-D, 1881-1956 RC. Web. 04/06/2021. http://www.Research Source.amdigital.co.uk/Documents/Details/CMS_I_Part9_Reel186_Vol1. Image 551. © [2021] Adam Matthew Digital Limited

(9) CEZMS Anniversary meetings, jubilee etc, 1930, 1938-1957 RC. Web. 14/08/2021. http://www.ResearchSource.amdigital.co.uk/Documents/Details /CMS_I_Part9_Reel210_Vol1. Image 76 © [2021] Adam Matthew Digital Limited

(10) CEZMS Miscellaneous leaflets, 1930s-1950s. 1930-1959. RC. 1935 edition written by Miss A M Robinson Editor & Superintendant of Publication Department 1926-1949 Web. 14/08/2021. http://www.ResearchSource.amdigital.co.uk/Documents/Details /CMS_I_Part6_Reel121_Vol2. Images 174-178. © [2021] Adam Matthew Digital Limited

(11) CEZMS Annual reports 1889-1892 RC. Web 14/08/2021 http://www.Research Source.amdigital.co.uk/Documents/Details/CMS_I_Part5_Reel94_Vol1. Image 25. © [2021] Adam Matthew Digital Limited

* Note: Image 26 and 27 contain the contract terms and the bye laws the missionaries had to abide by. They signed up for a period of at least five years service unless illness prevented them, and if they married before the five years service they were to refund some of their expenditure to the mission society. If a CEZMS missionary married they would leave the society.

(12) Mildmay or the story of the First Deaconess Institution by Harriette Cooke published by Elliot Stock Paternoster Row 1893 p117-129

(13) August IW Vol 15, Issue 110. 1895. Web. 14/08/2021. https://www.church missionarysociety.amdigital.co.uk/Documents/Images/CMS_CRL_IW_1895_08/14#Artic les. Image 352. © [2021] Adam Matthew Digital Limited

(14) Nov. - Dec. IW, Vol 5, Issue 30. 1885. Web. 14/08/2021. http://www.church missionarysociety.amdigital.co.uk/Documents/Details/CMS_CRL_IW_1885_06. Image 327, 329, 330. © [2021] Adam Matthew Digital Limited

(15) CEZMS: Missionaries' blue packets, including name and address, arranged alphabetically: B-D, 1881-1956 RC. Web. 04/06/2021. http://www.Research Source.amdigital.co.uk/Documents/Details/CMS_I_Part9_Reel186_Vol1. Image 539. © [2021] Adam Matthew Digital Limited

(16) Ibid. Image 543

(17) Ibid. Image 549

(18) Ibid. Image 545

New Beginnings - Karachi

(1) History of the Church Missionary Society by Eugene Stock, volumes I and II (1899) RC. Web. 04/06/2021 http://www.ResearchSource.amdigital.co.uk/Documents/Details /CMS_III_Part1_Reel6_Vol1. Vol 2 Part Vi p204. Image 405. © [2021] Adam Matthew Digital Limited

(2) Until Shadows Flee Away by AD 1912 page 108

(3) CEZMS: Correspondence re: possible publications, (Possible Publications) 1880-1957, vol. 1. RC. Web. 04/06/2021 http://www.ResearchSource.amdigital.co.uk /Documents/Details/CMS_I_Part5_Reel86_Vol6. Image 162. © [2021] Adam Matthew Digital Limited

(4) Annual letters of the missionaries 1886-1890. CMS archive at CRL, UoB. Web 06/06/2021 http://www.ResearchSource.amdigital.co.uk/Documents/Details /CMS_III_Part4_Reel33_Vol1. Image 63. © [2021] Adam Matthew Digital Limited

(5) August IW, Vol 31, Iss. 302. 1911. Web. 06/06/2021. http://www.church missionarysociety.amdigital.co.uk/Documents/Details/CMS_CRL_IW_1911_08 Image 144. © [2021] Adam Matthew Digital Limited

(6) October IW Vol 21, Issue 1901. Web. 06/06/2021. http://www.church missionarysociety.amdigital.co.uk/Documents/Details/CMS_CRL_IW_1901_10 Image 231. © [2021] Adam Matthew Digital Limited

(7) July - August IW Vol 6, Iss.34 1886. Web. 15/08/2021. http://www.church missionarysociety.amdigital.co.uk/Documents/Details/CMS_CRL_IW_1886_04 Image 186. © [2021] Adam Matthew Digital Limited

(8) July - August IW Vol 7, Iss. 40 1887. Web. 15/08/2021 http://www.church missionarysociety.amdigital.co.uk/Documents/Details/CMS_CRL_IW_1887_04 Image 182. © [2021] Adam Matthew Digital Limited

(9) Ibid. Image 209

(10) CEZMS Annual reports 1884-1888 RC. Web. 15/08/2021. http://www.Research Source.amdigital.co.uk/Documents/Details/CMS_I_Part5_Reel93_Vol1. Image 297. © [2021] Adam Matthew Digital Limited

(11) July-August IW Vol 7 Iss. 40. 1887. Web. 15/08/2021 http://www.church missionarysociety.amdigital.co.uk/Documents/Details/CMS_CRL_IW_1887_04 Image 205. © [2021] Adam Matthew Digital Limited

(12) Ibid. Image 207

(13) August IW, Vol 14, Issue 98. 1894. Web. 05/08/2021 http://www.church missionarysociety.amdigital.co.uk/Documents/Details/CMS_CRL_IW_1894_08 Image 358. © [2021] Adam Matthew Digital Limited

(14) CEZMS Annual reports, 1889-1892 RC. Web. 05/08/2021. http://www.Research Source.amdigital.co.uk/Documents/Details/CMS_I_Part5_Reel94_Vol1. Image 127. © [2021] Adam Matthew Digital Limited

(15) CEZMS Annual reports, 1892-1896 RC. Web. 05/08/2021. http://www.Research Source.amdigital.co.uk/Documents/Details/CMS_I_Part5_Reel95_Vol1. Image 134. © [2021] Adam Matthew Digital Limited

(16) August IW. Vol 15, Iss.110. 189.5 Web. 05/08/2021.http://www.church missionarysociety.amdigital.co.uk/Documents/Details/CMS_CRL_IW_1895_08 Image 357, 352 © [2021] Adam Matthew Digital Limited

(17) August IW, 1894. Web. 05/08/2021. http://www.churchmissionary society.amdigital.co.uk/Documents/Details/CMS_CRL_IW_1894_08. Images 358, 359. © [2021] Adam Matthew Digital Limited

(18) July IW. Vol 20, Issue . 1900. Web. 14/08/2021 http://www.church missionarysociety.amdigital.co.uk/Documents/Details/CMS_CRL_IW_1900_07 Image 153. © [2021] Adam Matthew Digital Limited

(19) A Modern Tale of Sind p11 CEZMS: Leaflets and reports of CEZMS missions: Sindh, 1925, 1932-33. 1925-1933. RC. Web. 14/08/2021. http://www.Research Source.amdigital.co.uk/Documents/Details/CMS_I_Part6_Reel123_Vol6. Image 11. © [2021] Adam Matthew Digital Limited

(20) April IW. Vol 31, Issue 298. 1911. Web. 05/08/2021. http://www.church missionarysociety.amdigital.co.uk/Documents/Details/CMS_CRL_IW_1911_04 Image 80. © [2021] Adam Matthew Digital Limited

No Longer a Second

(1) August IW. 1894. Web. 05/08/2021. http://www.churchmissionary society.amdigital.co.uk/Documents/Details/CMS_CRL_IW_1894_08. Image 357. © [2021] Adam Matthew Digital Limited

(2) Possible Publications. Web. 04/06/2021. http://www.Research Source.amdigital.co.uk/Documents/Details/CMS_I_Part5_Reel86_Vol6. Images 175 &141 © [2021] Adam Matthew Digital Limited

(3) August IW. 1895 Web. 05/08/2021. http://www.churchmissionary society.amdigital.co.uk/Documents/Details/CMS_CRL_IW_1895_08. Image 353. © [2021] Adam Matthew Digital Limited

(4) September IW. Vol 18, Iss . 1898. Web. 05/08/2021. http://www.church missionarysociety.amdigital.co.uk/Documents/Details/CMS_CRL_IW_1898_09 Image 221. © [2021] Adam Matthew Digital Limited

(5) March IW. Vol 19, Issue . 1899. Web. 05/08/2021 http://www.church missionarysociety.amdigital.co.uk/Documents/Details/CMS_CRL_IW_1899_03 Image 61. © [2021] Adam Matthew Digital Limited

(6) Students and the Missionary Problem. The Masses of India address delivered at the International Student Missionary Conference London 2-6 January 1900 by The Rev. E P Rice London Missionary Society Bangalore, page 365 Web. 02/08/2021 https://archive.org/details/studentsmissiona00inteiala/page/364/mode/2up

(7) June IW. Vol 17, Issue 132. 1897. London: CEZMS. Adam Matthew, Marlborough, CMS Periodicals, Web. 05/08/2021 http://www.churchmissionarysociety. amdigital.co.uk/Documents/Details/CMS_CRL_IW_1897_06 Image 18. © [2021] Adam Matthew Digital Limited

(8) August IW. 1895 Web. 05/08/2021 http://www.churchmissionarysociety. amdigital.co.uk/Documents/Details/CMS_CRL_IW_1895_08. Image 356. © [2021] Adam Matthew Digital Limited

(9)Annual reports 1892-1896 RC. Web 05/08/2021 http://www.Research Source.amdigital.co.uk/Documents/Details/CMS_I_Part5_Reel95_Vol1. Image 479. © [2021] Adam Matthew Digital Limited

(10) June IW, Vol 16, Issue 120. 1896. Web. 14/08/2021 http://www.church missionarysociety.amdigital.co.uk/Documents/Details/CMS_CRL_IW_1896_06 Image 142 © [2021] Adam Matthew Digital Limited

(11) August IW. Vol 16, Iss 122. 1896. Web. 14/08/2021 http://www.church missionarysociety.amdigital.co.uk/Documents/Details/CMS_CRL_IW_1896_08 Image 186. © [2021] Adam Matthew Digital Limited

(12) 'Zenana: Or Woman's Work in India', November 1905 - October 1911 RC. Web. 14/08/2021. http://www.ResearchSource.amdigital.co.uk/Documents/Details /CMS_II_Part4_Reel41_Vol1. Image 12. © [2021] Adam Matthew Digital Limited

(13) The Bible and the Flag Brian Stanley published by Apollos 1990 page 161 and 'Zenana: Or, Woman's Work in India', November 1905 - October 1911 RC. Web. 15/08/2021. http://www.ResearchSource.amdigital.co.uk/Documents/Details /CMS_II_Part4_Reel41_Vol1. Image 53. © [2021] Adam Matthew Digital Limited

(14) Annual letters of the missionaries, 1897-1898. CMS archive at CRL, UoB. Source. Web. 07/06/2021. http://www.ResearchSource.amdigital.co.uk/Documents/Details /CMS_III_Part4_Reel37_Vol1. Image 143. © [2021] Adam Matthew Digital Limited

(15) August IW. Vol 17, Iss. 134. 1897. Web. 14/08/2021 http://www.church missionarysociety.amdigital.co.uk/Documents/Details/CMS_CRL_IW_1897_08 Image 181, 182 © [2021] Adam Matthew Digital Limited

(16) Ibid. Images 178 179

(17) Ibid. Images 179, 180

(18) June IW. 1897. Web. 14/08/2021 http://www.churchmissionary society.amdigital.co.uk/Documents/Details/CMS_CRL_IW_1897_06. Image19. © [2021] Adam Matthew Digital Limited

(19) Ibid. Image 142

(20) CEZMS Annual reports 1897-1900 RC. Web. 14/08/2021 http://www.Research Source.amdigital.co.uk/Documents/Details/CMS_I_Part5_Reel96_Vol1. Image 144. © [2021] Adam Matthew Digital Limited

(21) August IW. 1897. Web. 14/08/2021 http://www.churchmissionary society.amdigital.co.uk/Documents/Details/CMS_CRL_IW_1897_08. Image 180. © [2021] Adam Matthew Digital Limited

(22) July IW. Vol 17, Issue 133. 1897. Web. 14/08/2021 http://www.church missionarysociety.amdigital.co.uk/Documents/Details/CMS_CRL_IW_1897_07 Image 168. © [2021] Adam Matthew Digital Limited

(23) September IW. Vol 18, Issue . 1898. Web. 14/08/2021 http://www.church missionarysociety.amdigital.co.uk/Documents/Details/CMS_CRL_IW_1898_09. Images 221, 222. © [2021] Adam Matthew Digital Limited

(24) August IW. Vol 18, Issue . 1898. Web. 14/08/2021 http://www.church
missionarysociety.amdigital.co.uk/Documents/Details/CMS_CRL_IW_1898_08 Images
180, 181 © [2021] Adam Matthew Digital Limited
(25) Behind the Pardah by Irene Barnes 1897 page 108 Published by Thomas Y Crowell
& Company
(26) September IW Vol 16, Iss 123. 1896 Web14/08/2021 http://www.church
missionarysociety.amdigital.co.uk/Documents/Details/CMS_CRL_IW_1896_09 Image
210 © [2021] Adam Matthew Digital Limited
(27) April India's Women, Vol 50, Iss. 519 1930 London: CEZMS. Adam Matthew,
Marlborough, CMS Periodicals Web 14/08/2021 http://www.church
missionarysociety.amdigital.co.uk/Documents/Details/CMS_CRL_IW_1929-1930_16.
Image 83. © [2021] Adam Matthew Digital Limited
(28) March IW, Vol 19, Issue . 1899. Web. 14/08/2021 http://www.church
missionarysociety.amdigital.co.uk/Documents/Details/CMS_CRL_IW_1899_03 Image
61. © [2021] Adam Matthew Digital Limited
(29) Map of the C.M.S. Mass Movement Areas in India. Image Type: Map Image From:
The Mission Hospital Volume: 35 Issue: 405 Date: Oct 1931 Copyright: Church Mission
Society Web. 14/09/2021 https://www.churchmissionarysociety.amdigital.co.uk/Image
Gallery/Image/CMS_CRL_Mission_1931_10/1# © [2021] Adam Matthew Digital Limited
(30) December IW Vol. 55 Iss.587 1935. Web. 14/08/2021http://www.church
missionarysociety.amdigital.co.uk/Documents/Details/CMS_CRL_IW_1935_12 Image
220. © [2021] Adam Matthew Digital Limited
(31) August IW. Vol 14, Issue 98. 1894. Web. 20/09/2021.http://www.church
missionarysociety.amdigital.co.uk/Documents/Details/CMS_CRL_IW_1894_08 Image
351. © [2021] Adam Matthew Digital Limited

Orphans and Villages

(1) Annotated register of missionaries vol. 1. 1804-1904. at the CMS Oxford Web
14/08/2021 http://www.ResearchSource.amdigital.co.uk/Documents/Details
/CMS_III_Part1_Reel1_Vol1. Image 403. © [2021] Adam Matthew Digital Limited
(2) December The Church Missionary Intelligencer, Vol. 26 Iss . 1901. London CMS
Adam Matthew, Marlborough CMS Periodicals Web. 14/08/2021 http://www.church
missionarysociety.amdigital.co.uk/Documents/Details/CMS_OX_Intelligencer_1901_12.
Image 942 © [2021] Adam Matthew Digital Limited
(3) A Modern Tale of Sind CEZMS Web. 07/06/2021. http://www.Research
Source.amdigital.co.uk/Documents/Details/CMS_I_Part6_Reel123_Vol6. Images 37, 38.
© [2021] Adam Matthew Digital Limited
(4) March IW Vol 23, Issue . 1903. Web. 14/08/2021 http://www.church
missionarysociety.amdigital.co.uk/Documents/Details/CMS_CRL_IW_1903_03 Images
53, 54. © [2021] Adam Matthew Digital Limited
(5) Possible publications Web. 14/08/2021 http://www.ResearchSource.amdigital.co.uk
/Documents/Details/CMS_I_Part5_Reel86_Vol6. Image 165. © [2021] Adam Matthew
Digital Limited
(6) October IW, Vol 21, Issue. 1901. Web. 14/08/2021 http://www.church
missionarysociety.amdigital.co.uk/Documents/Details/CMS_CRL_IW_1901_10 Image
230. © [2021] Adam Matthew Digital Limited
(7) December IW. Vol 21, Issue. 1901. Web. 14/08/2021 http://www.church
missionarysociety.amdigital.co.uk/Documents/Details/CMS_CRL_IW_1901_12 Image
273. © [2021] Adam Matthew Digital Limited
(8) July IW. Vol 24, Issue 1904. Web. 14/08/2021 http://www.church
missionarysociety.amdigital.co.uk/Documents/Details/CMS_CRL_IW_1904_07 Image
156. © [2021] Adam Matthew Digital Limited
(9) March IW. Vol 25, Issue 1905. Web. 14/08/2021 http://www.church
missionarysociety.amdigital.co.uk/Documents/Details/CMS_CRL_IW_1905_03 Images
60-62. © [2021] Adam Matthew Digital Limited

(10) March IW. Vol 27, Issue 249. 1907. Web. 14/08/2021 http://www.church missionarysociety.amdigital.co.uk/Documents/Details/CMS_CRL_IW_1907_03. Images 36, 37. © [2021] Adam Matthew Digital Limited

(11) August IW. Vol 30, Issue 290. 1910. Web. 14/08/2021 http://www.church missionarysociety.amdigital.co.uk/Documents/Details/CMS_CRL_IW_1910_08. Images 125, 126. © [2021] Adam Matthew Digital Limited

(12) March IW Vol 30 Issue 285 1910. Web. 14/08/2021 http://www.church missionarysociety.amdigital.co.uk/Documents/Details/CMS_CRL_IW_1910_03 Images 42, 43. © [2021] Adam Matthew Digital Limited

(13) July IW. Vol 21, Issue . 1901. Web. 14/08/2021 http://www.church missionarysociety.amdigital.co.uk/Documents/Details/CMS_CRL_IW_1901_07 Image 154. © [2021] Adam Matthew Digital Limited

(14) 'Zenana: Or, Woman's Work in India', Nov. 1905 - Oct. 1911. RC. Web. 29/06/2021. http://www.ResearchSource.amdigital.co.uk/Documents/Details /CMS_II_Part4_Reel41_Vol1. Image 193. © [2021] Adam Matthew Digital Limited

(15) CEZMS: Annual reports 1905-1908. RC. Web. 14/08/2021 http://www.Research Source.amdigital.co.uk/Documents/Details/CMS_I_Part5_Reel98_Vol1. Image 32. © [2021] Adam Matthew Digital Limited

(16) July IW. Vol 23, Issue. 1903. Web. 14/08/2021 http://www.church missionarysociety.amdigital.co.uk/Documents/Details/CMS_CRL_IW_1903_07 Image 153. © [2021] Adam Matthew Digital Limited

(17) November IW Vol 23, Issue . 1903. Web. 14/08/2021 http://www.church missionarysociety.amdigital.co.uk/Documents/Details/CMS_CRL_IW_1903_11 Image 246. © [2021] Adam Matthew Digital Limited

(18) Annual reports 1905-1908. Web. 14/08/2021 http://www.Research Source.amdigital.co.uk/Documents/Details/CMS_I_Part5_Reel98_Vol1. Image 32. © [2021] Adam Matthew Digital Limited

(19) November IW. Vol 26 Iss. 245 1906 Web 14/08/2021 http://www.church missionarysociety.amdigital.co.uk/Documents/Details/CMS_CRL_IW_1906_11 Image 172. © [2021] Adam Matthew Digital Limited

(20) November IW Vol 27 Issue 257 1907 Web. 14/08/2021 http://www.church missionarysociety.amdigital.co.uk/Documents/Details/CMS_CRL_IW_1907_11. Images 170, 171. © [2021] Adam Matthew Digital Limited

(21) The Madras weekly mail pg. 706 25 December 1902 Web. 10/08/2021. https://www.britishnewspaperarchive.co.uk/viewer/bl/0003345/19021225 /037/0006 Image © THE BRITISH LIBRARY BOARD. ALL RIGHTS RESERVED.

(22) December IW Vol 27 Iss. 258 1907 Web. 14/08/2021 http://www.church missionarysociety.amdigital.co.uk/Documents/Details/CMS_CRL_IW_1907_12 Image 191. © [2021] Adam Matthew Digital Limited

(23) June IW. Vol 28, Issue 264. 1908. Web. 14/08/2021 http://www.church missionarysociety.amdigital.co.uk/Documents/Details/CMS_CRL_IW_1908_06 Image 95. © [2021] Adam Matthew Digital Limited

(24) July IW. Vol 28, Issue 265. 1908. Web. 14/08/2021 http://www.church missionarysociety.amdigital.co.uk/Documents/Details/CMS_CRL_IW_1908_07 Image 107. © [2021] Adam Matthew Digital Limited

(25) August IW. Vol 28, Iss. 266. 1908. Web. 14/08/2021 http://www.church missionarysociety.amdigital.co.uk/Documents/Details/CMS_CRL_IW_1908_08 Images 115, 116. © [2021] Adam Matthew Digital Limited

(26) March IW. Vol 23, Issue. 1903. Web. 14/08/2021 http://www.church missionarysociety.amdigital.co.uk/Documents/Details/CMS_CRL_IW_1903_03 Image 53. © [2021] Adam Matthew Digital Limited

(27) November IW. Vol 23, Iss. 1903. Web. 14/08/2021 http://www.church missionarysociety.amdigital.co.uk/Documents/Details/CMS_CRL_IW_1903_11 Image 250. © [2021] Adam Matthew Digital Limited

(28) July IW. Vol 24, Issue . 1904. Web. 14/08/2021 http://www.church missionarysociety.amdigital.co.uk/Documents/Details/CMS_CRL_IW_1904_07 Image 157. © [2021] Adam Matthew Digital Limited
(29) November IW. 1907. Web. 14/08/2021 http://www.churchmissionary society.amdigital.co.uk/Documents/Details/CMS_CRL_IW_1907_11. Image 171. © [2021] Adam Matthew Digital Limited
(30) July IW. 1904. Web. 14/08/2021 http://www.churchmissionary society.amdigital.co.uk/Documents/Details/CMS_CRL_IW_1904_07. Image 156. © [2021] Adam Matthew Digital Limited

Widows and War
(1) Thing as they are - Mission work in southern India by Amy Carmichael 1901, page 66, London: Morgan and Scott 1905
(2) A Modern Tale of Sind. Web. 07/06/2021 http://www.ResearchSource. amdigital.co.uk/Documents/Details/CMS_I_Part6_Reel123_Vol6. Image 36. © [2021] Adam Matthew Digital Limited
(3) September IW Vol 35 Iss 351 1915. Web. 14/08/2021 http://www.church missionarysociety.amdigital.co.uk/Documents/Details/CMS_CRL_IW_1915_09 Image 170. © [2021] Adam Matthew Digital Limited
(4) June IW. 1919. Web. 14/08/2021 http://www.churchmissionary society.amdigital.co.uk/Documents/Details/CMS_CRL_IW_1919-1920_06. Image 59. © [2021] Adam Matthew Digital Limited
(5) CEZMS: Leaflets and reports of CEZMS missions: Karachi, 1922/23, 1931/32, 1934/35. (Leaflets 1922-1935) RC. Web. 07/06/2021. http://www.Research Source.amdigital.co.uk/Documents/Details/CMS_I_Part6_Reel122_Vol15. Image 45, 46. © [2021] Adam Matthew Digital Limited
(6) Possible publications Web. 15/08/2021. https://www.research source.amdigital.co.uk/Documents/Images/CMS_I_Part5_Reel86_Vol6/168. Image 169. © [2021] Adam Matthew Digital Limited
(7) June IW. 1918. Web. 14/08/2021 http://www.churchmissionarysociety. amdigital.co.uk/Documents/Details/CMS_CRL_IW_1917-1918_17. Image 54. © [2021] Adam Matthew Digital Limited
(8) June IW. Vol , Issue . 1919. Web. 14/08/2021 http://www.church missionarysociety.amdigital.co.uk/Documents/Details/CMS_CRL_IW_1919-1920_06. Image 59. © [2021] Adam Matthew Digital Limited
(9) 'History of the Church Missionary Society' by Eugene Stock, volume IV 1916. CMS archive at CRL, UoB. Web. 14/08/2021 http://www.ResearchSource.amdigital.co.uk /Documents/Details/CMS_III_Part1_Reel8_Vol1. Image 305. © [2021] Adam Matthew Digital Limited
(10) The Call of a World Task in War Time J Lovell Murray page 82 Education Secretary Student Volunteer Movement Published by New York Student Volunteer Movement 1918. Web. 30/07/2021 https://babel.hathitrust.org /cgi/pt?id=wu.89100093657&view=1up&seq=92&skin=2021
(11) CEZMS: Annual reports, 1913-1919 RC. Web. 30/07/2021 https://www.research source.amdigital.co.uk/Documents/Images/CMS_I_Part5_Reel100_Vol1/505. Image 506. © [2021] Adam Matthew Digital Limited
(12) Possible publications. Web. 07/06/2021. https://www.research source.amdigital.co.uk/Documents/Images/CMS_I_Part5_Reel86_Vol6/168. Image 169. © [2021] Adam Matthew Digital Limited
(13) Annual reports 1913-1919 Web. 30/07/2021 https://www.research source.amdigital.co.uk/Documents/Images/CMS_I_Part5_Reel100_Vol1/540. Image 541. © [2021] Adam Matthew Digital Limited
(14) June IW. 1919. Web. 14/08/2021 https://www.churchmissionarysociety. amdigital.co.uk/Documents/Images/CMS_CRL_IW_1919-920_06/14#Articles. Image 59. © [2021] Adam Matthew Digital Limited

(15) Annual reports 1913-1919 Web. 30/07/2021 https://www.research source.amdigital.co.uk/Documents/Images/CMS_I_Part5_Reel100_Vol1/540 . Image 541. © [2021] Adam Matthew Digital Limited

(16) June IW 1919. Web. 14/08/2021 https://www.churchmissionarysociety. amdigital.co.uk/Documents/Images/CMS_CRL_IW_1919-1920_06/14#Articles Image 60. © [2021] Adam Matthew Digital Limited

(17) August IW. Vol 31, Issue 302. 1911. Web. 14/08/2021 https://www.church missionarysociety.amdigital.co.uk/Documents/Images/CMS_CRL_IW_1911_08/3#Articl es. Images 144 -146 © [2021] Adam Matthew Digital Limited

(18) July IW. Vol 31, Issue 301. 1911. London: CEZMS.   Adam Matthew, Marlborough, CMS Periodicals, Web. 14/08/2021 http://www.church missionarysociety.amdigital.co.uk/Documents/Details/CMS_CRL_IW_1911_07 Image 131. © [2021] Adam Matthew Digital Limited

(19) October IW. Vol 33, Iss 328. 1913 Web. 14/08/2021. http://www.church missionarysociety.amdigital.co.uk/Documents/Details/CMS_CRL_IW_1913_10 Image 195. © [2021] Adam Matthew Digital Limited

(20) August IW. Vol 35, Issue 350. 1915. Web. 14/08/2021 http://www.church missionarysociety.amdigital.co.uk/Documents/Details/CMS_CRL_IW_1915_08. Images 154, 155. © [2021] Adam Matthew Digital Limited

(21) Annual reports, 1913-1919 Web. 30/07/2021 https://www.research source.amdigital.co.uk/Documents/Images/CMS_I_Part5_Reel100_Vol1/540 . Image 541. © [2021] Adam Matthew Digital Limited

(22) June IW 1916. Web. 30/07/2021 https://www.churchmissionarysociety .amdigital.co.uk/Documents/Images/CMS_CRL_IW_1916_06/14#Articles. Image 105 © [2021] Adam Matthew Digital Limited

(23) June IW. 1919. Web. 14/08/2021 https://www.churchmissionarysociety .amdigital.co.uk/Documents/Images/CMS_CRL_IW_1919-1920_06 /15#Articles Image 60. © [2021] Adam Matthew Digital Limited

(24) August IW. Vol 31, Iss 302. 1911. Web. 14/08/2021 https://www.church missionarysociety.amdigital.co.uk/Documents/Images/CMS_CRL_IW_1911_08/3#Articl es. Image 144. © [2021] Adam Matthew Digital Limited

(25) March IW. Vol 40, Iss 401. 1920. Web. 14/08/2021 http://www.church missionarysociety.amdigital.co.uk/Documents/Details/CMS_CRL_IW_1919-1920_14. Image 41. © [2021] Adam Matthew Digital Limited

(26) December IW Vol 31 Iss 306 1911. Web. 14/08/2021 http://www.church missionarysociety.amdigital.co.uk/Documents/Details/CMS_CRL_IW_1911_12 Images 223, 224. © [2021] Adam Matthew Digital Limited

(27) March IW. Vol 33, Iss 321. 1913. Web. 14/08/2021 http://www.church missionarysociety.amdigital.co.uk/Documents/Details/CMS_CRL_IW_1913_03 Images 52 -54. © [2021] Adam Matthew Digital Limited

(28) May IW. Vol 36, Issue 359. 1916. Web. 14/08/2021 http://www.church missionarysociety.amdigital.co.uk/Documents/Details/CMS_CRL_IW_1916_05 Image 84. © [2021] Adam Matthew Digital Limited

(29) May IW. Vol 34, Issue 335. 1914. Web. 14/08/2021 http://www.church missionarysociety.amdigital.co.uk/Documents/Details/CMS_CRL_IW_1914_05 Image 85. © [2021] Adam Matthew Digital Limited

(30) September IW Vol 35 Iss 351 1915 Web 14/08/2021 http://www.church missionarysociety.amdigital.co.uk/Documents/Details/CMS_CRL_IW_1915_09 Image 169. © [2021] Adam Matthew Digital Limited

(31) October IW. Vol 39, Issue 396. 1919. Web. 14/08/2021 http://www.church missionarysociety.amdigital.co.uk/Documents/Details/CMS_CRL_IW_1919-1920_09. Images 101,102. © [2021] Adam Matthew Digital Limited

(32) September IW. 1915. Web. 14/08/2021 http://www.churchmissionarysociety. amdigital.co.uk/Documents/Details/CMS_CRL_IW_1915_09 Image 170. © [2021] Adam Matthew Digital Limited

(33) July-August IW Vol 36 Issue 361 1916. Web. 14/08/2021 http://www.church missionarysociety.amdigital.co.uk/Documents/Details/CMS_CRL_IW_1916_07. Image 132. © [2021] Adam Matthew Digital Limited
(34) September IW Vol 39 Iss 395 1919. Web 14/08/2021 http://www.church missionarysociety.amdigital.co.uk/Documents/Details/CMS_CRL_IW_1919-1920_08. Image 92. © [2021] Adam Matthew Digital Limited
(35) October IW. Vol 37, Issue 374. 1917. Web. 14/08/2021 http://www.church missionarysociety.amdigital.co.uk/Documents/Details/CMS_CRL_IW_1917-1918_09. Image 117. © [2021] Adam Matthew Digital Limited
(36) November IW Vol 33 Issue 329 1913. Web. 14/08/2021 http://www.church missionarysociety.amdigital.co.uk/Documents/Details/CMS_CRL_IW_1913_11. Image 208. © [2021] Adam Matthew Digital Limited
(37) October IW. 1919. Web. 14/08/2021 http://www.churchmissionary society.amdigital.co.uk/Documents/Details/CMS_CRL_IW_1919-1920_09. Image 107. © [2021] Adam Matthew Digital Limited
(38) March IW. 1913. Web. 14/08/2021 http://www.churchmissionarysociety. amdigital.co.uk/Documents/Details/CMS_CRL_IW_1913_03 Image 52. © [2021] Adam Matthew Digital Limited
(39) Ibid. Image 53
(40) October IW 1919. Web. 14/08/2021 http://www.churchmissionarysociety. amdigital.co.uk/Documents/Details/CMS_CRL_IW_1919-1920_09. Image 102. © [2021] Adam Matthew Digital Limited
(41) May IW 1914. Web. 15/08/2021 http://www.churchmissionarysociety. amdigital.co.uk/Documents/Details/CMS_CRL_IW_1914_05 Image 84. © [2021] Adam Matthew Digital Limited
(42) November IW Vol 29 Iss. 281 1909. Web. 25/08/2021http://www.church missionarysociety.amdigital.co.uk/Documents/Details/CMS_CRL_IW_1909_11 Image 164. © [2021] Adam Matthew Digital Limited

Trials and Honour

(1) CEZMS: Correspondence with missions (incoming and outgoing): India: Punjab and Sind, 1921. RC. Web. 08/06/2021. http://www.ResearchSource.amdigital.co.uk /Documents/Details/CMS_I_Part8_Reel148_Vol2. Image 143. © [2021] Adam Matthew Digital Limited
(2) Ibid. Image 142
(3) Ibid. Image 139
(4) Ibid. Image 141
(5) CEZMS: Correspondence with missions (incoming and outgoing): India: Punjab and Sind, 1922-1923. RC. Web. 07/06/2021. http://www.ResearchSource.amdigital.co.uk /Documents/Details/CMS_I_Part8_Reel149_Vol1. Images 142, 143, 144 © [2021] Adam Matthew Digital Limited
(6) Ibid. Image 145
(7) Ibid. Image 40
(8) Ibid. Images 106 - 109
(9) Ibid. Image 151
(10) Ibid. Image 38
(11) CEZMS: Correspondence with missions (incoming and outgoing): India: South India/Madras, 1922-1924 RC. Web. 14/08/2021 http://www.Research Source.amdigital.co.uk/Documents/Details/CMS_I_Part8_Reel163_Vol1. Image 283. © [2021] Adam Matthew Digital Limited
(12) October IW. Vol 41, Iss. 418. 1921.Web. 14/08/2021 http://www.church missionarysociety.amdigital.co.uk/Documents/Details/CMS_CRL_IW_1921_09 Image 150. © [2021] Adam Matthew Digital Limited
(13) Correspondence with missions 1921. Web. 08/06/2021. http://www.Research Source.amdigital.co.uk/Documents/Details/CMS_I_Part8_Reel148_Vol2. Image 120. © [2021] Adam Matthew Digital Limited

(14) July IW. Vol 44, Issue 451. 1924. Web. 14/08/2021 http://www.church missionarysociety.amdigital.co.uk/Documents/Details/CMS_CRL_IW_1924_07 Image 112. © [2021] Adam Matthew Digital Limited

(15) February IW Vol 45 Issue 457 1925 Web. 14/08/2021 https://www.church missionarysociety.amdigital.co.uk/Documents/Images/CMS_CRL_IW_1925-1926_02/18#Articles. © [2021] Adam Matthew Digital Limited

(16) CEZMS: Correspondence with missions (incoming and outgoing): India: Punjab and Sind, 1924-1926. RC. Web. 09/06/2021. http://www.ResearchSource.amdigital.co.uk/Documents/Details/CMS_I_Part8_Reel150_Vol1. Image 91 © [2021] Adam Matthew Digital Limited

(17) Ibid. Image 92

(18) Ibid. Image 77

(19) Ibid. Image 282

(20) September IW Vol 45 Issue 464 1925 Web. 14/08/2021. http://www.church missionarysociety.amdigital.co.uk/Documents/Details/CMS_CRL_IW_1925-1926_09. Image 174. © [2021] Adam Matthew Digital Limited

(21) CEZMS: Annual reports, 1920-1927 RC. Web. 14/08/2021. http://www.Research Source.amdigital.co.uk/Documents/Details/CMS_I_Part5_Reel102_Vol1. Image 192. © [2021] Adam Matthew Digital Limited

(22) November IW Vol 47 Issue 490 1927 Web. 14/08/2021. http://www.church missionarysociety.amdigital.co.uk/Documents/Details/CMS_CRL_IW_1927-1928_11. Images 206, 217. © [2021] Adam Matthew Digital Limited

(23) July IW. Vol 48, Issue 498. 1928. Web. 14/08/2021. http://www.church missionarysociety.amdigital.co.uk/Documents/Details/CMS_CRL_IW_1927-1928_19. Image 124. © [2021] Adam Matthew Digital Limited

(24) October IW. 1921. Web. 14/08/2021. http://www.church missionarysociety.amdigital.co.uk/Documents/Details/CMS_CRL_IW_1921_09 Images 147, 150. © [2021] Adam Matthew Digital Limited

(25) CEZMS: Leaflets 1922-1935. RC. Web. 07/06/2021. http://www.Research Source.amdigital.co.uk/Documents/Details/CMS_I_Part6_Reel122_Vol15. Images 3, 5,6,7. © [2021] Adam Matthew Digital Limited

(26) Ibid. Image 8

(27) Ibid. Images 9-13

(28) November IW. 1927. Web. 23/08/2021. http://www.churchmissionary society.amdigital.co.uk/Documents/Details/CMS_CRL_IW_1927-1928_11. Image 207. © [2021] Adam Matthew Digital Limited

(29) Annual reports 1920-1927. Web. 14/08/2021. http://www.Research Source.amdigital.co.uk/Documents/Details/CMS_I_Part5_Reel102_Vol1. Image 192. © [2021] Adam Matthew Digital Limited

(30) Correspondence with missions 1924-1926. Web. 09/06/2021. http://www.ResearchSource.amdigital.co.uk/Documents/Details/CMS_I_Part8_Reel150_Vol1. Image 316. © [2021] Adam Matthew Digital Limited

(31) CEZMS: Leaflets 1922-1935. RC. Web. 07/06/2021. http://www Research Source.amdigital.co.uk/Documents/Details/CMS_I_Part6_Reel122_Vol15. Image 5. © [2021] Adam Matthew Digital Limited

(32) Leaflets 1922-1935. Web.07/06/2021. http://www.ResearchSource. amdigital.co.uk/Documents/Details/CMS_I_Part6_Reel122_Vol15. Image 10. © [2021] Adam Matthew Digital Limited

(33) October IW. Vol 44, Iss. 453. 1924 Web. 14/08/2021 http://www.church missionarysociety.amdigital.co.uk/Documents/Details/CMS_CRL_IW_1924_09 Images 178, 179.© [2021] Adam Matthew Digital Limited

(34) Possible Publications. Web. 07/06/2021 http://www.ResearchSource. amdigital.co.uk/Documents/Details/CMS_I_Part5_Reel86_Vol6. Image 146. © [2021] Adam Matthew Digital Limited

(35) CEZMS: Correspondence with missions (incoming and outgoing): India: Punjab and Sind, 1927-1930. RC. Web. 09/06/2021. http://www.ResearchSource.amdigital.co.uk /Documents/Details/CMS_I_Part8_Reel151_Vol1. Image 179. © [2021] Adam Matthew Digital Limited

(36) Ibid. Image 180

(37) July IW. Vol 49, Iss. 510. 1929. Web. 14/08/2021. http://www.church missionarysociety.amdigital.co.uk/Documents/Details/CMS_CRL_IW_1929-1930_07. Image 125. © [2021] Adam Matthew Digital Limited

(38) Correspondence with missions 1927-1930. Web. 09/06/2021. http://www.ResearchSource.amdigital.co.uk/Documents/Details/CMS_I_Part8_Reel151_ Vol1. Image 493. © [2021] Adam Matthew Digital Limited

(39) Ibid. Image 423

(40) Ibid. Image 424

(41) Ibid. Image 424

(42) Ibid. Image 415

(43) Ibid. Image 414

(44) Ibid. Image 409

(45) Ibid. Image 378

(46) Ibid. Image 405

(47) DoM RC Web 04/06/2021 http://www.ResearchSource.amdigital.co.uk/Documents /Details/CMS_I_Part9_Reel193_Vol5. Image 4. © [2021] Adam Matthew Digital Limited

(48) Correspondence with missions 1927-1930. Web. 09/06/2021. http://www.ResearchSource.amdigital.co.uk/Documents/Details/CMS_I_Part8_Reel151_ Vol1. Image 377. © [2021] Adam Matthew Digital Limited

(49) CEZMS: Correspondence with missions (incoming and outgoing): India: Punjab and Sind, 1931-1933. RC. Web. 09/06/2021. http://www.Research Source.amdigital.co.uk/Documents/Details/CMS_I_Part8_Reel152_Vol1. Image 139. © [2021] Adam Matthew Digital Limited

(50) Ibid. Image 152

(51) February IW. 1925. Web. 14/08/2021 http://www.churchmissionary society.amdigital.co.uk/Documents/Details/CMS_CRL_IW_1925-1926_02. Image 24. © [2021] Adam Matthew Digital Limited

(52) Ibid. Image 25

(53) Ibid. Image 26

(54) May IW. Vol 45, Issue 460. 1925. Web. 14/08/2021 http://www.church missionarysociety.amdigital.co.uk/Documents/Details/CMS_CRL_IW_1925-1926_05. Image 91. © [2021] Adam Matthew Digital Limited

Financial Pressures and Jubliee

(1) June IW. Vol 52, Issue 545. 1932. Web. 15/08/2021 http://www.church missionarysociety.amdigital.co.uk/Documents/Details/CMS_CRL_IW_1932_06 Image 112.© [2021] Adam Matthew Digital Limited

(2) Leaflets 1922-1935. RC. Web. 17/08/2021 http://www.ResearchSource. amdigital.co.uk/Documents/Details/CMS_I_Part6_Reel122_Vol15. Image 30. © [2021] Adam Matthew Digital Limited

(3) October IW. Vol 52, Iss. 549. 1932. Web. 15/08/2021 http://www.church missionarysociety.amdigital.co.uk/Documents/Details/CMS_CRL_IW_1932_10 Image 205. © [2021] Adam Matthew Digital Limited

(4) Leaflets 1922-1935. Web. 07/06/2021. http://www.ResearchSource. amdigital.co.uk/Documents/Details/CMS_I_Part6_Reel122_Vol15. Images 26, and 27. © [2021] Adam Matthew Digital Limited

(5) February IW. Vol 55, Iss. 577. 1935. Web. 15/08/2021 http://www.church missionarysociety.amdigital.co.uk/Documents/Details/CMS_CRL_IW_1935_02Image 40. © [2021] Adam Matthew Digital Limited

(6) June IW. 1932. Web. 15/08/2021 http://www.churchmissionarysociety.
amdigital.co.uk/Documents/Details/CMS_CRL_IW_1932_06. Image 112. © [2021]
Adam Matthew Digital Limited

(7) "RIOT IN KARACHI." *The Sydney Morning Herald (NSW : 1842 - 1954)* 23 March
1935: 16. Web. 20/08/2021 http://nla.gov.au/nla.news-article17163148. The National
Library of Australia

(8) Leaflets 1922-1935. Web. 07/06/2021. http://www.ResearchSource.amdigital.co.uk
/Documents/Details/CMS_I_Part6_Reel122_Vol15. Image 24. © [2021] Adam Matthew
Digital Limited

(9) Ibid. Image 27

(10) Ibid. Image 28

(11) Ibid. Image 25

(12) Ibid. Image 23

(13) Ibid. Image 40

(14) Ibid. Image 42

(15) Ibid. Image 45

(16) CEZMS: Correspondence with missions (incoming and outgoing): India: Punjab &
Sind 1934-1936 RC. Web 07/06/2021 http://www.ResearchSource.amdigital.co.uk
/Documents/Details/CMS_I_Part8_Reel153_Vol1. Image 224. © [2021] Adam Matthew
Digital Limited

(17) November IW. Vol 55, Issue 586. 1935. Web. 15/08/2021 http://www.church
missionarysociety.amdigital.co.uk/Documents/Details/CMS_CRL_IW_1935_11. Image
197. © [2021] Adam Matthew Digital Limited

(18) December IW Vol 55 Issue 587 1935. Web.15/08/2021 http://www.church
missionarysociety.amdigital.co.uk/Documents/Details/CMS_CRL_IW_1935_12. Images
219, 220. © [2021] Adam Matthew Digital Limited

(19) February IW. Vol 56, Issue 589. 1936. Web. 15/08/2021 http://www.church
missionarysociety.amdigital.co.uk/Documents/Details/CMS_CRL_IW_1936_02. Images
23, 24. © [2021] Adam Matthew Digital Limited

(20) May IW. Vol 55, Issue 580. 1935. Web. 15/08/2021 http://www.church
missionarysociety.amdigital.co.uk/Documents/Details/CMS_CRL_IW_1935_05 Image
86. © [2021] Adam Matthew Digital Limited

(21) March IW. Vol 58, Iss. 614. 1938. Web. 15/08/2021 http://www.church
missionarysociety.amdigital.co.uk/Documents/Details/CMS_CRL_IW_1938_03 Image
50. © [2021] Adam Matthew Digital Limited

(22) May IW. Vol 58, Issue 616. 1938. Web. 15/08/2021 http://www.church
missionarysociety.amdigital.co.uk/Documents/Details/CMS_CRL_IW_1938_05 Image
83. And November IW. Vol 58, Issue 622. 1938. Web. 15/08/2021 http://www.church
missionarysociety.amdigital.co.uk/Documents/Details/CMS_CRL_IW_1938_11. Image
174. © [2021] Adam Matthew Digital Limited

(23) July IW. Vol 59, Issue 630. 1939. Web. 15/08/2021 http://www.church
missionarysociety.amdigital.co.uk/Documents/Details/CMS_CRL_IW_1939_07. Images
102, 103. © [2021] Adam Matthew Digital Limited

(24) CEZMS: Correspondence with missions (incoming and outgoing): India: Punjab and
Sind, 1940-1946. RC. Web. 07/06/2021 http://www.ResearchSource.amdigital.co.uk
/Documents/Details/CMS_I_Part8_Reel155_Vol1. Image 59 . © [2021] Adam Matthew
Digital Limited

(25) Ibid. Image 55

(26) Correspondence 1940-46. Web. 07/06/2021. http://www.Research
Source.amdigital.co.uk/Documents/Details/CMS_I_Part8_Reel155_Vol1. Images 46, 47,
48. © [2021] Adam Matthew Digital Limited

(27) Ibid. Image 51

(28) Ibid. Image 43

(29) Ibid. Image 32

(30) Ibid. Image 9, 10

(31) CEZMS: Probation forms of missionaries, A-Z, n.d. 1880-1957. RC. Web. 28/08/2021https://www.researchsource.amdigital.co.uk/Documents/Images/CMS_I_P art9_Reel193_Vol4/29. © [2021] Adam Matthew Digital Limited
(32) Correspondence 1940-46. Web. 07/06/2021. http://www.Research Source.amdigital.co.uk/Documents/Details/CMS_I_Part8_Reel155_Vol1. Image 8. © [2021] Adam Matthew Digital Limited
(33) Ibid. Image 11
(34) Ibid. Image 12
(35) Ibid. Image 13
(36) Ibid. Image 16
(37) November LE. Vol 60, Issue 10. 1940. Web. 25/08/2021. http://www.church missionarysociety.amdigital.co.uk/Documents/Details/CMS_CRL_IW_1940_10. Image 160. © [2021] Adam Matthew Digital Limited
(38) May IW. 1935. Web. 15/08/2021 http://www.churchmissionary society.amdigital.co.uk/Documents/Details/CMS_CRL_IW_1935_05. Image 85. © [2021] Adam Matthew Digital Limited
(39) February IW. 1936. Web. 15/08/2021 http://www.churchmissionary society.amdigital.co.uk/Documents/Details/CMS_CRL_IW_1936_02. Image 23. © [2021] Adam Matthew Digital Limited
(40) July IW. 1939. Web. 15/08/2021 http://www.churchmissionary society.amdigital.co.uk/Documents/Details/CMS_CRL_IW_1939_07. Image 103. © [2021] Adam Matthew Digital Limited

Journey's End
(1) December IW Vol 59 Iss. 635 1939. Web. 25/08/2021. http://www.church missionarysociety.amdigital.co.uk/Documents/Details/CMS_CRL_IW_1939_12 Image 178 © [2021] Adam Matthew Digital Limited)
(2) December LE. Vol 61, Iss. 11. 1941. Web 15/08/2021 http://www.church missionarysociety.amdigital.co.uk/Documents/Details/CMS_CRL_IW_1941_11 Image 176. © [2021] Adam Matthew Digital Limited
(3) January LE. Vol 62, Issue 1. 1942. Web. 15/08/2021 http://www.church missionarysociety.amdigital.co.uk/Documents/Details/CMS_CRL_IW_1942_01 Images 15, 16. © [2021] Adam Matthew Digital Limited
(4) September LE. Vol 62, Iss. 8 1942. Web. 25/08/2021. http://www.church missionarysociety.amdigital.co.uk/Documents/Details/CMS_CRL_IW_1942_08 Image 122. © [2021] Adam Matthew Digital Limited
(5) February LE. Vol 63, Issue 2. 1943. Web. 25/08/2021. http://www.church missionarysociety.amdigital.co.uk/Documents/Details/CMS_CRL_IW_1943_02 Image, unpaginated (next to image 17) © [2021] Adam Matthew Digital Limited
(6) Ibid. 31
(7) Ibid. 21
(8) DoM. Web. 04/06/2021 http://www.ResearchSource.amdigital.co.uk/Documents /Details/CMS_I_Part9_Reel193_Vol5 Images 19,20,21 © [2021] Adam Matthew Digital Limited
(9) *Note: Arya Samaj is a reform movement of modern Hinduism. February LE. Vol 63, Issue 2. 1943. Web. 25/08/2021. http://www.churchmissionarysociety.amdigital.co.uk /Documents/Details/CMS_CRL_IW_1943_02. Image 31. © [2021] Adam Matthew Digital Limited
(10) March LE. Vol 64, Issue 3. 1944. Web. 25/08/2021 http://www.church missionarysociety.amdigital.co.uk/Documents/Details/CMS_CRL_IW_1944_03 Article From recent letters next to image 40. © [2021] Adam Matthew Digital Limited
(11) May-June LE. Vol 64, Issue 5. 1944. Web. 25/08/2021. http://www.church missionarysociety.amdigital.co.uk/Documents/Details/CMS_CRL_IW_1944_05. Images 56, 57. © [2021] Adam Matthew Digital Limited

(12) February LE. 1943. Web. 25/08/2021. http://www.churchmissionarysociety.amdigital.co.uk/Documents/Details/CMS_CRL_IW_1943_02. Images 17,18, 19. © [2021] Adam Matthew Digital Limited

(13) February LE. 1943. Web. 25/08/2021. Headquarters Notes page ii http://www.churchmissionarysociety.amdigital.co.uk/Documents/Details/CMS_CRL_IW_1943_02. © [2021] Adam Matthew Digital Limited

(14) November Homes of the East, Vol 39, Issue 183. 1942. London: CEZMS. Adam Matthew, Marlborough, CMS Periodicals, Web 15/08/2021 http://www.churchmissionarysociety.amdigital.co.uk/Documents/Details/CMS_CRL_Homes_1940-1943_17. Image 44. © [2021] Adam Matthew Digital Limited

(15) July LE. Vol 67, Iss 6. 1947 Web 15/08/2021 http://www.churchmissionarysociety.amdigital.co.uk/Documents/Details/CMS_CRL_IW_1946-1947_16. Image 125. © [2021] Adam Matthew Digital Limited

(16) September LE. Vol 67, Issue 7. 1947. Web.15/08/2021 http://www.churchmissionarysociety.amdigital.co.uk/Documents/Details/CMS_CRL_IW_1946-1947_17. Image 140. © [2021] Adam Matthew Digital Limited

(17) October LE. Vol 64, Iss 8. 1944. Web. 15/08/2021 http://www.churchmissionarysociety.amdigital.co.uk/Documents/Details/CMS_CRL_IW_1944_08 Image 91.© [2021] Adam Matthew Digital Limited

(18) October LE Vol 67 Issue 8 1947. Web. 15/08/2021 http://www.churchmissionarysociety.amdigital.co.uk/Documents/Details/CMS_CRL_IW_1946-1947_18. Image 160. © [2021] Adam Matthew Digital Limited

(19) West Pakistan: Sub Files 1-2, 1935-1949. CMS archive at CRL, UoB. Web. 10/06/2021. http://www.ResearchSource.amdigital.co.uk/Documents/Details/CMS_VI_Part9_Reel187_Vol2. Image 272. © [2021] Adam Matthew Digital Limited

(20) Annual reports, 1941-1957 RC. Web. 15/08/2021 http://www.ResearchSource.amdigital.co.uk/Documents/Details/CMS_I_Part6_Reel106_Vol1. Image 392. © [2021] Adam Matthew Digital Limited

(21) DoM Web. 04/06/2021 http://www.ResearchSource.amdigital.co.uk/Documents/Details/CMS_I_Part9_Reel193_Vol5. Image 18. © [2021] Adam Matthew Digital Limited

(22) CEZMS: Correspondence with missions (incoming and outgoing): India: Punjab and Sind, 1947-1950. RC. Web. 10/06/2021. http://www.ResearchSource.amdigital.co.uk/Documents/Details/CMS_I_Part8_Reel156_Vol1. Image 341. © [2021] Adam Matthew Digital Limited

(23) DoM Web. 04/06/2021 http://www.ResearchSource.amdigital.co.uk/Documents/Details/CMS_I_Part9_Reel193_Vol5. Image 18. © [2021] Adam Matthew Digital Limited

(24) Annual reports, 1941-1957 Web. 15/08/2021 http://www.ResearchSource.amdigital.co.uk/Documents/Details/CMS_I_Part6_Reel106_Vol1. Image 480. © [2021] Adam Matthew Digital Limited

(25) Correspondence with missions 1947-1950. Web. 10/06/2021. http://www.ResearchSource.amdigital.co.uk/Documents/Details/CMS_I_Part8_Reel156_Vol1. Image 341. © [2021] Adam Matthew Digital Limited

(26) DoM. Web. 04/06/2021 http://www.ResearchSource.amdigital.co.uk/Documents/Details/CMS_I_Part9_Reel193_Vol5. Image 16. © [2021] Adam Matthew Digital Limited

(27) Ibid. Image 15

(28) Ibid. Image 14

(29) September LE Vol. 70 Issue 7 1950. Web. 15/08/2021 https://www.churchmissionarysociety.amdigital.co.uk/Documents/Images/CMS_CRL_IW_1950-1951_07/11?searchId=#Articles. Image 133. © [2021] Adam Matthew Digital Limited

(30) DoM. Web. 04/06/2021 http://www.ResearchSource.amdigital.co.uk/Documents/Details/CMS_I_Part9_Reel193_Vol5. Image 7. © [2021] Adam Matthew Digital Limited

(31) Ibid. Image 12

(32) CEZMS: Correspondence and policy, 1888-1957; Staff, 1940. RC. Web. 28/08/2021. http://www.ResearchSource.amdigital.co.uk/Documents/Details/CMS_I_Part4_Reel66_Vol1. Image 48 © [2021] Adam Matthew Digital Limited

(33) May LE. Vol 72, Issue 3. 1952. Web. 15/08/2021 http://www.church
missionarysociety.amdigital.co.uk/Documents/Details/CMS_CRL_IW_1952-1953_03.
Images 39, 40. © [2021] Adam Matthew Digital Limited
(34) CEZMS: Annual reports and statistical returns from missionaries, 1955-1956. RC.
Web. 27/08/2021. http://www.ResearchSource.amdigital.co.uk/Documents/Details
/CMS_I_Part9_Reel181_Vol1. Images 21, 22. © [2021] Adam Matthew Digital Limited
(35) Punjab and Sindh Mission: Sub Files 1-4, 1955-1959. CMS archive at CRL, UoB.
Web. 27/08/2021. http://www.ResearchSource.amdigital.co.uk/Documents/Details
/CMS_VI_Part9_Reel186_Vol1. Image 149. © [2021] Adam Matthew Digital Limited
(36) Note: "The Christ of the Indian Road" is the title of an influential book by American
Methodist missionary, E. Stanley Jones, published in 1925. Possible Publications. Web.
10/06/2021. http://www.ResearchSource.amdigital.co.uk/Documents/Details
/CMS_I_Part5_Reel86_Vol6. Image 161. © [2021] Adam Matthew Digital Limited
(37) Correspondence 1934-1936. UoB. Web. 10/06/2021. http://www.Research
Source.amdigital.co.uk/Documents/Details/CMS_I_Part8_Reel153_Vol1. Image 467. ©
[2021] Adam Matthew Digital Limited
(38) Ibid. Image 468
(39) November Homes of the East, Vol 39, Issue 183. 1942. London: CEZMS. Adam
Matthew, Marlborough, CMS Periodicals, Web. 15/08/2021http://www.church
missionarysociety.amdigital.co.uk/Documents/Details/CMS_CRL_Homes_1940-
1943_17. Image 45. © [2021] Adam Matthew Digital Limited
(40) November LE. Vol 66, Issue 9. 1946. Web. 15/08/2021 https://www.church
missionarysociety.amdigital.co.uk/Documents/Images/CMS_CRL_IW_1946-
1947_09/9#Articles © [2021] Adam Matthew Digital Limited
(41) DoM. Web. 04/06/2021 http://www.ResearchSource.amdigital.co.uk/Documents
/Details/CMS_I_Part9_Reel193_Vol5. Image 6. © [2021] Adam Matthew Digital Limited

Bibliography

The Bible and the Flag by Brian Stanley published by Apollos 1990

The Bulwark or Reformation Journal, volume 8 - 11 published by Seeleys, Jackson & Halliday and J Nisbet & Co. 1858 -1862

Captain Jane of the Guides adapted from Professor Jane by C I Davidson and Lieutenant Jane of the Guides by Blanche Brenton Carey published by Church of England Zenana Missionary Society

Crockford's Clerical Directory 1868 Biographical and statistical book of reference for facts relating to the clery and the church published by London: Horace Cox 1868

Echoes From the Harp of France by H M Carey Caen: printed by Domin, Hôtel des Monnaies 1858

Evenings with Grandpapa or The Admiral on Shore Naval Stories for Children, From the Fireside Stories of the Late Vice Admiral Sir Jahleel Brenton by Harriet M. Carey published by Dean & Son 1860

Extracts Relating to the Zulu War of 1879 from The Graphic an illustrated weekly newspaper January to December 1879 published by Debinair Publishing Ltd. 2005

Mildmay or the Story of the First Deaconess Institution by Harriette Cooke by Elliot Stock Paternoster Row 1893

Records of the Church of England Zenana Missionary Society Finding Number: CEZ Printed 29 May 2019. Cadbury Research Library: Special Collections, University of Birmingham.

Things as they are by Amy Carmichael London: Morgan and Scott 1905

Printed in Great Britain
by Amazon

18334055R00120